Interpreters of the prologue to Judges have wrestled with its structure. The book opens with a notice of Joshua's death, but in chapter 2 verse 6, Joshua is in the land of the living, dismissing the people to take their allotted territory. Verse 8 then records his death. Obviously, there is a chronological flashback at some point. Many see it occurring at 2:6 and, consequently, propose a two-part prologue: 1:1–2:5; 2:6–3:4. There are variations on this, with some seeing the flashback at 2:1 or even earlier. Still others eliminate the need for a flashback by reading "Moses," rather than "Joshua" in 1:1, albeit with no textual support.

Yohannes Sahile has proposed an insightful new solution to the problem of the Prologue's structure. He argues for a single prologue that has four flashback units (1:8–16, 20; 2:6–10; 2:22–3:4) embedded within the main narrative. The purpose of this structure, he argues, is to contrast the faithfulness and success of an earlier generation (Joshua's) with the disobedience and failure of a later generation (post-Joshua). In three cases, *wayyiqtol*-initiated clauses appear at the beginning of the flashback unit. This is potentially problematic, since normally *wayyiqtol* indicates pure sequence. But Sahile offers a plausible explanation in each case, arguing there are contextual indicators that signal the flashback. Though this proposal is novel, it deserves consideration by the scholarly guild.

Robert B. Chisholm, Jr., PhD
Chair and Senior Professor of Old Testament Studies,
Dallas Theological Seminary, USA

The Structure and Function of the Prologue of Judges

A Literary-Rhetorical Study of Judges 1:1–3:6

Yohannes Tesfaye Sahile

MONOGRAPHS

© 2017 by Yohannes Tesfaye Sahile

Published 2017 by Langham Monographs
An imprint of Langham Creative Projects

Langham Partnership
PO Box 296, Carlisle, Cumbria CA3 9WZ, UK
www.langham.org

ISBNs:
978-1-78368-307-9 Print
978-1-78368-309-3 Mobi
978-1-78368-308-6 ePub
978-1-78368-310-9 PDF

Yohannes Tesfaye Sahile has asserted his right under the Copyright, Designs and Patents Act, 1988 to be identified as the Author of this work.

All rights reserved. No part of this publication may be reproduced, stored in a retrieval system or transmitted, in any form or by any means, electronic, mechanical, photocopying, recording or otherwise, without the prior written permission of the publisher or the Copyright Licensing Agency.

Unless otherwise indicated, all Scripture translations in this work are the author's own.

British Library Cataloguing in Publication Data
A catalogue record for this book is available from the British Library

ISBN: 978-1-78368-307-9

Cover & Book Design: projectluz.com

Langham Partnership actively supports theological dialogue and an author's right to publish but does not necessarily endorse the views and opinions set forth here or in works referenced within this publication, nor can we guarantee technical and grammatical correctness. Langham Partnership does not accept any responsibility or liability to persons or property as a consequence of the reading, use or interpretation of its published content.

To my children,
Ebenezer, Eyosias, and Batseba

Contents

Abstract xi
Acknowledgments xiii
Abbreviations xv
Chapter 1 1
   Introduction
      Need for Study 1
         Issues 2
      Survey of Scholarship 3
         Scope of the Prologue 3
         Organization of the Prologue 5
      Thesis 8
      Method 9
      Overview 12
Chapter 2 15
   Structure of the Prologue
      Exposition: Israel at the Beginning of the Test (1:1–2) 15
      Complication: Israel in the Middle of the Test (1:3–36) 23
         Simeon 30
         Judah 31
         House of Joseph 34
         Summary 35
      Change: Warning for Israel's Failure (2:1–10) 35
      Unraveling: Israel's Failure and Its Consequence (2:11–3:4) .. 39
         Structure of 2:11–21 43
         The New Generation (2:11–14a) 44
         The New and Subsequent Generations (2:14b–19) 45
         The New Generation (2:20–21) 46
      Ending: Israel at the End of the Test (3:5–6) 54
Chapter 3 57
   Flashback in the Prologue
      Temporally Overlaid *Wayyiqtol* Clauses in Biblical Hebrew ... 57
         Clarification of Terms 57
         Survey of Scholarship 59
         Identifying Temporally Overlaid *Wayyiqtol* Clauses 75

    Examples of Temporally Overlaid *Wayyiqtol* Clauses 82
    Flashbacks in Judges 1:1–3:6..91
        Evaluation of Judah's Success (Judg 1:8–16, 20).........................91
        Comparison between Two Generations (Judg 2:6–10)...............102
        Comment on the Period of Testing (Judg 2:23–3:4) 107
        Summary 110

Chapter 4 111
Function of the Prologue – Part One
    Joshua as a Prequel to Judges...111
        Joshua 21:43–24:33..112
        Joshua 22 115
    Judges as Sequel to Joshua..117
        Success of a Judahite Family..118
        Failure of the Tribes 120
        Summary 128

Chapter 5 129
Function of the Prologue – Part Two
    The Prologue versus the Central Section 129
        Chronological Relationship 129
        Logical Relationship 130
        Summary 135
    The Prologue versus the Epilogue..135
        The Epilogue as a Unit...136
        Allusion to Joshua 22...139
        Summary 146

Chapter 6 147
Conclusion and Implication

Appendix 1 153
A Translation and a Syntactical Analysis of Judges 1:1–3:6
    Wayyiqtol Clauses 153
    Non-*Wayyiqtol* Clauses..155
    Exposition (1:1–2) 156
    Complication 1:3–36..157
        The Tribe of Simeon (v. 3) 157
        Judah (with Simeon) (vv. 4–7)..158
        Flashback (vv. 8–16) 159
        Judah *with Simeon* (vv. 17–19)..162
        Flashback (v. 20)...163

The Tribe of Benjamin (v. 21)	163
The Tribes of Joseph (vv. 22–29)	163
The Tribe of Zebulun (v. 30)	165
The Tribe of Asher (vv. 31–32)	165
The Tribe of Naphtali (v. 33)	166
The Tribe of Dan (vv. 34–36)	166
Change (2:1–5)	166
Flashback (2:6–10)	167
Unraveling (2:11–21)	168
Comment on the Period of Testing (2:22–3:4)	171
Author's Intrusion (2:22)	171
Flashback (2:23–3:4)	172
Ending (3:5–6)	173
Appendix 2	**175**
Examples of Temporally Overlaid wayyiqtol Clauses	
Genesis 12:1	175
Joshua 4:12	177
1 Samuel 17:13	178
1 Kings 13:12	180
Jonah 4:5 (JPS)	181
Genesis 5:6	183
Appendix 3	**185**
Outline of the Book of Joshua	
Bibliography	**187**

Abstract

This dissertation argues that with respect to structure, the prologue of Judges is a single introduction covering Judges 1:1–3:6, which has a five-stage plot structure: *exposition* (1:1–2), *complication* (1:3–36), *change* (2:1–10), *resolution* (2:11–3:4) and *ending* (3:5–6). Four flashbacks that refer to the period before Joshua's death are inserted at four stages in the narrative (1:8–16, 20; 2:6–10; and 2:23–3:4). These flashbacks are used to evaluate and/or explain what was said in the verses that preceded them (1:4–7; 1:17–19; 1:21–2:5; 2:11–22). The flashbacks capture how the generation before Joshua's death proactively obeyed the Lord by continually seeking to take possession of the land. However, according to the verses that directly speak of the period after Joshua's death (1:4–7; 1:17–19; 1:21–2:5; and 2:11–21) the generation after his death did not *intend* to take possession of the land, which the Lord viewed as disobedience to his ways. As for its function, the prologue is an etiological introduction to the book of Judges. It explains how Israel's situation, as described in the central section, came to be. It was Israel's failure, during the period of testing, to dispossess completely the inhabitants that caused Israel's constant suffering at the hands of the surrounding nations. Instead of dispossessing the inhabitants, Israel lived and made a covenant with them (1:3–7; 1:17–19; 1:21–2:5). Then Israel was lured into worshipping the gods of the inhabitants. Israel's idolatry angered the Lord, who used the surrounding nations to punish Israel (2:11–15). Having compassion on Israel, the Lord would then raise up leaders, who would not only deliver them from their enemies, but also would sometimes attempt to stop them from worshiping other gods. Unfortunately, Israel did not listen to the leaders the Lord raised up for them (2:16–17). The death of each leader meant even greater sin for Israel (2:19).

Acknowledgments

I am grateful for the involvement of Drs Robert B. Chisholm, Richard A. Taylor, and Trent C. Butler in this project. I would like to especially thank Dr Chisholm for his consistent encouragement and guidance in the writing of this dissertation. Both Chisholm and Taylor have demonstrated a Christ-like character and excellence in scholarship that I will continually attempt to imitate.

I am thankful for ILSP for the scholarship I have been receiving during my study at Dallas Theological Seminary. Without this scholarship I would not have been able to get such invaluable training.

There are many individuals and organizations that stood with me throughout my theological training at ABC, NEGST/AIU and here at DTS. I would like to acknowledge the support of Judith Schauer, Bill Ellison, Dr Kifle and Merge Admassu, Roger and Lois Linn, Brad and Megan Wynne, CLA, Pastor Dr Bedilu Yirga, EEBC church leadership and members. I am forever grateful for the support I received from all these and other individuals and organizations.

Above all I am thankful to my Lord and Savior whose faithfulness and kindness continue to overwhelm me.

(Ps 48:15) כִּי זֶה אֱלֹהִים אֱלֹהֵינוּ עוֹלָם וָעֶד הוּא יְנַהֲגֵנוּ עַל־מוּת׃

ይህ አምላክ ከዘላለም እስከ ዘላለም አምላካችን ነውና፤ እስከ መጨረሻው የሚመራንም እርሱ ነው (መዝ 48፡15)

For this God is our God for ever and ever:
He will be our guide *even* unto death. (Ps 48:15 ASV)

Abbreviations

AB	Anchor Bible
ABD	*Anchor Bible Dictionary.* Edited by D. N. Freedman. 6 vols. New York. 1992
AYB	Anchor Yale Bible
BETL	Bibliotheca Ephemeridum Theologicarum Lovaniensium
BH	Biblical Hebrew
BHK	*Biblia Hebraica*, ed. by R. Kittel
BHQ	*Biblia Hebraica Quinta*
BHS	*Biblia Hebraica Stuttgartensia*
BIS	Biblical Interpretation Series
BN	*Biblische Notizen*
BO	Berit Olam: Studies in Hebrew Narrative and Poetry
BRS	Biblical Resources Series
DOTHB	*Dictionary of Old Testament: Historical Books*
DOTWPW	*Dictionary of the Old Testament: Wisdom, Poetry and Writings*
ELS	English Language Series
FOTL	Forms of the Old Testament Literature
HALOT	Koehler, L., W. Baumgartner, and J. J. Stamm, *The Hebrew and Aramaic Lexicon of the Old Testament*. Translated and edited under the supervision of M. E. J. Richardson. 5 vols. Leiden, 1994–2000
HAOL	*Historia Actual Online*

HEB	Hebrew
HSMM	Harvard Semitic Museum Monographs
ICC	International Critical Commentary
ISBL	Indiana Studies in Biblical Literature
JBL	*Journal of Biblical Literature*
JBQ	*Jewish Bible Quarterly*
JPS	Jewish Publication Society
JPTSup	Journal of Pentecostal Theology Supplemental Series
JQR	*Jewish Quarterly Review*
JSNTSup	Journal for the Study of the New Testament: Supplement Series
JSOT	*Journal for the Study of the Old Testament*
JSOTSup	Journal for the Study of the Old Testament: Supplement Series
JSS	*Journal of Semitic Studies*
MT	Masoretic Text
NAC	New American Commentary
NET	New English Translation
NICOT	New International Commentary on the Old Testament
NIDOTTE	*New International Dictionary of Old Testament Theology and Exegesis.* Edited by W. A. VanGemeren. 5 vols. Grand Rapids, 1997
NIVAC	NIV Application Commentary
NRSV	New Revised Standard Version
OT	Old Testament
OTL	Old Testament Library
ResQ	*Restoration Quarterly*
SBF Analecta	Studium Biblicum Franciscanum. Analecta
SBLMS	Society of Biblical Literature Monograph Series
SubBi	Subsidia biblica

TDOT	*Theological Dictionary of the Old Testament.* Edited by G. J. Botterweck and H. Ringgren. Translated by J. T. Willis, G. W. Bromiley, and D. E. Green. 8 vols. Grand Rapids, 1974–
TynBul	*Tyndale Bulletin*
VT	*Vetus Testamentum*
VTSup	Supplements to Vetus Testamentum
WBC	Word Biblical Commentary
ZAH	*Zeitschrift für Althebräistik*
ZAW	*Zeitschrift für die alttestamentliche Wissenschaft*

CHAPTER 1

Introduction

This chapter introduces the subject matter and the need for this study. It will then present a survey of previous studies on the subject. After the survey, it will briefly summarize the thesis of this dissertation. A discussion of the methodology used and the assumptions that inform this study will be followed by an overview of the organization of this dissertation, which will conclude this introductory chapter.

The focus of this dissertation is Judges 1:1–3:6. The dissertation will analyze the structure of this passage, its meaning based on that structure, its function in relation to the book of Joshua, and its function within the entire book of Judges based on this meaning.

Need for Study

Before the publication of Matthias Ederer in 2011, there was not a single work devoted to Judges 1:1–3:6 in its entirety.[1] Even after the publication of

---

1. Matthias Ederer, *Ende und Anfang: Der Prolog des Richterbuchs (Ri 1,1–3,6) in "Biblischer Auslegung,"* Herder's Biblical Studies, ed. Hans-Josef Klauck and Erich Zenger, vol. 68 (Freiburg: Herder, 2011). Erder explains: Ri 1,1–3,6 ist in der neueren Forschung nur selten (alleiniger) Gegenstand einer umfangreichen Studie. Die einzige Monographie neueren Datums, die sich auf den "Richterprolog" konzentriert, ist die Untersuchung von M. RAKE mit einer an der Redaktionsgeschichte des Textes interessierten Fragestellung. Diese nimmt Ri 1 (bzw. Ri 1,1–2,5) eingehender in den Blick, während Ri 2,6–3,6 lediglich am Rande behandelt wird. Daneben ist auf insgesamt fünf Monographien zu verweisen, die innerhalb der letzten 20 Jahre erschienen sind und sich – mit unterschiedlichen Herangehensweisen und verschiedener Akzentsetzung – dem Richterbuch (als Ganzem) zumeist aus synchroner Perspektive annähern. Innerhalb dieser Studien sind dem Richterprolog und seiner Funktion für das Buchganze jeweils längere Kapitel gewidmet. Jenseits der genannten Monographien werden Ri 1,1–3,6 bzw. Teile dieses Textes vor allem in Kommentaren und in kleineren Beiträgen behandelt. Ein Großteil dieser Beiträge ist einem historisch-kritischen Paradigma

his book, Ederer's observation remains true. Several studies have been published on the book of Judges as a whole in the past few years, and yet there has not been a study which focuses solely on Judges 1:1–3:6. Unlike other introductory sections of biblical books, which are significant mainly for the particular book of which they are part, a proper study of Judges 1:1–3:6 is significant not only for the obvious implication of understanding the book of Judges but for understanding the book of Joshua as well.

Issues

There are some issues one faces when reading the prologue of Judges. The first issue has to do with its structure. Where does it begin and where does it end? Is it a coherent unit? How is it organized? Is the prologue a double introduction, wherein the two introductions have different "perspectives"?[2] How are the sub-units related to each other? And particularly, what is the relationship of 2:1–5 to 1:1–36 and to 2:6–3:6?

In the processes of analyzing the structure, the exegete depends on his/her understanding of grammar and syntax. In the study of the prologue, one's understanding of how the verbal system in BH works has important implications. In this regard, one's view of the meaning and function of the *wayyiqtol* will affect one's interpretation of significant texts, such as Judges 2:6–10.

Once the structure is analyzed, questions of literary device arise. What kinds of literary devices does the author use? Are there allusions, differing points of view, foreshadowings, flashbacks? What are the rhetorical functions of these literary styles?

Finally, issues of the prologue's function within the book need to be addressed. Is its purpose to evaluate the events in Joshua and serve as an epilogue? Does it summarize the book of Judges? What is the relationship between the theme(s) of the prologue and the theme(s) of the book as a whole? All of these issues will be addressed in this dissertation.

---

verpflichtet. M. RAKE fasst die Tendenzen der Forschung (für Ri 1,1–2,5 als ihrem primaren Untersuchungsgegenstand) wie folgt zusammen: "Im Laufe der Forschungsgeschichte ist das literarkritische dem historischen und das histonsche schließlich dem redaktions- und kompositionsgeschichtlichen Interesse an Ri 1 gewichen."

2. J. Clinton McCann, *Judges*, Interpretation: A Bible Commentary for Teaching and Preaching, ed. James Luther Mays (Louisville: John Knox, 2001), 27.

Survey of Scholarship

This section briefly surveys previous studies on the prologue of Judges. However, the focus here is on how others have viewed its structure. Structure refers to both the scope and the organization of the prologue.[3]

Scope of the Prologue

Scholars are divided in their view of the extent of the prologue. For some, the prologue ends at 2:5.[4] Mayes gives three reasons for separating this section from the central section, which covers 2:6–16:31: (1) There is no mention of the works of the judges; (2) There is no mention of Israel's relationship with foreigners outside the land; (3) These verses focus on the tribes.[5]

Block offers four additional arguments raised by those who take 2:5 as the end of the prologue: (1) These verses report events whereas 2:6–3:6 are "overtly theological and sermonic." (2) Joshua's death in 2:6–9, though it was already mentioned in 1:1, suggests a break. (3) 2:6–3:6 and 3:7–16:31 share common features both "stylistically and theologically." (4) Though not all, some of these scholars argue that 1:1–2:5 is a later addition because Joshua's death in 1:1 happened after his dismissal of the people in 2:6.[6]

Block then refutes ending the prologue at 2:5 by giving five reasons: (1) 2:1–5 resembles 2:6–3:6 in content and style. (2) The "*waw*-consecutive" at 2:6 necessitates a reading of 2:6–10 "in light of and as a continuation" of 2:1–5. (3) The references to Joshua's death at 1:1 and in 2:6–10 have different form and function. (4) Despite the similar style of 2:6–3:6 and 3:7–16:31, including 1:1–2:5 with 2:6–23 heightens its importance for interpreting the central section. (5) The current chapter division makes more sense.

Other scholars take 2:23 as the end.[7] Here are the reasons Butler offers for ending the prologue at 2:23: (1) The disjunctive syntax at 3:1; (2) the

---

3. Trent C. Butler, *Judges*, WBC, ed. Bruce M. Metzger et al., vol. 8 (Nashville, TN: Thomas Nelson, 2009), 10.

4. A. D. H. Mayes, *Judges* (Sheffield: Sheffield Academic Press, 1995), 13; Gregory T. K. Wong, *Compositional Strategy of the Book of Judges: An Inductive, Rhetorical Study*, VTSup, vol. 111 (Leiden: Brill, 2006), 23.

5. He uses these same reasons for distinguishing the epilogue (17:1–21:25) from the central section.

6. Daniel I. Block, *Judges, Ruth*, NAC, ed. E. Ray Clendenen, vol. 6 (Nashville, TN: Broadman & Holman, 1999), 76.

7. Butler, *Judges*, 12.

different genre of 3:1–6; (3) and the change of topic after 3:1 (i.e. Joshua is absent, different nations are in focus).

Still others consider the prologue to end at 3:4.[8] Stemmer argues that הִנִּיחַ in 3:1 connects 3:1–4 with 2:23 that begins with וַיַּנַּח.[9] He concludes that 3:5 begins the "proper book of Judges." However, he does not clearly communicate why he considers 3:5 rather than 3:7 to be the opening verse of the central section.[10]

A number of OT scholars take 3:6 as the end of the prologue.[11] This dissertation agrees with those scholars who take 3:6 to be the end of the prologue. Despite using a similar statement in 2:11 and 3:7 as well as a similar pattern in 2:11–19 and 3:7–11, 3:7–11 differs from 2:11–19 in that whereas 3:7–11 narrates one-time events, 2:11–19 summarizes all of the one-time events of 3:7–16:31 in both a summary as well as an iterative form.[12]

The main reason behind ending the prologue at 3:6 is because 1:1–3:6 contains a plot that presents the events "by grasping them together into successive wholes."[13] The plot of the story of the Israelites that begins in 1:1–2 with an exposition does not "end" or "conclude" until 3:5–6. As the analysis in the second chapter of this dissertation will show, a reading of Judges 1:1–3:6 as a narrative with a five-stage plot structure – *exposition*, *complication*, *change*, *unraveling*, and *ending* – demonstrates that the prologue is a single narrative, not a double introduction.

---

8. Nathan Stemmer, "The Introduction to Judges, 2,1–3,4." *JQR* 57, no. 3 (1967): 239.

9. Ibid., 241.

10. He began his article by stating "the reasons for this will be given later on," but reasons were not given (ibid., 239).

11. Barry G. Webb, *The Book of the Judges: An Integrated Reading*, JSOTSup Series, vol. 44 (Eugene, OR: Wipf & Stock, 2008), 8. Though at the beginning of his study Wong considered the limit to cover 1:1–2:5, he concluded his study with a proposal that limits the central section to 3:12–16:31 and by implication limits the introductory material from 1:1–3:11. He argued, ". . . what was previously considered the central section of the book should perhaps be redefined to include only the primarily redacted portion of Judges found in 3:12–16:31" (Wong, *Compositional Strategy*, 257).

12. See the discussion on pp. 51–52 where it is argued that the use of plural and the lack of specific names mark 2:14b–19 as a pattern and so as iterative.

13. Webb, *Judges: An Integrated Reading*, 116–117.

A narrative, which is a recounting of one or more events, "must have a continuant subject and constitute a whole."[14] This whole has a structure with a beginning, a middle, and an end.[15] The prologue has a subject – the Israelites – in the beginning (1:1–2), the middle (1:3–3:4), and the end (3:5–6).

Organization of the Prologue

Despite the difference in scholars' views of the extent of the prologue, it seems there is a tendency to see its organization as a two-part introduction. Even those who consider 2:5 as the end see another introduction extending up to 2:23 or 3:6 – though serving as such only for the central section.[16] Included among the two-part organizations is Butler's division of 1:1–36 and 2:1–23.[17] Frolov divides it into 1:1–26 and 1:27–3:6.[18] However, most scholars who take 1:1–3:6 as the limit see a double introduction consisting of 1:1–2:5 and 2:6–3:6.[19]

One of the major reasons why scholars differ in their division of the prologue lies in their understanding of where the author inserts the flashback to the time when Joshua was still alive. This is because despite the report of his death in Judges 1:1, which clearly marked the events that follow as happening after his death, Joshua was alive in Judges 2:6. It is clear then that somewhere between 1:1 and 2:6 the narrative retreats to the time before Joshua died in order for him to be alive again in 2:6.

For instance, Frolov considers 1:27–3:6 as occurring before the events of 1:1–26, i.e. before Joshua's death. He argues against taking 2:6 as introducing the flashback to the time of Joshua. He suggests that 2:6 is part of the

---

14. Gerald Prince, *A Dictionary of Narratology* (Lincoln, NE: University of Nebraska Press, 1987), 58.

15. Ibid., 59.

16. The central section includes 3:1–16:31 if 2:23 is taken as the end of the introduction or 3:7–16:31 if 3:6 is taken as the end of the introduction.

17. Butler, *Judges*, 12. With minor modification from Butler, Block divides the prologue into 1:1–36, 2:1–23, and 3:1–6 (Block, *Judges, Ruth*, 77).

18. Serge Frolov, "Joshua's Double Demise (Josh. 24:28–31; Judg. 2:6–9): Making Sense of a Repetition." *VT* 58 (2008): 315–323.

19. Amit divides it into 1:1–2:5 and 2:11–3:6 with 2:6–10 functioning as a transitional unit (Yairah Amit, *The Book of Judges: The Art of Editing*, BIS, ed. R. Alan Culpepper and Rolf Rendtorff, vol. 38 [Leiden: Brill, 1999], 135).

flashback that started with 1:27–33.[20] He builds his argument by making the following four "observations" from 1:27–33: (1) Out of 15 main clauses, only eight are *wayyiqtols*, which are normally used to narrate consecutive events. (2) The "plain perfects"[21] that open the report on each tribe digress the narrative and move the story's temporal clock to a time when Joshua was still alive. He particularly regards verse 27 as the beginning of a new section, considering the syntax of the verse (*waw-לא-perfect*) as signaling a major break.[22] (3) The narrator "implicitly specifies the scale of the regression by opening it with somewhat modified but easily recognizable quotations of Joshua xvii 11–13 (Judg. i 27–28) and Josh. xvi 10 (Judg. i 29)." (4) He claims that the asyndetic clauses in 1:30–33 signal discontinuity.

The first observation cannot be a criterion for identifying flashback. If 1:27–33 were indeed a flashback, one disjunctive *qatal* could be enough to introduce it and *wayyiqtols* could carry the narrative forward.

The second observation seems to go against his own criterion of clauses that disrupt the narrative. He says, "[p]erfect main clauses outside quoted speech are disruptive unless the use of the form is attributable to rhetorically motivated shift of the subject or the object to the forefront or the presence of the negative particle לא before the verb."[23] The presence of the negative particle לא before the verb necessitates the change from *wayyiqtol* to *qatal*.

The construction לא + *qatal* has three possible functions: (1) it provides a summary; (2) it contrasts as a background or "off-line" comment; and (3) it occasionally could be a "momentous negation" that "furthers the narrative along in the same way that a *wayyiqtol* verbal form would."[24] In Judges 1:27–33, the construction לא + *qatal* is used to provide a negative summary statement on each tribe that constitutes the house of Joseph–Ephraim and

---

20. Frolov, "Joshua's Double Demise," 318.

21. They are actually negated, not plain perfects.

22. Serge Frolov, *Judges*, FOTL, ed. Rolf P. Knierim and Marvin A. Sweeney, vol. 18 (Grand Rapids: Eerdmans, 2013), 57–59.

23. Ibid., 6.

24. Roy L. Heller, *Narrative Structure and Discourse Constellations: An Analysis of Clause Function in Biblical Hebrew Prose*, Harvard Semitic Studies, ed. Jo Ann Hackett and John Huehnergard, vol. 55 (Winona Lake, IN: Eisenbrauns, 2004), 24. So Robert E. Longacre, *Joseph – A Story of Divine Providence: A Text Theoretical and Textlinguistic Analysis of Genesis 37 and 39–48*, 2nd ed. (Winona Lake, IN: Eisenbrauns, 2003), 79.

Manasseh. It would also be correct to say that it moves the narrative of the account of the house of Joseph, which began in verse 22, forward.

Frolov's third observation is a solid criterion for identifying flashbacks, but it also is not without fault. Though taking quotation as a criterion for identifying flashbacks is appropriate, Judges 1:27–28 cannot be considered a direct quotation of Joshua 17:11–13 and so cannot be a flashback. Since the quoted material contains a negated clause, one cannot ascertain that the author is referring to a flashback to a time before Joshua's death. When bounded events – achievements and/or accomplishments such as *dispossessing*, which is the topic of 1:27–33 – are negated, they become temporally unbound because "if there is no actualization, the situation cannot be interpreted as having boundaries."[25] Since Ephraim still did not take possession of his inheritance even after the time of Joshua, the way of describing his failure to take possession of the land cannot change. It would still be described with לֹא plus *qatal*.[26] Again, the change from *wayyiqtol* in Judges 1:22–26 to *weqatal* in 1:27 is primarily due to the presence of the negative לֹא.

As for the fourth observation, the asyndetic clauses of 1:30–33 do not signal discontinuity. Rather, they can be attributed to the genre of these verses – and verses 3–36 as a whole – being a *list*. Verses 3–36 lists the tribes' involvement or lack of involvement in the conquest after the death of Joshua.[27]

Therefore, Judges 1:27 cannot be a point of major break that moves the narrative clock back to the time when Joshua was still alive. Following 1:1–2, verses 27–36 speak of events that took place after Joshua's death.[28] Frolov, however, is correct in arguing that Judges 2:6–10 is not an isolated flashback. This dissertation will argue for three more flashbacks inserted in Judges 1:1–3:6.

---

25. Renaat Declerck, *When-Clauses and Temporal Structure* (London and New York: Routledge, 1997), 214.

26. The author of Judges, however, could be said to have given some signals dropping בְּנֵי from Josh 17:12 and 16:10 in Judg 1:27 and 29. If this is so, then whereas he refers to the earlier generation with בְּנֵי, he refers to the present generation without it.

27. See pp. 23–26 for a discussion of vv. 3–36 as a list.

28. Susanne Gillmayr-Bucher, *Erzählte Welten im Richterbuch: Narratologische Aspekte eines polyfonen Diskurses*, BIS, ed. Paul Anderson and Yvonne Sherwood, vol. 116 (Leiden: Brill, 2013), 42.

Those who consider the prologue as being made up of 1:1–2:5 and 2:6–3:6 argue for such organization not only on the basis of where they think the flashback is found but also on their understanding of the different emphasis of the two introductions. It is often said that whereas the so-called first introduction (1:1–2:5) focuses on political issues, the second introduction (2:6–3:6) focuses on religious issues. Though these two sections clearly differ in emphasis, the conclusion that there are two introductions does not seem to be the best interpretation of those distinctions, for two reasons: (1) The "two introductions" speak of two separate events that have a cause–effect relationship with each other. Taking them as two introductions would be appropriate if the events described were identical. If it were so, it could be said that the author chose to view the same event from two different angles. (2) In the first introduction, there are many religious overtones 1:1–2, 4, 19, 22; 2:1–5. The second introduction also consists of many political reports as in 2:6, 14b–16, 18, 2:20–3:4.

Thesis

This dissertation proposes a structure that is actually based on the plot structure of the narrative of the prologue of Judges. The prologue is a single-narrative story with a five-stage plot structure: an *exposition* (1:1–2), a *complication* (1:3–36), a *change* (2:1–10), an *unraveling* (2:1–3:4) and an *ending* (3:5–6). Into this single-plot narrative are inserted four flashbacks at four stages in the narrative (1:8–16, 20, 2:6–10, and 2:23–3:4) to evaluate the events preceding the flashbacks (1:4–7, 17–19; 2:1–5, and 2:21–22 respectively).

The prologue of the book of Judges is a single narrative that tells the story of the Israelites in relation to the inhabitants of the land of Canaan during the period of testing, which began with the death of Joshua and ended before the appearance of the first judge. It reports how the Israelites failed to completely dispossess the inhabitants of Canaan from their allotted land despite the Lord's clear command to do so. Though the Lord warned them in 2:1–5 that their failure would result in their entrapment by the Canaanites' gods, the Israelites failed to act on the warning and ended up being lured by foreign gods, and as a result enraged the Lord.

The Lord then punished Israel by declaring that he would not continue to dispossess the Canaanites. He also allowed the Canaanites to repeatedly attack and rule over Israel during the period of the judges. The Lord in his mercy gave Israel judges who would deliver them from their enemies, but he never again continued to dispossess the Canaanites, who remained to live with the Israelites, intermarry with them, and lure the Israelites to continue worshipping their gods.

With regard to the function of the prologue, this dissertation argues that the prologue is an etiological introduction to the book of Judges. It explains how Israel's situation as described in the central section came to be: That is, it gives the cause of Israel's constant suffering at the hands of the surrounding nations. The prologue argues that their suffering was the result of their failure, during the period of testing, to completely dispossess the inhabitants. It also serves as a bridge between the end of Joshua and the central section of Judges.

Method

This dissertation is a literary-rhetorical study that gives attention to such narratives features as: narrative structure, recurring themes, differing points of view, allusion, and flashback. Basically, it agrees with Webb's approach, which is a literary analysis of the book of Judges in its canonical form. Webb describes his method:

> The analysis was guided throughout by two basic questions: How precisely is the text structured? and, what does it mean as a complex whole? Basic to the methodology was the assumption that these two questions are inextricably related to one another, although it was with the latter, not the former, that the analysis was ultimately concerned.[29]

This dissertation differs from Webb in two ways: (1) This basic methodology is applied only to the prologue; whereas, Webb employs it to the entire book. (2) Unlike Webb, who focuses on the second question, this dissertation focuses on the structure of the prologue since, as Webb himself agrees, our understanding of its meaning depends on our understanding of its structure. A different structure for the prologue will be proposed and a

---

29. Webb, *Judges: An Integrated Reading*, 208.

discussion of its implications for understanding the meaning and function of the prologue will be offered.

In the discussion of the structure, both genre and syntax are given their due place. In the exegetical undertaking of any given text, one needs to begin with a structural analysis of the text. Frolov encourages both form-critics and exegetes with these sound statements that argue for the key role that structure plays in form-critical and exegetical analysis of a biblical text:

> Although the form of the communication is by no means reducible to its structure, the importance of the latter is difficult to overestimate: no form-critical investigation (and indeed no other exegetical project) can proceed until the studied fragment is positioned vis-à-vis the hierarchy of the literary units that make up the received HB.[30]

Judges 1:1–3:6 is a narrative text. Analysis of a narrative text such as Judges 1:1–36 should be done on two levels, as noted by Osborne.[31] First, one has to study the text at the macro level, which deals with the whole. The analysis at this level depends on what Ska calls "dramatic criteria," which focus on the plot.[32] Second, after the structure at the macro level has been identified, the text should be studied at the micro level, which deals with subsections that make up the whole. Osborne adds, "Each story is broken up into its 'actantial' units, its individual elements or actions. These are charted to determine how the characters interact and how the conflict ebbs and flows within both the single story and the larger narrative of which it is a part."[33] Analyzing the narrative at the micro level could be done using the four "modes of narrative":[34] (1) straight narrative,[35] (2) scenic narrative,[36] (3) description, and (4) comment. This level should be done together with

---

30. Frolov, *Judges*, 4.
31. Grant R. Osborne, *The Hermeneutical Spiral: A Comprehensive Introduction to Biblical Interpretation*, rev. and expanded ed. (Downers Grove, IL: IVP Academic, 2006), 216–217.
32. Jean Louis Ska, *"Our Fathers Have Told Us": Introduction to the Analysis of Hebrew Narratives*, SubBi, vol. 13 (Rome: Editrice Pontificio Instituto Biblico, 2000), 2.
33. Osborne, *Hermeneutical Spiral*, 217.
34. Jacob Licht, *Storytelling in the Bible*, 2nd ed. (Jerusalem: Magnes Press, 1986), 29–30.
35. It can also be referred to as "telling" or "reporting."
36. This can also be referred to as "showing."

genre analysis, since the author could use "different genre elements and markers within or even across various narrative elements."[37]

The narrative of Judges 1:1–3:6 has a clear plot. By following the narrative's plot, the following five-stage structure can be observed in the prologue of Judges:[38]

Exposition: The Israelites faced the test (1:1–2).

Complication: The Israelites fought back, but only enough to scare the enemy, not to dispossess them, and so failed the test (1:3–36).

Change: The Lord warned the Israelites what would happen if they continued to let the Canaanites live with them and make covenants with them (2:1–10).

Unraveling: Having failed to listen to the Lord's warning, the Israelites began to worship the gods of the inhabitants of the land and angered the Lord, who declared his decision never to dispossess the inhabitants of the land. This resulted in the following pattern: suffering under the surrounding nations, deliverance through judges, and relapse into sin at the death of a judge (2:11–3:4).

Ending: The Israelites lived and intermarried with the inhabitants of the land of Canaan and worshipped their gods (3:5–6).

Structuring the prologue based on the narrative plot shows that 1:1–3:6 is a single narrative. The narrative, whose subject is the Israelites according to 1:1, is a whole with a beginning, middle, and end, and does not conclude until 3:6. The subunits such as 1:3–36 or 2:1–10 should be studied in light of the narrative of which they are a part.

In analyzing the narrative structure, both at the macro and micro levels, due attention is given to syntax in order to better follow the plot of the narrative. This is in keeping with Butler's caution: "As so often, conversation

---

37. Butler, *Judges*, 37.

38. Amit calls this five-stage plot structure a pediment structure that is "arranged symmetrically and governed by a concentric structure" (Yairah Amit, *Reading Biblical Narratives: Literary Criticism and the Hebrew Bible*, trans. Yael Lotan [Minneapolis: Fortress, 2001], 47).

dominates much of the narrative, yet the major syntactical thread remains easy to follow."[39] In analyzing BH narrative, clauses are grouped into two categories: *wayyiqtol* and non-*wayyiqtol* clauses. The latter include verbal clauses (those governed by *qatal*, *yiqtol*, or *weqatal*) and non-verbal clauses (*participles, verbless,* or *incomplete*).[40] This dissertation begins with the assumption that *wayyiqtol* is the default narrative verb in BH. This means that *wayyiqtol* clauses mark the foreground of narrative prose. Foreground refers to "that which is focused on, underlined, emphasized; that which comes to the fore against a background."[41] Background, on the other hand, refers to "that part of literary composition concerned with fleshing out given events or characters, contextualizing them in time, place and circumstances."[42]

Since a key feature of narrative is temporal progression, an important step in understanding the structure of a given narrative text is analyzing temporal relationship at the clausal level. In this dissertation, *wayyiqtol* is not viewed as solely sequential.[43] The author approaches BH narrative with the assumption that it is paragraph blocks, not necessarily each *wayyiqtol* clause, that move BH narrative forward.[44]

Overview

This dissertation is organized into six chapters. Chapter 1 discusses introductory matters. Chapter 2 is a study of the structure of the prologue. The dissertation follows the plot structure of the narrative of the prologue of Judges. The plot structure will show that the prologue is a single, unified narrative trajectory that begins after the death of Joshua in 1:1 and ends with a summary of the failure of Israel in 3:5–6. Chapter 3 discusses flashbacks in

---

39. Ibid., 10.
40. Heller, *Narrative Structure and Discourse Constellations*, 26.
41. Prince, *A Dictionary of Narratology*, 33.
42. Ziony Zevit, *The Anterior Construction in Classical Hebrew*, SBLMS, ed. Terence E. Fretheim, vol. 50 (Atlanta, GA: Scholars Press, 1998), 33.
43. So Geiger Gregor, "Erzählte Welt und *Wayyiqtol*," in Ἐν πάσῃ γραμματικῇ καὶ σοφίᾳ: *En pāsē grammatikē kai sophiā*, SBF Analecta, ed. Gregor Geiger, vol. 78 (Milan: Edizioni Terra Santa, 2011), 149–150. Gregor lists the following functions of the *wayyiqtol* as cases where the *wayyiqtol* cannot be regarded as successive: *Wiederaufnahme* – "resumptive," *Gleichzeitigkeit* – "simultaneous," *Plusquamperfekt* – "pluperfect," *Zusammenfassung* – "summary," *logischer, nicht chronologischer Sukzession* – "logical, not chronological succession."
44. Heller, *Narrative Structure and Discourse Constellations*, 431, n. 8.

Biblical Hebrew. The chapter is divided into two sections. The first section will briefly survey the contribution of scholars on the use of *wayyiqtol* verb form in temporally overlaid clauses. It will then summarize the criteria that should be used to identify the *wayyiqtol* clause as temporally overlaid. The second section will apply these criteria to the prologue of Judges and identify four flashbacks that are introduced with a temporally overlaid *wayyiqtol* clause. Chapter 4 discusses the first part of the function of the prologue. It will discuss how the prologue functions in relation to the book of Joshua. Chapter 5 discusses the function of the prologue within the book of Judges itself. It will discuss the prologue's relationship to the central section and the epilogue. Chapter 6 summarizes the conclusion and implications of this study. There are also three appendices. The first contains the author's translation and syntactical analysis of Judges 1:1–3:6. The second offers examples of temporally overlaid *wayyiqtol* clauses. The third contains a structural outline of the book of Joshua.

CHAPTER 2

Structure of the Prologue

This chapter is an analysis of Judges 1:1–3:6 based on its plot structure. The narrative text of the prologue can be divided into a five-stage plot: *Exposition* (1:1–2), *Complication* (1:3–36), *Change* (2:1–10), *Unraveling* (2:11–3:4), and *Ending* (3:5–6). It will be shown that the narrative follows a trajectory of events that took place after the death of Joshua into which four flashbacks to the lifetime of Joshua were inserted at four stages in the narrative. After the "interruption" from these flashbacks, the narrative returns to the same trajectory. The flashbacks will only be mentioned in this chapter and discussed in detail in the next chapter.

Exposition: Israel at the Beginning of the Test (1:1–2)

Judges 1:1–2 function as the *exposition* of the prologue of Judges.[1] These two verses are important to a proper understanding of the prologue, which

---

1. Younger divides v. 2 into two parts and takes v. 2a "Judah will go up" together with v. 1. He then concludes that 1–2a makes up the introduction to the prologue. He takes v. 2b "I have given the land into their [sic] hands" as part of the story of Judah in vv. 2b–21 (K. Lawson Younger, *Judges, Ruth*, NIVAC, ed. Terry Muck [Grand Rapids: Zondervan, 2002], 64). His division, however, is problematic work because v. 2b is part of the Lord's speech. It is very unlikely that the narrative would be divided in the middle of a character's speech. On the other hand, Stone includes v. 3 as part of 1:1–2 (Joseph Coleson, Lawson G. Stone, and Jason Driesbach, *Joshua, Judges, Ruth*, Cornerstone Biblical Commentary, ed. Philip W. Comfort, vol. 3 [Carol Stream, IL: Tyndale House, 2012], 223). He argues that 1:1–3 introduce both the whole book and 1:4–21. However, v. 3 is different from vv. 1–2 in both content and form. Whereas in vv. 1–2 all Israel is in view, v. 3 shifts to two tribes only. The former reports the dialogue between all Israel and the Lord in a cultic setting. The latter captures Judah's request and Simeon's response in the context of forming a coalition. Whereas the former introduces the prologue, the latter starts off the subunit that focuses on the tribes.

in turn will enlighten one's understanding of the rest of the book. Niditch argues "to make sense of the first chapter of Judges is immediately to come to terms with challenges presented by the book as a whole."[2] It can also be said that to make sense of these first two verses is to come to terms with the challenges faced in the prologue itself. One's understanding of these two verses affects one's understanding of the prologue as a whole. Rather than approach these verses with a presupposition about the Israelites based on the end of Joshua, one must attempt to approach them with simple questions: What does the *exposition* tell us about the Israelites? What prompted their inquiry? What exactly is their inquiry?

Amit notes that an *exposition* "provides readers with the primary information and basic background materials to enable them to enter the world of the story, at least at the start."[3] She then lists three elements that an *exposition* may contain: (1) the central characters, (2) the temporal and/or geographical setting, or (3) "the prevailing conditions and customs in the story's setting."[4] The *exposition* of the prologue of Judges contains these three elements.

The central characters in the prologue are the Israelites. The *exposition* begins (1:1–2) and the *ending* closes (3:5–6) by speaking about them. The Israelites are the grammatical and the logical subjects of both the beginning and end of the prologue.

Despite the mention of individual tribes in 1:3–36, individual tribes are not the central characters of the prologue. Walsh notes:

> [i]ndividuals within the group are not differentiated and only the group itself has any real role . . . Occasionally, however – especially if the group's role is a bit more substantial – one member of the group will act as representative of the whole. That individual is not really a "character" in his or her own right, but is only, so to speak, the face of the group.[5]

---

2. Susan Niditch, *Judges: A Commentary*, OTL, ed. William P. Brown, Carol A. Newsom, and David L. Petersen (Louisville, KY: Westminster John Knox, 2008), 35.

3. Yairah Amit, *Reading Biblical Narratives: Literary Criticism and the Hebrew Bible*, trans. Yael Lotan (Minneapolis: Fortress, 2001), 33.

4. Ibid.

5. Jerome T. Walsh, *Old Testament Narrative: A Guide to Interpretation* (Louisville, KY: Westminster John Knox, 2009), 25.

The central characters in all of the prologue, including 1:3–36, are the Israelites as a nation. As the analysis of 1:3–36 will reveal, the author named the individual tribes to highlight the failure of all of Israel.

The *exposition* also offers the temporal setting in the phrase ויהי אחרי מות יהושע. When taken at face value, this phrase simply informs the reader that what follows took place after Joshua died. Scholars have noticed that this phrase means more than just what the translation of the words communicate. For Niditch, it "draws attention to the important events or narrative transition which are to follow."[6] For Chisholm, like Niditch, it "signals an important transition in the life of Israel. An important era had ended; a new challenge awaited the people."[7] Both of them see the phrase more as a transition. Younger, on the other hand, takes it as "a stylistic way of recapitulating briefly the previous book before interpreting it further."[8] Webb takes it as linking "what follows to what has preceded it . . . But the same words also separate what follows from what has gone before."[9]

Without reading into the phrase, the following three functions can be seen. First, it indicates the chronological order of events. The events in the book of Judges took place after Joshua's death. This first function is the most obvious meaning, and yet it plays an important role in identifying flashbacks that are from the lifetime of Joshua. The second function is found in the author's rhetoric throughout the prologue of Judges. The author, as will be argued repeatedly, compares the people and events in the book of Judges with those in the book of Joshua. If nothing else, the reader should be ready to read Judges in comparison with Joshua.[10] Third, the phrase shows that what comes after 1:1 is an important development in the story of the Israelites. This last function of the phrase will be made more clear in two of the flashbacks that the author uses in 2:6–10, and 2:22–3:4.

---

6. Niditch, *Judges*, 32 n.a.

7. Robert B. Chisholm, *A Commentary on Judges and Ruth*, Kregel Exegetical Library (Grand Rapids: Kregel, 2013), 119.

8. K. Lawson Younger, *Judges, Ruth*, NIVAC, ed. Terry Muck (Grand Rapids: Zondervan, 2002), 64.

9. Barry G. Webb, *The Book of Judges*, NICOT, ed. R. K. Harrison and Robert L. Hubbard (Grand Rapids: Eerdmans, 2012), 92–93.

10. See chapter 4 for a discussion of Judges as a sequel to Joshua.

The third element of the *exposition* is the "prevailing condition or custom in the story's setting."[11] According to the *exposition* the story is set at the beginning of the period of testing. Two things in the *exposition* suggest that the test has already began:

(1) Joshua is dead. The author views the death of Joshua as signaling the beginning of the testing period. The inquiry of the Israelites, "who will go up for us," suggests that not only Joshua, but even "the elders who outlived him" (cf. 2:10), are dead at this point.[12] As 2:6–10 will make evident, the events of chapter 1 could not have taken place while the elders were alive. The omission of the death of the elders was due to the author's need to emphasize not only the role Joshua played in the lives of the Israelites but also the literary function of his death.[13]

(2) Israel is at war. It is often argued that in these verses the Israelites are proactively inquiring of the Lord about Israel's task of completing the conquest now that Joshua is dead.[14] Gerhard Hauch, for instance, claims that these verses "come laden with the memory of YHWH's promise to drive out the remaining nations (Jos 23:4–5) and the memory of the Israelites [sic] inability to see through the Gibeonite guise because they failed to inquire of YHWH (Jos 9:14)."[15]

However, the author's use of שאל plus ביהוה, Judah's use of גורל and Bezek being the first battle field that Judah went to, suggest that Israel is facing an imminent enemy threat. The construction שאל plus ביהוה "X inquired of the Lord" occurs twelve times in the OT and these occurrences are found only in Judges and Samuel. The inquiry was made by the Israelites in Judges 1:1; 20:23, 27; 1 Samuel 10:22; Ahimelech in 1 Samuel 22:10; David in 1 Samuel 23:2, 4; 30:8; 2 Samuel 2:1; 5:19, 23; and Saul in 1 Samuel 28:6. Fuhs notes: "[T]he setting in life of the expression *šā'al beyhwh*

---

11. Amit, *Reading Biblical Narratives*, 33.
12. All Scripture translations in this work are the author's own.
13. See pp. 104–105.
14. Israel is seen positively in these verses, only to be found at fault beginning from v. 6 or even from v. 3 according to some scholars (Mark J. Boda, "Judges," in *Numbers to Ruth*, ed. Tremper Longman III and David E. Garland, rev. ed, vol. 2, Expositor's Bible Commentary [Grand Rapids: Zondervan, 2012], 1069).
15. Gerhard Hauch, "Text and Contexts: A Literary Reading of the Conquest Narrative (Jos 1–11)" (PhD diss., Princeton Theological Seminary, 1991), 188.

is the Yahweh war (9 of 12 times)."[16] The three exceptions are 1 Samuel 10:22; 22:10; and 2 Samuel 2:1. In these verses inquiry is directed to the Lord in a non-war context for some kind of guidance such as "where is X?" or "Where should I go?"

As Fuhs correctly noted, the other nine occurrences of the phrase שאל plus ביהוה are in the context of war but not necessarily "Yahweh war." What is interesting is that in all of these occurrences the inquirers came to the Lord in reaction to the threat of war. There is not a single instance where the inquirer was initiating a war.

In Judges 20:23 and 20:27 the Israelites inquired of the Lord in reaction to what the Benjamites did (this is clearly not a "Yahweh war"). In 1 Samuel 23:2 and 4, David inquired of the Lord twice when he had learned that the Philistines were fighting in Keilah. In 1 Samuel 28:6, Saul inquired of the Lord when he saw the camp of the Philistines that was at Shunem. In 1 Samuel 30:6, David inquired of the Lord because the Amalekites had attacked and destroyed Ziklag and had taken everyone captive. In 2 Samuel 5:19 and 23, David inquired of the Lord when the Philistines came to attack him and camped in the valley of Rephaim. In all of these instances the inquirer is reacting to the threat of war.

Auld interprets Judges 1:1–2 in light of other instances in Judges that use the root חלל "to begin":

> These verses anticipate the rather fuller questioning of God before and during the battle against Benjamin in chapter 20 (see especially vv. 18, 23, and 27–28). Who will have pride of place in the front line? Who will have the honour of making a beginning? This interest in priority, initiative, and getting things going is echoed at other points in the book too, like 10:18 – "Who is the man that will *begin* to fight against the Ammonites? He shall be head over all the inhabitants of Gilead." Then it is said during the promise of Samson's birth:"he shall *begin* to deliver Israel from the hand of the Philistines" (13:5).[17]

---

16. H. F. Fuhs, "שאל," in *TDOT*, ed. G. Johannes Botterweck, Helmer Ringgren, and Heinz-Josef Fabry, trans. Douglas W. Stott, vol. 14 (Grand Rapids: Eerdmans, 2004), 259.

17. A. Graeme Auld, *Joshua, Judges, and Ruth*, Daily Study Bible: Old Testament, ed. John C. L. Gibson (Louisville, KY: Westminster John Knox, 1984), 134.

In all of these instances that Auld mentions, however, the Israelites were not initiating a war but reacting to one. The honor is in being in the front line, not in initiating a war. Judges 10:7 speaks of how the Lord turned the Israelites over to the Philistines and the Ammonites. This is the context in light of which 10:18 and 13:5 should be read. Judges 1:1 is not as an exception. Here too the phrase שאל plus ביהוה implies that Israel is facing an imminent enemy threat.

One can make the same conclusion when looking at the use of גורל. A study of גורל reveals that it is used in verse 3 as a military allotment, rather than an allotted territory. In the Pentateuch גורל occurs only in Leviticus and Numbers. It is used with regard to only one topic in both books. In Leviticus 16:8–10 it is used with regard to the lot that determines which goat was for the Lord and which one was for Azazel. All of the occurrences in Numbers (26:52; 33:54; 34:13; 36:2–3) deal with the process of the allocation of land in Canaan but never to the land itself.

Within the former prophets גורל occurs only in Joshua and Judges. All of the occurrences in Joshua are within the sections dealing with land allotment (Josh 13–19, 21). Here גורל is a technical term referring to the processes of allotting the land, never to the allotted land itself. Van Dam quotes Numbers 36:2–3, Joshua 14:2, and Joshua 15:1 as instances where גורל is used to refer to "the land that has been acquired by the use of lot and thus connotes inheritance."[18] However, examining these three texts reveals that גורל is used to refer to the process of allotting the land, not to the allotted land itself.[19] The allotted land itself is referred to with נחלה in Joshua.

The three other occurrences of גורל are found in the book of Judges – twice in 1:3 and once in 20:9. Niditch understands the גורל in 20:9 as referring to "a military allotment or enlistment roll," but she takes the one at 1:3 as referring to "a portion of territory, an inheritance believed to be

---

18. Cornelis Van Dam, "גורל," in *NIDOTTE*, ed. Willem A. VanGemeren, vol. 1 (Grand Rapids: Zondervan, 1997), 826.

19. A translation of Num 36:2–3 can show that גורל is used for the process, not the land: "They said, 'The Lord commanded my Lord to give the land as inheritance (בנחלה) by lot (בגורל) to the Israelites and my Lord was commanded by the Lord to give the inheritance of Zelophehad our brother to his daughters. Now when they marry from among the sons of the tribes of the Israelites, the inheritance from the inheritance (נחלתן מנחלת) of our father will be reduced and will be added upon the inheritance of the tribe they marry into and it will be reduced from our allotted inheritance.'"

assigned by divine designation."²⁰ The use of גורל as indicated above, its undebatable use in 20:9 as a military allotment, and the imminent threat in the context of 1:1–7 indicate that its use in 1:3 is also to refer to Judah's military allotment. In using the term, Judah was asking Simeon to go with him into the battle as determined by the military allotment. Judah then promised to do the same when the lot would fall on Simeon. The fact that there was another lot in 20:9 shows that Judah was speaking of the possibility for another tribe to be elected by lot for another military campaign. This interpretation is also supported by Judah's statement regarding his purpose: ונלחמה "so that we may fight." This was the same purpose for the Israelites in 1:2, להלחם "to fight." What is clear in both is seeking help to fight back an imminent enemy.

Besides the use of שאל plus ביהוה and גורל, identification of the first place that Judah went to suggests that Israel's inquiry was for help to fight back the imminent enemy threat. The first place Judah went for battle was at Bezek. The only other time Bezek is mentioned is in 1 Samuel 11:8. Based on Saul's statement here (i.e. a calculation of how long it takes him to go from Bezek to Jabesh), Bezek has been identified as Khirbet Ibzik or Khirbet Salhab.²¹ Garstang argues that "the introduction of Perizzites into the narrative seems also to point in the same general direction, for these people are encountered elsewhere only as inhabiting the wooded highlands to the north and east of Shechem."²² Neither of these sites was part of the territory allotted to either Judah or Simeon, as they are far to the north.²³ Butler asks: "If this [Khirbet Ibzik or Khirbet Salhab] is the correct location for Bezek, it brings mystery into the narrative. Why were Judah and Simeon so far north?"²⁴

Several proposals have been given in answer to such a question. Amit proposes, ". . . this may be a case of a war waged by the northern tribes which

---

20. Niditch, *Judges*, 33.

21. Adam Zertal, "*Bezek*," in *ABD*, ed. David Noel Freedman, vol. 1 (New York: Doubleday, 1992), 717–718.

22. John Garstang, *Joshua–Judges: The Foundations of the Bible* (Grand Rapids: Kregel, 1978), 207–208.

23. Serge Frolov, *Judges*, FOTL, ed. Rolf P. Knierim and Marvin A. Sweeney, vol. 18 (Grand Rapids: Eerdmans, 2013), 42.

24. Trent C. Butler, *Judges*, WBC, ed. Bruce M. Metzger et al., vol. 8 (Nashville, TN: Thomas Nelson, 2009), 21.

Judah claimed for itself, possibly because of the similarity between the name Adoni-bezek and 'Adoni-zedek,' who was the king of Jerusalem during the conquest, or to present itself as a tribe which also warred on behalf of other tribes."[25] Aharoni claims: "Judah evidently belongs to the later wave of conquest which entered Canaan about the middle of the thirteenth century . . . That is, the Judahites destroyed one of the Canaanite cities in the region of Manasseh when they passed through the Ephraimite hill country."[26] Zertal offers the following observation:

> The historical background of the Bezek battle against the Canaanites is not clear. It is possible that clans of Judah and Simeon moved up from the Jordan Valley to be met at Bezek by the Canaanites, and from there they continued S as a part of an overall movement of Israelite clans from the N mountains to Jerusalem and the Judahite territory.[27]

The best explanation, however, for why Judah and Simeon went so far north to fight an enemy in an area which belonged to neither of them is found when one considers what the Israelites were inquiring of the Lord. As argued above Israel was facing an imminent enemy threat. Judah was elected to lead that battle against such enemy. Frolov rightly concludes, "The only way to make sense of this move is to surmise that the Judahites, aided by the Simeonites, start by attacking an enemy of all Israel."[28]

Therefore, the battle at Bezek also confirms that Israel was not initiating a war but reacting to one. What should be considered is how the Canaanites would react to the death of Joshua. If during his lifetime nations in both the south and north tried to push Israel out of Canaan but failed because of the leadership of Joshua, would the nations sit quietly after Israel's leader died? The answer is a resounding "no." The Canaanites would try to take advantage of Joshua's death. Indeed they did. They were ready to fight Israel and were waiting at Bezek. Stevenson agrees:

---

25. Yairah Amit, *The Book of Judges: The Art of Editing*, BIS, ed. R. Alan Culpepper and Rolf Rendtorff, vol. 38 (Leiden: Brill, 1999), 145, n. 31.

26. Yohanan Aharoni, *The Land of the Bible: A Historical Geography*, trans. A. F. Rainey (Philadelphia, PA: Westminister, 1967), 197.

27. Zertal, "Bezek," 718.

28. Frolov, *Judges*, 46.

A continuation of conquest wars would be necessary because it appears that "after the death of Joshua" (1:1) the Canaanites revived against a weakened and complacent Israel, who simply did not see the urgency of carrying out the absolute *herem* law, much less the other requirements of Yahweh regarding their interaction with the Canaanites (Deut 7:15, 16).[29]

In summary, it can be said that the prevailing situation, which the *exposition* states or implies, is that Israel is at the beginning of the period of testing. The test began after the death of Joshua. It also began with a threat of a common enemy which would face Israel at Bezek.

The *exposition* also hints at the purpose of the test. The *intention* of the Lord in putting Israel to the test is captured in 1:2 in his promise to give Judah the land. Though Israel's inquiry was prompted by the imminent enemy threat at Bezek, the Lord's *intention* for Israel was not simply to defeat the imminent enemy but to engage in a follow up conquest to take possession of their allotted land. When looking at Joshua, except for the battle against Jericho and Ai, both the southern and northern campaigns were reactions to a war initiated by the Canaanites. Israel started with a battle against the common enemy followed by conquest of the land. The Lord expects Israel to engage in the conquest of the land after fighting the common enemy at Bezek.

The *exposition* leaves the readers wondering: Would the Israelites *go up* to fight back against their imminent enemy? Would they, after fighting the imminent enemy, engage in a follow up battle to *take possession of* their allotted territories? These questions prompt the reader to keep reading.

Complication: Israel in the Middle of the Test (1:3–36)

After the *exposition*, the next stage in the plot structure of a narrative is *complication*. This is the stage that captures the events that brought about a change in the state of the characters or the situations described or implied

---

29. Jeffery S. Stevenson, "Judah's Successes and Failures in Holy War: An Exegesis of Judges 1:1–20." *ResQ* 44, no. 1 (2002): 46.

in the *exposition*.[30] The *complication* explains how the state of the Israelites changed from what was seen in the *exposition* (1:1–2) to what will be seen in the *change* (2:1–5). Without the *complication* one cannot understand the accusation of the messenger of the Lord in 2:1–3 nor truly evaluate Israel's response in 2:4–5.

The *complication* runs from verse 3 through the end of the chapter. Since 2:1 speaks of all Israel, as opposed to individual tribes on whom 1:3–36 focuses, 2:1 should be seen as beginning a new subsection in the single narrative of 1:1–3:6.

Though 1:3–36 is narrative in broad terms, identifying the narrow classification of its genre contributes to a proper exegesis of this text. Younger takes it as a conquest account that can be compared to the Assyrian summary inscriptions.[31] Some scholars, on the other hand, take only parts of these verses as a conquest account or report. Frolov takes only verses 1–26 as a "*story-shaped conquest account* or *conquest quasi-account*"[32] and sees verses 27–33 as a *list*.[33] Chisholm and Webb take only verses 27–36 as *conquest report*.[34] Niditch objects by noting the difference between Judges 1 and the Assyrian summary inscriptions – whereas Judges 1 uses third person reports, the Assyrian summary inscriptions use first person.

Judges 1:3–36 does fit the form of a conquest report despite some obvious differences with the Assyrian summary inscriptions. These verses report the conquest account of the Israelites by listing each tribe's success and/or failure. As Frolov rightly noted, conquest accounts and lists share common characteristics "in their tendency to string the notices on specific victories without attempting to relate them to each other or to arrange them in a meaningful fashion."[35] There are several signals in these verses that mark them as a list.

---

30. Amit, *Reading Biblical Narratives*, 47.

31. K. Lawson Younger, "Judges 1 in Its Near Eastern Literary Context," in *Faith, Tradition, and History: Old Testament Historiography in Its Near Eastern Context*, ed. A. R. Millard, James K. Hoffmeier, and David W. Baker (Winona Lake, IN: Eisenbrauns, 1994), 208–227.

32. Frolov, *Judges*, 41.

33. Ibid., 60.

34. Chisholm, *Judges and Ruth*, 118. Webb, *Book of Judges*, 118.

35. Frolov, *Judges*, 40. Frolov uses this argument to distinguish vv. 1–26 from vv. 27–33, stating that in the former, "implicit causal links can be traced between all military campaigns recounted in Judg 1:1–26."

The first signal is the report about Simeon in verse 3. At first sight, the verse looks as if it simply introduces the conquest report of Judah (vv. 4–20). However, two observations can be made against such a view:

(1) Although Judah's inquiry is given in a speech form, which marks it as a *scenic narrative*, Simeon's response is not.[36] Rather, it is narrated as a report. The narrator chooses to capture Simeon's response by narrating what he did, not what he said. This takes the reader from the *scene* where the dialogue between the two tribes took place to a summary report of Simeon's participation in the battle. (2) Despite the statement, "Simeon went with him," the narrator adds, "Judah went up." The latter is implied in the former. The logical continuation of "Simeon went with him" is "and the Lord gave the Canaanites and Perizzites in their hands." The addition of "Judah went up" signals that the narrator is interested in structuring the report by listing each tribe's contribution and/or lack of it.

(2) The second signal is the use of גם "too" in verse 22. This word is "a mark of coordination" that connects the *going up* of the house of Joseph with that of Judah.[37] These two tribes are the only two that *went up*. Though Simeon *went* (הלך) with Judah, the word *went up* (עלה) is not used.

(3) The third signal is the asyndetic constructions in verses 30–33. The reports about the tribes of Zebulun (v. 20), Asher (v. 31), and Naphtali (v. 33) begin with an asyndetic construction. The use of *waw* in verse 27 and verse 29 is due to the fact that in these verses the failure of the two tribes are contrasted with their success which is reported in verses 22–26. The *house of Joseph*, Ephraim and Manasseh, were portrayed in a *seemingly* positive manner as having *gone up* against Bethel. In verse 27 and verse 29 their failure is being reported as a contrast to the positive portrayal. The use of *wayyiqtol* in listing the report about Simeon, Judah, house of Joseph and Dan suggests that these are developments after the death of Joshua. The negative reports are also developments after Joshua's death but the change from *wayyiqtol* to *qatal* is due to the presence of לא.

---

36. A *scenic narrative* is a narrative that contains direct speech. Cf. Gregory T. K. Wong, *Compositional Strategy of the Book of Judges: An Inductive, Rhetorical Study*, VTSup, vol. 111 (Leiden: Brill, 2006), 145–146.

37. Robert E. Longacre, *Joseph – A Story of Divine Providence: A Text Theoretical and Textlinguistic Analysis of Genesis 37 and 39–48*, 2nd ed. (Winona Lake, IN: Eisenbrauns, 2003), 100.

The above three signals support the argument that 1:3–36 is a conquest report. This reporting-list, however, differs from other conquest reports, such as Joshua 10:28–43, in that both the success and failure of the tribes are reported, that is, that the tribes went up (עלה) to fight and/or whether or not they took possession of (ירשׁ) their allotted inheritance. The two are not necessarily identical. The former is supposed to lead to the latter. This difference from other conquest reports that report only success is, at least partly, because 1:3–36 is a *complication*.

As discussed above, the *exposition* hinted at two prevailing themes as found in the inquiry of the Israelites and in the response of the Lord: *going up* (עלה) and *taking possession of* (ירשׁ). And as Amit rightly noted, "[t]he elements making exposition are usually quite functional, serving the process of events."[38] Therefore, the events narrated in the *complication* are directly tied to the two themes that were mentioned in the *exposition*. These two themes are used in conjunction with the tribal names to form the structure of the *complication*.

The conquest report which is structured as a list can be summarized as below:

(1) Simeon *went* with Judah . . . (v. 3)
(2) Judah
    2.1 He *went up* . . . (vv. 4–16)
    2.2 But he did not *take possession of* . . . (vv. 17–20)
(3) Sons of Benjamin did not *take possession of* . . . (v. 21)
(4) House of Joseph[39]
    4.1 They too *went up* . . . (vv. 22–26)
    4.2 But they did not *take possession of* . . . (vv. 27–29)
(5) The rest of Israel did not *take possession of* . . . (vv. 30–36)

The list begins with a summary report for each tribe followed by statements that clarify the summary. Chisholm notes that verses 27–36 are organized with a summary statement first and then explanatory statements.[40] This is true of all in verses 3–36, and not just verses 27–36. This is particularly clear with the sons of Benjamin in verse 20. Like the other tribes in verses

---

38. Amit, *Reading Biblical Narratives*, 34.
39. This term refers to both Ephraim and Manasseh. So Frolov, *Judges*, 58.
40. Chisholm, *Judges and Ruth*, 114, n. 16.

30–36, the summary statement is only about *failure to take possession of the allotted land*. There is one summary statement for each tribe followed by additional statements that clarify or qualify the summary.

As for Judah and the house of Joseph, the summary statement is about both *going up* and *not taking possession of the allotted land*. Therefore, two summary statements can be found for each of these two tribes. For both of them, the first summary statement is regarding *going up*, whereas the second summary statement is regarding *taking possession of their allotted land*.

The report about Judah begins with a summary statement in verse 4 regarding his *going up*. Lindars comments, "[i]t seems best to treat v. 4 as editorial introduction to Judah's conquests, based on the tradition which follows in vv. 5–7; v. 8 as a separate tradition, added to the next item in Judah's progress."[41] Verse 4 summarizes what verses 5–7 elaborate. Verses 8–16 are flashbacks that are meant to help the reader evaluate the *seemingly positive* portrayal of Judah in verses 4–7.[42]

The mention of Simeon in verse 17 indicates that verses 17–18 continue with a summary report of a follow up battle which Judah and Simeon were engaged in after they fought the imminent enemy of all Israel at Bezek. According to Webb the "reappearance of Simeon suggests that the larger unit that opened in verse 3 is also coming to a close."[43] However, the report does not close for three more verses. The best way to see its function is as *resumptive* of the report of the coalition of Judah and Simeon that was interrupted in verses 8–16. After Judah and Simeon brought Adoni-bezek to Jerusalem, they now move to Zephath. The transition from the plural בני יהודה in verses 8–16 to the singular יהודה is another signal that the story is now picking up from verse 7. As in the case of verses 3–7, the singular form of the tribal name is used here in verses 17–19. In addition, whenever each individual tribe is the grammatical subject of the verbs in these verses, the verb is also in the singular form. However, when the coalition is the grammatical subject, then the verbs change to the plural form.

---

41. Barnabas Lindars, *Judges 1–5: A New Translation and Commentary*, ed. A. D. H. Mayes (Edinburgh: T&T Clark, 1995), 16.

42. See pp. 91–102 for a discussion of these verses as flashback.

43. Webb, *Book of Judges*, 107.

Sasson seems to agree, though with a slight difference: "v. 17 actually rehearses information provided earlier on Judah making common cause with Simeon. It thus strives to textually leapfrog the material on Adoni-bezeq and on Achsah sandwiched between 1:4 and 1:16."[44] Sasson takes the textual leapfrog from verse 3 to verse 17 because he does not consider Simeon to have been part of the battle against Adoni-bezek. He argues that the narrative ignores the coalition of Simeon and Judah in verses 4–16 until it is picked up again in verse 17.[45] He adds: "Henceforth, plurals attached to nouns and verbal forms seem associated solely with Judah and its warriors."[46] The use of the plural in verses 4–7 refers to the coalition of Judah and Simeon, not to Judah alone.[47] The use of a singular verb for Judah in verse 4a cannot be reconciled with the plural verbs and pronouns in these verses. The correct way to understand the change is to take them as referring to both Judah and Simeon.

Therefore, verses 17–18 are summary reports of follow up battles of Judah aided by Simeon to take possession of their allotted territories. The report concludes with a summary evaluation in verses 19–20.[48] According to verse 19 their victory is seen as partial, despite the Lord's enabling presence. The narrator introduces a flashback in verse 20 to Caleb's victory in taking possession of Hebron to show his total victory, unlike the present generation of his tribe.[49]

The report about the house of Joseph begins with a summary statement in verse 22.[50] This summary report is then elaborated with the scenic narrative of verses 23–26. Just as Judah's *seemingly positive* conquest report concluded with a negative summary statement, the narrator concludes the house of Joseph's *seemingly positive* report in verses 22–26 with negative

---

44. Jack M. Sasson, *Judges 1–12: A New Translation with Introduction and Commentary*, AYB, ed. John J. Collins, vol. 6D (New Haven: Yale University Press, 2014), 157.

45. Ibid., 129.

46. Ibid.

47. See the discussion on בני יהודה on pp. 92–95.

48. So Daniel I. Block, *Judges, Ruth*, NAC, ed. E. Ray Clendenen, vol. 6 (Nashville, TN: Broadman & Holman, 1999), 99.

49. See pp. 101–102 for a discussion of this verse as a flashback.

50. So Wong, *Compositional Strategy*, 150.

summary statements for each of the two tribes that make up the house of Joseph in verses 27–29.

Therefore, 1:3–36 is a conquest account that lists the tribes' success and/or failure which began with the report of the battle against Israel's common and immense enemy at Bezek. The tribes' success, if any, is first reported followed by a negative report of their failure. Each report, either positive or negative, is first summarized, followed by qualifying statements or scenic narratives when the summary is positive. The summary statements regarding each tribe make up the storyline of the conquest account. When the scenic reports and other supplementary materials are taken out of it, the following summary report remains:

> ³ᵇSimeon went with him [Judah]. ⁴ᵃJudah went up ⁴ᵇand the Lord handed the Canaanites and Perizzites in to their hands ⁴and they struck them at Bezek – ten thousand men. ¹⁷ᵃJudah went with Simeon his brother ¹⁷ᵇand they struck the Canaanites who lived in Zephath. ¹⁸ᵃJudah captured Gaza and its territory, and Ashkelon and its territory, and Ekron and its territory. ¹⁹ᵃYahweh was with Judah ¹⁹ᵇand he disposed the hill country ¹⁹ᶜbut he did not dispossess those living in the valley because they had chariots of iron. ²¹ᵃThe Jebusites who were living in Jerusalem – the sons of Benjamin did not dispossess. ²²ᵃThe house of Joseph, too, went up against Bethel ²²ᵇ*and Yahweh was with them.* ²⁷ᵃManasseh did not take possession of Beth Shan, and its surroundings, Taanach and its surroundings, nor those living in Dor and its surroundings, nor those who live in Ibleam and its surroundings, nor those living in Megiddo and its surroundings. ²⁷ᵇThe Canaanites managed to remain in this land. ²⁸ᵃWhenever Israel was strong, ²⁸ᵇthey put the Canaanites to forced labor. ²⁸ᶜbut certainly did not dispossess them. ²⁹ᵃEphraim did not dispossess the Canaanites who were living in Gezer. ²⁹ᵇThe Canaanites lived in their midst in Gezer. ³⁰ᵃZebulun did not dispossess those who were living in Kitron and those who were living in Nahalol. ³⁰ᵇThe Canaanites lived in their midst ³⁰ᶜand they became forced labor. ³¹Asher did not dispossess those who were living in Acco and those who

were living in Sidon and Ahlab nor did they take possession of Achzib nor Helbah nor Aphik nor Rehob. ³²Asher lived in the midst of the Canaanites who were living in the land because he did not dispossess them. ³³ᵃNaphtali did not dispossess the inhabitants of Beth-shemesh nor the inhabitants of Beth-anath ³³ᵇand they lived among the Canaanites who were living in the land. ³³ᶜNow the inhabitants of Beth-shemesh and Beth-anath were for him for forced labor. ³⁴The Amorites forced the sons of Dan to go to the hill country for they did not allow them to go to the plain. ³⁵ᵃThe Amorites managed to remain in Harheres, Aijalon, and Shaalbim. ³⁵ᵇThen the hand of the sons of Joseph became strong ³⁵ᶜand the Amorites became forced labor. ³⁶ *The border of the Amorites was from the ascent of Akrabbim, from Sela and on up.*⁵¹

Judges 1:3–36 is a complication first of all because it reports both the success and failure of the tribes. The complication can also be observed, not only in the report of both success and failure together, but also in the way both the seemingly positive reports and the negative reports are described or qualified. A close look at both the positive and negative reports helps clarify this point. The author uses different literary devices (e.g. flashback and allusion) to highlight the complication.

Simeon

The author has not directly commented on whether or not Simeon took possession of his inheritance. The only instance when Simeon is the subject of a verb is in verse 3: "Simeon *went* with him." This is a reference to his joining Judah in the battle against the coalition of the Canaanites and the Perrizzites. They both were the subjects of the verbs in verses 4b–7. Both were responsible for the victory over the common enemy.

The only other mention of Simeon is in verse 17. Here Simeon is not the subject of a verb. The summary report of verse 17 begins and ends with

---

51. Wong attempts to isolate what he refers to as "a surprisingly lucid and relatively coherent conquest report" by isolating the summary statements that are used to report from the descriptive and scenic material (Ibid., 145–150). The only major difference in the approach of the present author and that of Wong is that the present author views 1:8–16 and 1:20 as flashbacks.

Judah. The third masculine singular verb at the end of verse 17 refers to Judah. If it referred to Simeon, the author would have clearly indicated the change in the subject, as the author has done so far whenever he introduced a new subject. The chiastic structure of the *wayyiqtols* of this verse shows that "he" refers to Judah.

    A   וילך יהודה . . . "Judah went . . ."
        B   ויכו . . . "they struck . . ."
        B'   ויחרימו . . . "they destroyed . . ."
    A'   ויקרא . . . "he called . . ."

Though Simeon partook in the battle against Zephath, he is here overshadowed by Judah. Here too Simeon is given credit for joining Judah but is not portrayed as a tribe that is proactively seeking to take possession of its allotted land. Unlike Judah who was engaged in the conquest without Simeon in verse 18, Simeon did not engage in the conquest without Judah.

Judah

The report on Judah is given in two stages. In the first stage, Judah's victory in the battle at Bezek is given. The battle report begins with Judah's request addressed to Simeon so that Simeon may join him. The author does not intend this request to be a negative comment.[52] As it will be clear from 2:22, the measurement of success or failure of any tribe should be whether or not they passed the test of dispossessing the inhabitants from the territories allotted to the tribes. A reader may observe one tribe doing better than another; however, the author does not compare tribes.

Joined by Simeon, Judah *went up* and won the battle against the coalition of Canaanites and Perizzites. Then Judah mutilated Adoni-bezek, who was the leader of the coalition. By the Canaanite standard – as Adoni-bezek confessed – Judah was victorious. However, their task was to destroy all the inhabitants. Keeping Adoni-bezek alive is clearly an indication of Judah's failure.

Judah then brought Adoni-bezek to Jerusalem, which ended the battle report on Bezek. As Gullaume rightly noted, "[a]s the conquest of Jerusalem isn't mentioned, the simplest answer is that Juda [*sic*] was at home in

---

52. Cf. Stevenson, "Judah's Successes and Failures," 46.

Jerusalem before the campaign and brought its prisoner back to its home base."[53] This then allows the reader to understand why Judah brought the mutilated Adoni-bezek to Jerusalem. Gaster argues that the statement "cut off his thumbs and big toes 'was' designed to prevent his ever again taking up arms or marching to war."[54] This does not answer why they did not kill him, since killing him would seem to be a better option if their intention was to keep him from taking up arms. A better explanation is given by Boling, who suggests that their purpose was "instilling fear at Jerusalem."[55] He then adds, "Similar practices involving decapitated bodies are mentioned in the Mari texts and in classical sources and are widespread among preliterate and semiliterate cultures."[56]

The goal of instilling fear, however, was not for a new battle against Jerusalem. From the words of Adoni-bezek himself, one can assume that the goal of instilling fear was to rule one's subjects. Judah was already living with the Jebusites in Jerusalem according to Joshua 15:63. It seems, then, that Judah wanted to continue living with the Jebusites, but at the same time wanted to do so by earning their respect and fear. To that end, Judah kept a mutilated king alive.[57] The verb that closes the anecdote on Adoni-bezek is וַיָּמָת (v. 7). When compared to Joshua, who in Joshua 11:17 captured kings and executed them (וַיְמִיתֵם), the use of the *qal* stem as opposed to the *hiphil* signals that the death of Adoni-bezek was not tied to Judah. Judah failed to follow in the footsteps of its leader. It also failed to obey the Lord's direct command to destroy the Canaanites by keeping Adoni-bezek alive.

Keeping Adoni-bezek alive was only one of the weaknesses of Judah. The lack of any attempt to dispossess the Jebusites, with whom they lived in Jerusalem (Josh 15:63), is another failure. The author will evaluate Judah's

---

53. Philippe Guillaume, "An Anti-Judean Manifesto in Judges 1?" *BN* 95 (1998): 13.

54. Theodor H. Gaster, *Myth, Legend, and Custom in the Old Testament: A Comparative Study with Chapters from Sir James G. Frazer's Folklore in the Old Testament* (Gloucester, MA: Peter Smith), 416.

55. Robert G. Boling, *Judges: Introduction, Translation, and Commentary*, AB, ed. William Foxwell Albright and David Noel Freedman, vol. 6A (Garden City, NY: Doubleday, 1975), 55.

56. Ibid.

57. Adoni-bezek's statement is best understood as a request, which Judah granted. Adoni-bezek had mutilated other kings, as Judah did. However, by confessing that he kept the kings alive, he seems to "request" that Judah might keep him alive too.

actions using a flashback that runs in verses 8–16. The flashback will add to the complication by overshadowing the present day Judah with a better picture of their ancestors.

The second stage of the report on Judah is found in verses 17–20. Here again, Judah joined Simeon. Unlike the report in the first stage, which simply records victory over the enemy, here Judah not only defeated the enemy but also took possession of Zephath and three other cities. The battle at Bezek was meant to initiate a battle against all the foreigners who live in the allotted inheritances of each tribe. This second stage ends with positive and negative comments that show Judah's partial success. The positive comment is that Judah took possession of the hill country. The negative comment is that Judah did not take possession of the coastal plain.

The negative comment implies that Judah achieved only partial success by taking possession of three coastal plain cities. In light of this, the positive comment about taking possession of the hill country should be understood not as a reference to Hebron and Debir that Caleb had taken possession of, but as referring to the rest of the hill country that was part of Judah's allotment as mentioned in Joshua 15:48–60. The implication, whether or not this was historically accurate, is that Judah took possession of the entire hill country that was allotted to him but not the coastal plain. Judah's weakness here is also hinted at by the author when he changed his point of view to that of the Judahites.[58] By mentioning the Lord's presence with Judah, the author not only interprets their success as being the result of the Lord's presence, he also highlights Judah's failure – Judah did not always depend on the Lord. Despite the Lord's enabling presence, Judah feared the iron chariots of the coastal people and refrained from taking possession of their allotted land.

The author will use Caleb, in a flashback (v. 20), as a standard to measure the success of Judah. Although Caleb took possession of all of the land that was allotted to him, Judah did not. Judah after the death of Joshua seems to be characterized by failure to take total possession of his allotment by (1) letting the inhabitants live (vv. 3–7), and (2) failing to take possession of all of his allotted lands (vv. 18–19).

---

58. Cf. Chisholm, *Judges and Ruth*, 130.

House of Joseph

The report on the house of Joseph is covered in verses 22–29. Like the report on Judah, the report on the house of Joseph is given in two stages. The first involves a battle against Bethel. By using עלה, the narrator portrays the house of Joseph positively. Instead of using an evaluative flashback, as he did for Judah in verses 8–16, or changing the point of view in verse 19, the narrator uses *allusion* in verses 22–26 to allow the reader to evaluate the *seemingly positive* report on the house of Joseph. This *allusion*, triggered by a mention of spies, is to the conquest of Jericho. Since the command to destroy Jericho was given, the comparison between the two accounts cannot be with regard to the extent of the destruction. Jericho was a total destruction. Bethel, however, still stands. Other than making some observations on the difference between the two accounts, it is difficult to find the weakness of the house of Joseph. The command was to take possession of the land, and they did. The clear report on the failure of the house of Joseph is given in the second report (vv. 27–29). Despite their success in defeating Bethel, the house of Joseph – both Manasseh and Ephraim – failed to take possession of their allotted land.

The rest of the tribes also failed to dispossess their allotted land. The author further highlights the failure of these tribes by adding two qualifying statements: (1) They lived with the inhabitants of the land. Not only were they hesitant to dispossess the inhabitants from their allotted land, they also lived with them. The manner of living with the inhabitants changes from the inhabitants living among the tribes (so Manasseh, 1:27; Ephraim, 1:29; and Zebulun, 1:30) to the tribes living among the inhabitants (so Asher, 1:32; and Naphtali, 1:33) to a tribe being forced out of their allotted land (Dan, 1:34).

(2) Though the above qualifying statement implies that the tribes were weak, the second qualifying statement indicates otherwise. The statement that they forced the inhabitants to do hard labor is found for all tribes except for Ephraim and Asher. For example, in the midst of the report on the failure of Manasseh, the author inserts an embedded paragraph that captures what was true of all of Israel. He notes, "Whenever Israel was strong, they put the Canaanites to forced labor but certainly did not dispossess them" (1:28). This suggests that though there were times that Israel as a nation

gained military strength, it did not translate this strength into obedience by dispossessing the Canaanites. Therefore, the author clearly indicates that all of Israel failed to take initiative to dispossess the inhabitants from their allotted land despite their military strength.

Summary

In reading the *exposition* the reader is prompted to ask: Would the Israelites *go up* to fight their imminent enemy? Would they follow this up with an attempt to *take possession of* their allotted territories? These questions were answered in the *complication* with what looks like a "yes" and "no." The report about the sons of Benjamin, Zebulun, Naphtali, Asher, and Dan answers the question with a resounding "No!" However, the report on the tribe of Simeon, the sons of Judah, and house of Joseph was given with both "yes," and "no." These tribes did take possession of some of the allotted land but none totally took possession of all the territories given to them. The next few verses take the complication into a climax. Webb concludes:

> As chapter 1 progresses it gradually becomes apparent that the expectations created in the opening verses will not be fulfilled. Conquest gives way to co-existence as the Israelites begin to come to terms with entrenched Canaanites. The full significance of this does not become clear until the Israelites are confronted by Yahweh's messenger in 2:1–5 where the issue of "making an agreement with the inhabitants of the land" is taken up directly. It is in this confrontation that the first climax of the narrative is reached.[59]

Change: Warning for Israel's Failure (2:1–10)

The *change* is the third stage in the development of the plot of a narrative. Judges 2:1–5 constitute the *change* in the narrative plot of the prologue. These verses capture the change in the state of the characters from what was stated or implied in the *exposition*.

---

59. Barry G. Webb, *The Book of the Judges: An Integrated Reading*, JSOTSup Series, vol. 44 (Eugene, OR: Wipf & Stock, 2008), 116.

According to Amit the *change* is "the heart of the story."⁶⁰ This is true of 2:1–5 for two reasons: (1) It captures the climax of the *complication*. (2) It is a Janus construction that looks back to the *complication* (1:3–36) and looks ahead to the *unraveling* (2:11–3:4). Block calls it a hinge between chapter 1 and 2:6–23.⁶¹ The play on words with עלה and the content of the accusation is said to suggest that it looks back and is a continuation of what precedes. The fact that it is a warning, which would become true in 2:11–21, relates it to what follows.

According to Frolov, the genre of 2:1–3 is prophetic announcement of judgment.⁶² There is, however, no judgment here. The speech best fits a lawsuit,⁶³ more specifically, a covenant-lawsuit, which "typically refers to YHWH's case against Israel for violation of the terms of the covenant between YHWH and Israel."⁶⁴ Common elements of a lawsuit are:⁶⁵

(1) Description of the scene of trial
(2) Accusation
(3) Defense
(4) Judgment

The first element is present in 2:1. Here the scene of the trial is given as Bochim, whose etiology would be given later. Along with the description of the trial scene, the author mentions the angel's movement from Gilgal. Martin comments on the rhetorical function of the mention of Gilgal: "In light of the associations of Gilgal as Joshua's victory headquarters and the

---

60. Amit, *Reading Biblical Narratives*, 47.
61. Block, *Judges, Ruth*, 109.
62. Cf. Frolov, *Judges*, 74.
63. George W. Ramsey, "Speech-Forms in Hebrew Law and Prophetic Oracles," *JBL* 96, no. 1 (1977): 45–46. For an argument against referring to these verses as a lawsuit, see, Michael De Roche, "Yahweh's Rîb Against Israel: A Reassessment of the So-Called "Prophetic Lawsuit" in the Preexilic Prophets," *JBL* 102, no. 4 (1983): 563–574. He suggests calling them "Rîb Oracles." He argues that these oracles involve only Yahweh and Israel; whereas, lawsuits involve three parties. He describes Rîb Oracles as those that describe "the ordinary experience of confronting someone with a complaint, there is no need to invoke judicial forms to interpret these passages and then try to formulate reasons why the oracles deviate from these same forms" (Ibid., 571).
64. Marvin A. Sweeney, *Isaiah 1–39: With an Introduction to Prophetic Literature*, FOTL, ed. Rolf P. Knierim and Gene M. Tucker, vol. 16 (Grand Rapids: Eerdmans, 1996), 541.
65. Kirsten Nielsen, *Yahweh as Prosecutor and Judge: An Investigation of the Prophetic Lawsuit (Rîb-Pattern)*, JSOTSup Series, vol. 9 (Sheffield: University of Sheffield Press, 1978), 25.

place of Israel's renewal and blessing, the movement of the angel of Yahweh from Gilgal to Bochim recalls the victories of Joshua as they stand in sharp contrast to the defeats just recounted in Judges Chapter 1."[66] Chisholm gives a better, though related, explanation by saying that "it suggests that the God who sent him was still residing in or had retreated to Joshua's campsite at the entry point of the land. This in turn reinforces the point that the conquest was far from complete and suggests that Israel's hold on the land was still quite tenuous."[67] Though Israel was no longer engaged in battle to take possession of the land, the Lord was still at Gilgal waiting for his people to continue the task of the conquest.

The second element of the lawsuit here is the accusation. Having reminded the reader that the Lord was waiting on Israel in Gilgal to finish the task of the conquest, he now spells out the accusation clearly. The accusation is stated as: "you have not listened to my voice. What is this you have done?" The Lord clearly spells out what voice they disobeyed. The voice refers to what he had said to them after they got into the land of Canaan. The Lord had told Israel, "You too shall not make any covenant with the inhabitants of this land; you shall break their altars" (v. 2). The accusation implies that the people had already made covenants with the inhabitants of the land and that they did not destroy their altars. None of these failures is clearly reported in the complication. In Judges 1, whenever the author spoke of the inhabitants of the land living with any of the tribes of Israel or the tribes of Israel living among the Canaanites, he could be suggesting that the two lived together as a result of a covenant they made with each other. The same statement could also signal that they did not destroy the altars. The best way to understand the accusation is, however, by taking it as the climax of the failure of all Israel to take possession of the land.

The third element, the defense, is missing. As mentioned earlier, it shows that the people had no excuse. The accusation does not make any distinction between a tribe who achieved partial success and one that did not. None of the tribes, not even Judah, defended themselves. A reader may clap for Judah, but the Lord would not. The test was not to take only parts of the land. All

---

66. Lee Roy Martin, "From Gilgal to Bochim: The Narrative Significance of the Angel of Yahweh in Judges 2:1," *Journal for Semitics* 18, no. 2 (2009): 339.

67. Chisholm, *Judges and Ruth*, 138.

of the tribes equally failed to listen to the Lord's voice. The fact that there is no distinction between the tribes here is also conveying the unity of Israel. The report in Judges 1 does not suggest a disintegrated Israel. The author's choice to focus on each tribe is to show that every single one of them failed to fully obey the Lord's command to destroy the Canaanites.

The fourth element, the judgment, is also not given. Instead, an earlier warning is repeated. The reminder functions as a renewed warning. The Lord had said that he himself would not drive out the inhabitants before Israel and that the gods of the nations would lure them. The implication is that his earlier warning would still be fulfilled if their situation were to remain unchanged. The omission of judgment suggests that the Lord was still giving them another chance, though they failed the test so far.

This leaves the reader to be hopeful that Israel would do better now and pass the test.[68] In fact, the reader may consider Israel's response in 2:4–5 as signs of repentance. The people wept. They changed the name of the scene of trial. They built an altar for the Lord. None of these responses, however, is what the Lord was looking for. Their "weeping" should have prompted them to change their practice. Instead, they simply changed the name of the place. They should have destroyed the altars of the Canaanites. Instead, they built one for the Lord. They added to the list of their failures by what they did in response to the warning.

Both Israel's attitude towards the Canaanites and the Lord's message towards Israel has changed in these verses. The attitude of the Israelites in the *exposition* was one that was willing to fight the Canaanites even if they were just trying to defend themselves from an imminent threat. Here they showed no sign of that. In the *exposition*, the Lord's message for them was a promise of victory. Here, his message to Israel was a warning that clearly spelled out how they would be judged if they did not change their ways.

In Judges 2:6–10, the author gives a flashback to Joshua's time to help the reader evaluate Israel's *seemingly positive* response.[69] After the evaluative flashback, the author proceeds to narrate the consequence of Israel's unwillingness to truly repent by returning to its former attitude.

---

68. Cf. Sasson, *Judges 1–12*, 207.
69. See pp. 102–107 for a discussion of 2:6–10 as flashback.

Unraveling: Israel's Failure and Its Consequence (2:11–3:4)

The *unraveling* is the fourth stage in the plot of the prologue. It captures "the consequences of the change."[70] Judges 2:11–21 picks up the same narrative trajectory of 2:1–5 after the brief "interruption" from the evaluative flashback in 2:6–10. The Lord had warned the Israelites at 2:3 by reminding them of his earlier warning that (1) the Canaanites would be thorns at their sides and (2) their gods would be a snare to them. In the *unraveling*, the Lord's warning came true: Israel was trapped by the gods, which led to the Lord's judgment to make the Canaanites thorns at their sides. The whole of 2:11–21 is a fulfillment of the warning of 2:1–3.[71]

The narrow genre of 2:11–21 is summary narrative[72] or "introductory summary report."[73] The summary, however, is of both one-time as well as repeated events. A distinction must be made between these in order to get a proper understanding of this summary narrative.

Before making a distinction between one-time and repeated events, the events themselves need to be identified. There are four major themes that capture the events of these verses: evil, judgment, compassion, and response. The first and the last are what the Israelites did, whereas the middle two are what the Lord did.

Israel's sin is summarized as "they did what was evil[74] in the eyes of the Lord."[75] As in Numbers 32:13, the phrase does not necessarily connote idolatry as idolatry is not always tied to this statement in the central section.

---

70. Amit, *Reading Biblical Narratives*, 47. Several scholars have made a similar observation. Sweeney, for instance, argues that whereas Judg 1:1–2:5 report the failure of the tribes to expel the Canaanites from the land, Judg 2:11–23/3:6 report the consequence of this failure (M. A. Sweeney, "Davidic Polemics in the Book of Judges," *VT* 47, no. 4 [1997]: 520).

71. Cf. Webb, *Book of Judges*, 140.

72. Frolov, *Judges*, 74.

73. Butler, *Judges*, 39.

74. Heb: אֶת־הָרַע בְּעֵינֵי יְהוָה. "The article on *hārā'* (lit., the evil) may imply both a specific and consummate evil, namely, apostasy from Yahweh . . . although it may simply be an articular usage with an abstract noun" (Younger, *Judges, Ruth*, 88).

75. For a detailed discussion of the phrase, see Lawson Grant Stone, "From Tribal Confederation to Monarchic State: The Editorial Perspective of the Book of Judges" (PhD diss., Yale University, 1988), 291–305.

This is also true in Judges 3:12–30; 4:1–5:31, and 13:1–16:31. None of these instances mention idolatry.

In 2:11–13, however, this *evil* is said to have two sides: (1) serving other gods and (2) abandoning the Lord. These are two sides of the same coin.[76] One cannot be dogmatic about which comes first. Whereas in 3:7 *abandoning* (*forgetting*) the Lord comes first, in 10:6 *serving* other gods comes first. In analyzing the sequence of events in 2:11–22, these two events will be considered as a single event: the Israelites did evil. This is the first stage.

The Lord's judgment can also be divided into two: his anger and what he did to the Israelites. What he did to the Israelites can further be divided into what he said – that is, the pronouncement of judgment – and his deed – that is, a realization of the spoken judgment. Therefore, three stages can be identified in the theme of judgment that follow the first stage: his anger makes up the second stage; stage three is the announcement of judgment; and stage four is the realization of judgment.

The theme of compassion has only one event: delivering Israel through the raising up of judges. This is the fifth stage. Israel's relapse into its evil despite the Lord's compassion and/or the judges' deliverance is the sixth stage.

The words used to describe events in 2:11–21 can be grouped under the four major themes and their subdivisions as in table 1 on the following page. The columns represent subsequent events in the development of Israel's story during the period of judges. The rows do not represent subsequent events; rather, each row simply reiterates the event/state mentioned in the row above it in the same column. Each row renews the emphasis on the event/state either by using the exact verb (e.g. עזב at 12a and 13a) or a synonymous root (כעס at 12d and חרה at 14a). The story moves forward in a linear manner only as one moves across the columns. First, Israel sinned (2:11–12c, 13). This then brought the Lord's wrath upon Israel (2:12d, 14a, 20a) who first announced his judgment (2:20b–21), which was then realized throughout the period of Judges (2:14b–19).

---

76. Younger, *Judges, Ruth*, 88.

Table 1: Events in 2:11–21

Evil		Judgment			Compassion	Response
Abandon	Idolatry	Anger	Speech	Realization		
	11b עבד					
12a עזב	12b + c הלך + חוה	12d כעס				
13a עזב	13b עבד	14a חרה		14–15 נתן/מכר יד יהוה	16 קום	17 לא שמע סור + לא עשה
					18 קום	19b שוב + שחת לא נפל
		20a חרה	20b–21 אמר			

Stone rightly observes that scholars too often assume that the cycle begins in 2:11 and that all of verses 11–19 are cyclical.[77] He correctly concludes that such assumptions are not right. The assumption of a cyclical structure probably results from the six-fold repetition of 2:11a in the book's central section. One needs to ask whether the syntax and the content of 2:11–21 shows any such pattern. Even if 2:11a is repeated in the central section six more times, here at 2:11a or in the central section, it is always presented as a one-time event, not cyclical.

Stone observes, again rightly, that 2:11–13 "speaks of a single doing evil in Yahweh's eyes." He then claims that "the entire period is thus branded as a single, gigantic falling away."[78] He has, however, no lexical or syntactical basis to claim that a one-time event represents the whole period. Butler, on the other hand, sees verse 16 as beginning the cycle that involves the

---

77. Polzin extends the pattern (calling it cyclical, not circular) up to 2:22 (Robert Polzin, *Moses and the Deuteronomist: A Literary Study of the Deuteronomic History, Part One: Deuteronomy, Joshua, Judges*, ISBL, ed. Herbert Marks and Robert Polzin [New York: Seabury, 1980], 151).

78. Joseph Coleson, Lawson G. Stone, and Jason Driesbach, *Joshua, Judges, Ruth*, Cornerstone Biblical Commentary, ed. Philip W. Comfort, vol. 3 (Carol Stream, IL: Tyndale House, 2012), 232.

following generations and verses 11–15 as dealing with only the generation after Joshua, not the following generations.[79]

Sasson, like Butler, takes verse 16 as the beginning of the cycle and so translates verses 16–19 with the English modal "would."[80] He observes that since only one judge was raised at a time, the use of the plural should be understood either as distributive or repetitive. He prefers the latter. He says, "more attractive to me is that the plural here moves the narrative from an actual recital of what has happened ('one judge came and then another judge came') to one that is to happen at the time of description ('judges would come')."[81]

Frolov, though at first sight understanding the *wayyiqtols* in verses 11–16 as presenting "a string of punctual, one-time developments," later hesitates to take them as such, arguing that "the absence of any specifics, except for two names of foreign gods, and especially the fact that the narrator never names Israel's nemeses . . . and its deliverers . . . referring to both in the plural, strongly suggest that the text describes a recurrent pattern."[82]

Both Sasson and Frolov are right in seeing the plural as signaling a cycle instead of one-time event. In addition, Frolov is also correct in seeing the lack of any specifics as a sign of a cycle. These criteria make sense when one compares 2:11–21 with the subsequent sections (e.g. Judg 3:7–11) that describe the one-time developments of each period of judges. Judges 3:7, for example, is a one-time development. It captures the behavior of Israelites at the beginning of the judges' period before the Lord raised the first judge. Therefore, a one-time development means what happened at the time of a single period within the period of judges. If this is true of 3:7, it should be true of 2:11 too. Nothing in 2:11 signals that it is a summary of the period of judges. It captures how the Israelites behaved after the warning and their weeping at Bochim.

---

79. Butler, *Judges*, 45. He does not explain, however, how he arrived at his conclusion.
80. He does mention that v. 14 could be the beginning of the cycle (Sasson, *Judges 1–12*, 192).
81. Ibid., 192.
82. Frolov, *Judges*, 68–69.

It can be concluded that the *wayyiqtol* moves the story forward as punctual, one-time developments, describing what happened in a single period within the period of judges, unless the following is true of the *wayyiqtol* clause:

(1) A plural form is used for individuals or groups for whom the singular form is used in the central section. The use of the plural in שֹׁפְטִים verses 16–18, though only one judge is raised in each of episodes in the central section, suggest that verses 16–18 are summarizing the period of judges. The use of the singular in verse 17 and verse 19 has to do with the focus of these verses to summarize what was true in each individual judge. This confirms taking 2:16–19 as a pattern.

(2) There are no specific names. In the central section Israel's oppressors are named in every single period of judges. However, in 2:14b–15 the names of Israel's enemies are not given. Instead, general terms, not specific names, are used. The two nouns used in 2:14b–15 are אֹיֵב and שֹׁסִים. שֹׁסִים is not used again in the central section. אֹיֵב is used in the central section but never in the frameworks. This sets 2:14b–15 as a pattern that captures the whole period, not one specific period.

When these criteria are applied to 2:11–21, only 2:11–14a and 2:20–21 can be taken as presenting "a string of punctual, one-time developments." The use of specifics for the names of the other gods in 2:11 and 2:13 indicates that they are one-time events, not repeated patterns. Every *wayyiqtol* clause in 2:11–14a is similar to the *wayyiqtol* clauses of the frameworks of the central section that capture one-time developments. Therefore, it can be concluded that 2:11–14a capture one-time developments in the time of the first generation. Then beginning from 2:14b the period of judges as a whole is summarized. The following structure of the section can be identified when such a distinction is made between one-time events and cyclical events.

Structure of 2:11–21

The New Generation: One-time events (2:11–14a)
    Stage one: Evil (vv. 11–12c)
    Stage two: Anger (v. 12d)
    Stage one: Evil (v. 13)
    Stage two: Anger (v. 14a)

The New and Subsequent Generations: Cyclical events (2:14b–19)
    The Judges' period seen as a whole (v. 14b)
        Stage Four: Realization of Judgment
    Each Judges' period seen individually (v. 15)
        Stage Four: Realization of Judgment
    The Judges' period seen as a whole (vv. 16–17)
        Stage Five: Compassion (v. 16)
        Stage Six: Response (v. 17)
    Each Judge's period seen individually (vv. 18–19)
        Stage Five: Compassion (v. 18)
        Stage Six: Response (v. 19)
The New Generation: One-time events (2:20–21)
    Stage Two: Anger (v. 20a)
    Stage Three: Announcement of Judgment (vv. 20b–21)

A closer look at the text will clarify this distinction between one-time and cyclical events, as well as between the new generation and the subsequent generation. It will help the reader appreciate the *unraveling* of the narrative.

The New Generation (2:11–14a[83])

The *wayyiqtols* in these verses (vv. 11b–14a) are not always consecutive. Longacre argued that the *wayyiqtol* forms in 2:10–23 are "only weakly sequential in that synonyms and even repetitions of the same verb enlarge the series."[84] His comment is particularly true of verses 11–14a. The *wayyiqtol* at 2:11 is *consecutive*, not of 2:10 but of 2:5, and so it picks up the narrative from 2:5. Israel's lack of true response to the messenger's rebuke in 2:1–5 resulted in the realization of his warning, particularly the warning that the gods of the nations would lure them.

Verses 11b–12c explain Israel's *evil* (2:11a), and so the *wayyiqtols* in verses 11b–12c are either epexegetical and/or complementary. In verse 12d, the

---

83. Webb, Younger, and Chisholm analyze vv. 11–13 together (Webb, *Book of Judges*, 140–141; Younger, *Judges, Ruth*, 88; Chisholm, *Judges and Ruth*, 153–154). Verse 14a is included here because it is synonymous with 12d, which suggests that it is meant to be treated together with vv. 11–13.

84. Robert E. Longacre, "*Weqatal* Forms in Biblical Hebrew Prose: A Discourse-Modular Approach," in *Biblical Hebrew and Discourse Linguistics,* ed. Robert D. Bergen (Dallas, TX: Summer Institute of Lingusitics, 1994), 64.

consequence of Israel's evil is given. Here the *wayyiqtol* is consequential. In verse 13, the author reiterates Israel's evil. The *wayyiqtol* is clearly resumptive-reiterative, not sequential.

The author's decision to reiterate verses 11b–12c and 12d in verse 13 and verse 14a, respectively, is best understood when looking at the severity of the judgment from the Lord in verses 14b–19. In verse 13 the author uses identical verbs as in verses 11b–12c. In verse 14, the author returns to the Lord's anger against Israel's sin, but he uses another root that is synonymous to the one used in verse 12. Here too, the *wayyiqtol* is resumptive-reiterative.

Therefore, these verses summarize the one-time evil that Israel did after their weeping and sacrifice in 2:4–5. This brought the Lord's anger. The Lord had already given Israel a warning in 2:3. In his anger the Lord announced, not a warning as in 2:1–3, but his judgment, which is given in 2:20–21b. The author moves to the realization of the judgment in 2:14b–19, delaying the announcement so that his comment (i.e. 2:21b–3:4) on the announcement would not disrupt the flow of the narrative.

The New and Subsequent Generations (2:14b–19)

These verses capture the cyclical events of not just the first generation, but also of the subsequent generations of the period of the judges. Here the author develops his narration by first summarizing the events of the period of the judges as a whole. He then focuses on each generation as individual units. This has implications for how those verses are to be interpreted.

He begins by looking at the judgment over the whole period in verse 14b. This verse captures what was true when looking at the period of the judges as a whole. Not everything mentioned in this verse is necessarily true of each period. The author uses two verbs to describe the judgment: נתן and מכר. In the central section, the author exchanges these two verbs.

The author then narrates what was true of each individual period in verse 15. Israel, in each period, was no longer able to stand against their enemies. The statement "just as the Lord had spoken and just as he swore to them" has no parallel in 2:1–3. And since the audience is clearly identified as "to them," as opposed to "to their ancestors," the only parallel is 2:20–21b.[85] This suggests the Lord had indeed given a judgment speech before he executed his

---

85. See the discussion on these verses below.

judgment. It would be very unlikely for him to punish his people without announcing his judgment.[86]

Next the author summarizes the Lord's compassion and Israel's response in verses 16–19. He first looks at the period as a whole in verses 16–17. In verse 16 the Lord's compassion over the whole period is seen. In verse 17 Israel's response is summarized. This verse compares all the generations during the period of the judges with the generation of Joshua. These two verses (vv. 16–17) are general statements that were true of the period when seen as a whole. The things mentioned here were not necessarily true in each period. It is only the next two verses that summarize what was true of each period.

The implication of this observation is significant for understanding verse 17. The statement "they did not listen even to their judges" suggests that the judges were in good standing with the Lord, that is, they tried to lead the people in the right path. However, when looking at the central section, the judges were not always in good standing with the Lord. And this difference between verse 17 and the central section is in keeping with the interpretation of verse 17 as a general statement.

The statement "they quickly turned from the way which their fathers walked on" is also another general statement that looks at the period as a whole. Instead of comparing one period with another, as in verses 18–19, here the comparison is between the period of the judges and the period of the previous generation that includes Joshua and the elders.

After summarizing the whole period (vv. 16–17), the author now gives what was true of each period in verses 18–19. The main point of these verses is that the Lord persisted in saving Israel from its enemies by raising up a judge for them; and, Israel also persisted and even worsened in their stubbornness in the subsequent periods.

The New Generation (2:20–21)

Having finished the cyclical summary narrative (vv. 14b–19), the author does not begin to narrate the individual stories that the cycle hinted at

---

86. Cf. Amos 3:7.

(3:7–16:31). Rather, he now gives what can be considered as "supplementary material" in 2:20–3:6.[87]

That the Lord's speech began in verse 20a is clear, but where the speech ends is not as clear. Therefore, before making any comment on 2:20–3:6, the first issue that needs to be addressed is that of identifying the end of the Lord's speech.

Several scholars include verse 22 as the Lord's direct speech and consider verse 23 as the beginning of the author's comment.[88] Webb argues, "the explicit change of subject does not come until 23a, 'Yahweh left these nations.' It is here that the change to indirect speech is made and the commentary on Yahweh's speech begins."[89] However, the transition from direct to indirect speech can be clearly identified even before this verse.

The second alternative is taken by Boling, who ends the direct speech at the beginning of verse 22 with למען נסות בם את ישראל "so as to test Israel with them."[90] The parallel construction in 3:4, however, suggests that the rest of the verse should be taken together with this purpose clause. Both 2:22 and 3:4 follow a similar pattern: the first half of each verse contains the infinitive construct of נסה followed by בם את־ישראל and after the *'aṭnāḥ*, the second half of each verse contains an interrogative question. The content of the second half of each verse captures what the *test* was.

The third alternative is to end the speech in the middle of verse 21 at the word indicated by the *'aṭnāḥ*. The prepositional phrase מן־הגוים clearly belongs to the second half of the verse since *'aṭnāḥ* is used to divide the verse into two. Wessels argues, "The *'aṭnāḥ* appears below מפניהם, thus concluding one meaningful unit, so that it need not necessarily be semantically linked

---

87. Lindars, *Judges 1–5*, 108. Lindars claims, "2.20–23 at least must have been added before the Prelude [1.1–2.5] was included, because otherwise there would be no need for it." "Supplementary" does not necessarily mean later addition by an editor. Here it refers to additional material that explains or gives comment on the preceding material. It does not move the narrative forward.

88. E.g. Block, *Judges, Ruth*, 133; Chisholm, *Judges and Ruth*, 150; Frolov, *Judges*, 72; NIV.

89. Webb, *Judges: An Integrated Reading*, 242, n. 110.

90. Boling, *Judges*, 74.

with the next unit."[91] The comment then could begin in 2:21b with the prepositional phrase "from the nations."[92]

The fourth proposal, which is suggested by Lindars, is that the Lord's speech could possibly end with אשר עזב יהושע in verse 21.[93] The author then picks up the trajectory of the narrative from the Lord's speech and continues the narrative with וימת "and he [Joshua] died."

The fifth option and one that is adopted by a number of translations and by the present author is to extend the Lord's speech to the end of verse 21 and start the author's comment at verse 22.[94] One of the ways that direct speech is distinguished from indirect speech in Hebrew is by means of "the deictic relationship between the quotation and the frame," that is, "pronominal elements in direct speech must be determined with reference to the clause that frames the quotation."[95] In the phrase את־דרך יהוה (v. 22), יהוה is in the third person, and so it explicitly indicates a change of speaker.[96] The third person indicates the narrator as the speaker, whereas the first person indicates the Lord as the speaker. Therefore, the change of speaker signals that the author, not the Lord, is speaking in verse 22. The Lord's speech then consists of verses 20b–21.

Judges 2:20–21 begins with a statement that is identical with that of 2:14a, that is, ויחר־אף יהוה בישראל. Several scholars, including Webb and

---

91. J. P. H. Wessels, "Persuasions in Judges 2.20–3.6: A Celebration of Differences," in *The Rhetorical Analysis of Scripture: Essays from the 1995 London Conference*, JSNTSup Series, ed. Stanley E. Porter and Thomas H. Olbricht, vol. 146 (Sheffield: Sheffield Academic Press, 1997), 125.

92. In 2:1–4 the Lord speaks to Israel through his messenger. Within his speech is a quoted speech, which he had spoken at a previous time. This speech is introduced with ויאמר: "I will not break my covenant with you forever but you must not cut a covenant with the inhabitants of this land, their altars you must break." The *'atnāḥ* marks the end of the quoted speech. After the word marked with *'atnāḥ*, the Lord continues his present speech, which itself is of course a quoted speech by the author. In 1 Kgs 11:2 the phrase "from the nations" begins an independent sentence. In Judg 2:12 the author modified the phrase "other gods" with "from among the gods of the people who surround them." In Gen 1:3 God said, "Let there be light" and there was light. Here the direct speech ends with "light" where the *'atnāḥ* is and the author's comment on the direct speech continues in the second half of the verse.

93. Lindars, *Judges 1–5*, 110.

94. E.g. NRSV; JPS.

95. Cynthia L. Miller, *The Representation of Speech in Biblical Hebrew Narrative: A Linguistic Analysis*, HSMM, ed. Lawrence E. Stager and Peter Machinist, vol. 55 (Atlanta: Scholars Press, 1996), 62.

96. Wessels, "Persuasions in Judges 2.20–3.6," 126.

Frolov, take the two statements as referring to two separate events. They argue that whereas verse 14a introduces the Lord's anger towards the new generation at the beginning of the period of judges, verse 20a captures the Lord's anger at the end of the period which was directed at Israel's consistent rebellion during the period of the judges. They conclude that the speech was given at the end of the period.[97]

Neither the syntax nor the content of verse 20 allows taking the Lord's anger at verse 20a as his anger that was directed at Israel at the end of the period of the judges. With regard to syntax, verse 20 cannot be consecutive of verses 14b–19 since the latter represents digression – that is, the cyclical narrative of verses 14b–19 interrupts the narrative of the one-time events. As for content, no such anger is recorded in the book of Judges as occurring at the end of the period of Judges. In the central section (3:8 and 10:7), the statement is used only to introduce, never to conclude, the period of individual judges.

Judges 2:20a is best seen as resumptive of 2:14a, not consecutive of verses 14b–19. Sasson argues that the repetition of the identical statement at 2:14a and 2:20a could be accidental, but then denies its probability here because of their "proximity." He suggests, "renewed formulas may operate stylistically as resumptive phrases."[98]

Sasson gives two alternatives to understand this resumption. The first alternative is to take verses 14–15 and verses 20–23 as speaking of simultaneous judgments. In the former, the enemies are from without; whereas, in the latter they are from within. The second alternative is to take verse 14a and verse 20a as enclosing "an *interpolation* – material that at one time deemed tangential . . . but eventually slipped into the body of the text, together with

---

97. Frolov, who considers only vv. 17–19 as an interruption from a cyclical summary, argues that v. 20 picks up from v. 16 (Frolov, *Judges*, 68–69). However, as discussed above, the pattern includes vv. 14b–19. Stone argues that 2:20b–3:6 and 2:14–15 both have a cause-effect relationship with 2:16–19 and 2:11–13 respectively. In so doing, he sees 2:20ff. as continuing from v. 19 (Stone, *From Tribal Confederation to Monarchic State*, 306–307).

98. Sasson, *Judges 1–12*, 197. He says: "The repetition of phrases with exact language can be accidental, especially because Hebrew prose shares neither the English style's dread of duplication nor its absorption with shaping seamless transitions. Yet, when set within relative proximity of each, renewed formulas may operate stylistically as resumptive phrases (*Wiederaufnahme*)."

the resumptive phrase." The implication, he suggests, is that verses 6–13 continue into verses 20–23.

There are two problems with the first alternative: (1) Whereas verses 14–15 involve cyclical events, verses 20–22 capture a one-time speech-event. The former contains what the Lord did throughout the period of the judges. The latter contains what he said at the beginning of the period, even before the events of verses 14b–15. (2) More importantly, the phrase איביהם מסביב "enemies all around" does not necessarily mean outside forces as Sasson suggests. In Joshua 23:1, the phrase clearly refers to the inhabitants of the land. It is best to see the phrase as inclusive of forces both within and without.

The second alternative is the best choice except for taking verses 14–19 as interpolation. Verse 20a "represents a chronological movement in time because it narrates a singular event in which Yahweh speaks."[99] This singular event picks up the story from verse 14a after the interruption (vv. 14b–19). Therefore, the *wayyiqtol* in verse 20a can be considered as resumptive-reiterative.[100] It is resumptive because verse 20a repeats verse 14a. It is reiterative because what the Lord said (vv. 20b–21) reiterates what he did (vv. 14b–19). The Lord's statement in 2:21, "I will not continue to dispossess," explains why the Lord or the judges would not dispossess the inhabitants of the land throughout the period of the judges. What 2:16–19 stated regarding the judges was one of deliverance from the enemies, not the dispossessing them from the land.

Taking the *wayyiqtol* in 2:20a as resumptive implies that the speech was given at the beginning of the period of judges. The use of the phrase לא אוסיף "I will not continue" supports this conclusion. The Lord did not dispossess anyone from before Israel throughout the period of judges and so these words would not make any sense if taken as given at the end of the period of the judges.

The Lord's speech, the announcement that he would no longer dispossess the nations, echoes Joshua 23. In Joshua 23:5 Joshua had assured Israel that the Lord himself would dispossess the remaining nations. Then in Joshua 23:12–13 he also assured them that if they make any kind of alliance with

---

99. Jacobus Marais, *Representation in Old Testament Narrative Texts*, BIS, ed. R. Alan Culpepper and Rolf Rendtorff, vol. 36 (Leiden: Brill, 1998), 91.

100. So Longacre, "*Weqatal* Forms," 65.

the nations, the Lord would stop dispossessing them. The use of גַם, "also, too" in גַּם־אֲנִי suggests the Lord's refusal to dispossess the nations was a response to Israel's refusal to dispossess them.

The *unraveling* concludes with the author's comment in 2:22. Lindars takes the change of speaker in verse 22 as a sign of possible addition, probably by an editor.[101] He adds that "as a comment on Yahweh's speech in v. 21 rather than a continuation of it, it is best regarded as an explanatory addition."[102] Lindars then suggests a parallel example in Genesis 37:22, where the narrator picks up from the speech of Reuben with the intrusion: "Reuben said to them, 'Do not shed blood. Throw him into this pit here in the wilderness but do not lay a hand on him' – *in order to rescue him from their hand, in order to return him to his father*."[103]

Lindars is correct in arguing that verse 22 is a comment on the Lord's speech. However, it is not necessary to consider it as an addition by an editor. It is possible for the author himself to make this comment as a means of answering a possible question raised by the readers.[104] As the author reads his own text, he could envision some questions that his text may raise in the readers' mind.[105] He answers these questions with obtrusions. This obtrusion is a non-break-frame obtrusion. Paris defines such obtrusions as those in which "the narrator follows literary rules and refrains from interrupting the flow of action by waiting to comment until the completion of an episode or the entire story."[106] Break-frame obtrusions, on the other hand, are those that "always defy . . . literary standards because they interrupt plot and action sequences by disrupting the narrative framework."[107] Since the

---

101. Lindars, *Judges 1–5*, 109; so George F. Moore, *A Critical and Exegetical Commentary on Judges*, ICC, ed. S. R. Driver, A. Plummer, and C. A. Briggs (Edinburgh: T&T Clark, 1895), 75.

102. Lindars, *Judges 1–5*, 110.

103. Ibid., 111. Judg 21:19 could be another example. The direct speech ends and the author's intrusion starts with אֲשֶׁר, which JPS rightly takes as a parenthetical note. Here they are speaking to each other. It is unlikely that the note about the location is part of their conversation. Rather, the author must have added it for his readers. It is only at 21:20 that they speak to the Benjamites. So it cannot be their words to them either.

104. Christopher T. Paris, *Narrative Obtrusion in the Hebrew Bible* (Minneapolis: Fortress, 2014), 173.

105. Ibid.

106. Ibid., 105.

107. Ibid., 103.

author has delayed his comment until the end of the Lord's speech which also marks the end of the unraveling, the comment is best seen as non-break-frame obtrusion.

Syntactically the author's comment in verse 22 is either dependent on a verb in the preceding verses or it could be a form of ellipsis. Lindars suggests that it could be dependent on וַיֹּאמֶר in verse 20.[108] This would mean that the test of verse 22 began in the period of judges. This may be possible grammatically but not when one compares the content of verses 20–21 and verse 22. Whereas 2:20–21 speak of punishment for lack of obedience, verse 22 speaks of the test whose purpose was to know if they would obey. He already knew their disobedience when he spoke in 2:20–21. Therefore, it could not be referring to what the Lord intended to do as a result of their failure in 2:10–19.

Verse 22 could also be dependent on עזב.[109] If so, then the purpose stated in verse 22 is that of Joshua. He was the one who intended to test Israel. However, as Chisholm rightly noted, the presence of וַיָּמָת before verse 22 is problematic.[110] It would make more sense to put verse 22 before וַיָּמָת if verse 22 were dependent on עזב. The verb וַיָּמָת is usually translated as ". . . when he died" by scholars who take it as part of the direct speech. Webb does this by emending the text to במותו in order to avoid the awkwardness created by the *wayyiqtol*.[111] This emendation is, however, unnecessary, and what is worse, the implication of this emendation misses the author's main point. The emendation implies that Joshua left the nations unconquered at the time of his death. A reading of the book of Joshua, however, makes it clear that Joshua left the nations unconquered even while he was still alive. To abandon the nations in this context is to abandon one's pursuing after the enemy. Joshua was proactively seeking to destroy the enemy.

Verse 22 could also be a form of ellipsis. Two elements of the sentence are missing. This becomes clear when the verse is compared to 3:4.[112] The two verses are very similar as can be seen below:

---

108. Lindars, *Judges 1–5*, 111.
109. Webb, *Book of Judges*, 146, n. 24.
110. Chisholm, *Judges and Ruth*, 160, n. 27.
111. Webb, *Judges: An Integrated Reading*, 114, n. 10.
112. See pp. 107–108 for the structure of 2:22–3:4.

2:22 _____ לְמַעַן נַסּוֹת | בָּם אֶת־יִשְׂרָאֵל | _____ הֲשֹׁמְרִים הֵם
אֶת־דֶּרֶךְ יְהוָה לָלֶכֶת בָּם כַּאֲשֶׁר שָׁמְרוּ אֲבוֹתָם אִם־לֹא
3:4 וַיִּהְיוּ לְנַסּוֹת | בָּם אֶת־יִשְׂרָאֵל | **לָדַעַת** הֲיִשְׁמְעוּ
אֶת־מִצְוֺת יְהוָה אֲשֶׁר־צִוָּה אֶת־אֲבוֹתָם בְּיַד־מֹשֶׁה:

The first missing element in 2:22 is the verb וַיִּהְיוּ. The second missing element is the infinitive construct לָדַעַת just before the indirect question. With regard to the missing verb, it could be an example of what Miller calls backwards ellipsis, where the verb is deleted from the first line in poetry.[113] Miller does acknowledge that ellipsis occurs, if rarely, in narrative prose. Miller adds, "most importantly, backwards ellipsis of the verb never occurs."[114] Miller apparently missed the instance of backward ellipsis of the verb in 2 Kings 25:4, "Then the city was breached. All the soldiers *left* by night through the gate between the two walls, which is near the king's garden – the Chaldeans were all around the city; and he [the king] left for the Arabah."[115] In the Hebrew text the verb הלך is missing from "All the soldiers *left*" but present in "he *left* for the Arabah." This is a case of backwards ellipsis.

It seems impossible to have exact knowledge of the syntactical relation between 2:22 and the literary context. The similar construction in 3:4 leads to the conclusion that 2:22 represents an ellipsis inserted by the author. The author clarifies the situation: At his death Joshua left several nations unconquered; these God would use to test Israel as to whether or not they would keep the way of the Lord to go in it just as their fathers kept it. The author's comment in verse 22 then marks the Lord's speech as the end of a period, that is, the period of testing. The author elaborates on this period by means of a flashback in 2:23–3:4.[116]

---

113. C. L. Miller, "*Ellipsis*," in *DOTWPW*, ed. Tremper Longman III and Peter Enns (Downers Grove, IL: InterVarsity Press, 2008), 158.

114. Ibid., 159.

115. Cf. NRSV.

116. See pp. 107–110 for a discussion on 2:23–3:4 as a flashback to the time of Joshua.

Ending: Israel at the End of the Test (3:5–6)

The fifth and final stage in the development of the plot of the prologue of the book of Judges is the *ending*. After commenting on the whole period of testing (2:22–3:4), the author now concludes his narrative.

Webb argues that 3:5–6 is separate from the preceding passage because it does not contain the three keywords of that passage: נסה "to test," ידע "to know," and גוים "nations."[117] Another signal that this is a separate section is the change of topic from the *test* through the nations to *the Israelites*. The *ending* gives the result of the test, not the test itself.

Being the *ending* of the plot of the narrative of the prologue, verses 5–6 capture the new state in which Israel is found. This new state is very different from the state in which Israel was found in the *exposition* (1:1–2). At the beginning of the period of testing Israel was asking for the Lord's help to fight the Canaanites. The *ending* informs the readers that Israel's attitude towards the Canaanites has changed. Instead of considering them as enemies and fighting them, Israel lived and intermarried with them (1:3b–7, 17–19, 21–2:5) and worshipped their gods (2:11–13).

Chisholm argues that the mention of intermarriage with the Canaanites is additional material in the conclusion as, he argues, it is not mentioned until now. He then concludes, "[i]t is the missing piece in the puzzle that explains how the compromises of 1:1–2:5 led to the outright paganism of 2:6–3:6."[118] This is in keeping with the author's approach to storytelling as was observed throughout the prologue. Very important missing elements were given as the story progresses. One example of these missing elements is 2:21b–3:4, which clearly informs the reader that 1:1 began the test, what the test was, for whom the test was intended, and what the purpose of the test was. Without this information, the reader could not properly evaluate the characters in the story.

In Judges 3:5–6 the author now clearly exclaims: "Israel failed the test!" Verses 5–6 function as a report card, expressing the author's (and the Lord's) evaluation of Israel's performance in this divinely administered examination.

---

117. Webb, *Book of Judges*, 150.
118. Chisholm, *Judges and Ruth*, 162.

The verdict is clear: Israel has failed![119] As Webb rightly noted, the Lord's words in 2:20–23 imply that Israel failed the test.[120] The Lord's accusation in 2:20 connects the judgment with Israel's apostasy. So Israel's failure, according to the accusation in 2:20, seems to be only apostasy. However, the author clarifies this by mentioning that the apostasy was a result of Israel's decision to live alongside and intermarry with the Canaanites.

---

119. Block, *Judges, Ruth*, 140.
120. Webb, *Book of Judges*, 150.

CHAPTER 3

Flashback in the Prologue

In chapter 2 of this dissertation it was mentioned that though the prologue of Judges narrates events that took place after Joshua's death (Judg 1:1), inserted in the prologue are four flashbacks that backtrack the narrative to the time when Joshua was still alive. The present chapter is a detailed analysis of these flashbacks.

Temporally Overlaid *Wayyiqtol* Clauses in Biblical Hebrew

All of these four flashbacks are introduced with temporally overlaid *wayyiqtol* clauses. Since flashback is normally introduced with *pluperfect qatal,* this chapter will first discuss and defend the argument that it is normal, though not frequent, for a temporally overlaid *wayyiqtol* clause to introduce a flashback. This section begins with a survey of scholarship on temporally overlaid *wayyiqtol* clauses.

Clarification of Terms

In the process of reading the works of the scholars listed below under "Survey of Scholarship," the reader will notice that some scholars use grammatical/syntactical terms such as pluperfect (past perfect) and temporal overlay instead of flashback.

In general terms, flashback (also referred to as analepsis) is "a term which probably derives from the cinema, and which is now also used to describe any scene or episode in a play, novel, story or poem which is inserted to show events that happened at an earlier time."[1] More specifically, it is "a form of anachrony by which some of the events of a story are related at a point in the narrative after later story-events have already been recounted."[2] It is a literary device by which a narrator backtracks the narrative time "to refer to a prior action that now becomes relevant."[3] Martin calls a flashback "a 'harking back' technique, for it takes the form of retrospective unlinearity."[4] He gives fives different orders in which the flashback may be found: (1) where the effect is mentioned before the cause; (2) where the end is mentioned before the beginning; (3) where the present state is mentioned before the past; (4) where the latter is mentioned before the earlier; and (5) where a consequence is mentioned before its antecedent.[5] As Chisholm rightly observed, a flashback event can chronologically precede the episode or scene of the story being related or it can occur within the time-frame of the story.[6]

Syntactically, flashback is introduced with an anterior construction. Zevit distinguishes between two kinds of anterior constructions: (1) pluperfect (past perfect) construction when "a given action in the past had *commenced and concluded* before another action in the past," and (2) preperfect construction when, "a given action in the past had *commenced* but not *necessarily terminated* in the past prior to the beginning of another action."[7] The focus of this dissertation is only on instances when the anterior construction is used for the first kind of situation.

---

1. "*Flashback*," in *A Dictionary of Literary Terms and Literary Theory*, ed. J. A. Cuddon, 4th ed. (Oxford: Blackwell, 1998), 321.

2. Chris Baldick, "*Analypsis*," in *Oxford Dictionary of Literary Terms* (Oxford: Oxford University Press, 2008), 13.

3. Robert B. Chisholm, *A Commentary on Judges and Ruth*, Kregel Exegetical Library (Grand Rapids: Kregel, 2013), 82.

4. W. J. Martin, "'Dischronologized' Narrative," in *Congress Volume: Rome 1968*, VTSup, ed. G. W. Anderson et al., vol. 17 (Leiden: Brill, 1969), 182.

5. Ibid., 181–182.

6. Chisholm, *Judges and Ruth*, 82.

7. Ziony Zevit, *The Anterior Construction in Classical Hebrew*, SBLMS, ed. Terence E. Fretheim, vol. 50 (Atlanta, GA: Scholars Press, 1998), 15. Martin defines pluperfect as denoting "some event which had already occurred before some specific point of time in the past . . . A whole series of events is shifted one stage further back in relation to a secondary point of reference in the past" (Martin, "'Dischronologized' Narrative," 181). The primary point of reference for a speaker is the present.

Another phrase used for the anterior (pluperfect) construction is temporal overlay. Temporal overlay should be distinguished from "semantic and temporal overlap."[8] When a clause temporally overlaps with the preceding clause, the event it describes is chronologically within the time-frame of the event of the preceding clause. A temporally overlaid clause, however, is one whose event chronologically precedes the event of the immediately preceding clause.

This dissertation uses *temporal overlay* when referring to the syntax of a flashback. It will use the term *flashback* in analyzing the narrative.

Survey of Scholarship

Several scholars have contributed to the discussion on temporally overlaid *wayyiqtol* clauses. Although some scholars simply acknowledge that *wayyiqtol* could be used in temporally overlaid clauses, others, such as Randall Buth, have helped formulate the criteria that enable the reader to know when the *wayyiqtol* clause is temporally overlaid. The contribution, direct or indirect, of these scholars deserves to be noted.

S. R. Driver

Acknowledging that *wayyiqtol* is not just sequential/consecutive, Driver discusses cases where it is used to express parallel events. He refers to these as cases in which "the disregard of chronological sequence is only apparent." He then moves to discuss cases where "no temporal relation is implied at all, and association in *thought* is the principle guiding the writer rather than association in *time*." It is within this latter concept that he addresses the issue of the *wayyiqtol*'s pluperfect sense. He considers it "a moot and delicate question" to ask how far the *wayyiqtol* can have a *pluperfect* sense.[9]

---

8. Randall Buth, "Methodological Collision between Source Criticism and Discourse Analysis: The Problem of 'Unmarked Temporal Overlay' and the Pluperfect/Nonsequential *Wayyiqtol*," in *Biblical Hebrew and Discourse Linguistics,* ed. Robert D. Bergen (Dallas: Summer Institute of Linguistics, 1994), 138.

9. S. R. Driver, *A Treatise on the Use of the Tenses in Hebrew and Some Other Syntactical Questions,* BRS, ed. Astrid B. Beck and David Noel Freedman, 4th ed. (1892; repr., Grand Rapids: Eerdmans, 1998), 84–88.

Driver acknowledges that the *wayyiqtol* may follow a *pluperfective qatal* and continue that sense.[10] However, he argued against some scholars who suggested that the *wayyiqtol* could introduce a pluperfect idea.[11] In cases where the event of the *wayyiqtol* clause clearly precedes the event of the preceding clause chronologically, Driver prefers to emend the text, calling it "doubtful," an "uncertain passage to rely upon," and "obscure." For instance, in discussing 1 Kings 9:14, he calls the text "obscure" and comments that verse 14 "*seems* to be in continuation of 11a."[12]

Driver concludes that the only possibility for such a sense is at the beginning of a new section. Even then, he argues, it is not considered a true *pluperfect* because it can be rendered with the simple past tense in English. Driver concludes that in all other cases, such a reading of a *wayyiqtol* is "without a sound basis in logic or philology."[13] Exodus 18:2 is one example of temporally overlaid *wayyiqtol* clauses that Driver dismisses. However, a close look at the text will show that it is indeed a case of temporal overlay.

Exod 18:1 וַיִּשְׁמַע יִתְרוֹ כֹהֵן מִדְיָן חֹתֵן מֹשֶׁה אֵת כָּל־אֲשֶׁר עָשָׂה אֱלֹהִים לְמֹשֶׁה וּלְיִשְׂרָאֵל עַמּוֹ כִּי־הוֹצִיא יְהוָה אֶת־יִשְׂרָאֵל מִמִּצְרָיִם: (initiatory)
2 וַיִּקַּח יִתְרוֹ חֹתֵן מֹשֶׁה אֶת־צִפֹּרָה אֵשֶׁת מֹשֶׁה אַחַר שִׁלּוּחֶיהָ: 3 וְאֵת שְׁנֵי בָנֶיהָ אֲשֶׁר שֵׁם הָאֶחָד גֵּרְשֹׁם כִּי אָמַר גֵּר הָיִיתִי בְּאֶרֶץ נָכְרִיָּה: 4 וְשֵׁם הָאֶחָד אֱלִיעֶזֶר כִּי־אֱלֹהֵי אָבִי בְּעֶזְרִי וַיַּצִּלֵנִי מֵחֶרֶב פַּרְעֹה: (flashback)[14]
5 וַיָּבֹא יִתְרוֹ חֹתֵן מֹשֶׁה וּבָנָיו וְאִשְׁתּוֹ אֶל־מֹשֶׁה אֶל־הַמִּדְבָּר אֲשֶׁר־הוּא חֹנֶה שָׁם הַר הָאֱלֹהִים: (sequential)

Jethro, Moses' father-in-law, heard of the Lord's deliverance of Israel from Egypt (v. 1) and came to Moses (v. 5) and spoke to him (v. 6). The *wayyiqtol* clause in verse 2 is temporally overlaid, introducing a flashback

---

10. Ibid. Davidson agrees with Driver in taking the *wayyiqtol* as *pluperfective* when following a *pluperfective qatal*, carrying the sense of that *qatal*. It seems, however, that he is hesitant to accept that a *wayyiqtol* can have a pluperfect sense when it is not following a *pluperfective qatal* (A. B. Davidson, *Hebrew Syntax*, 3rd ed. [Edinburgh: T&T Clark, 1901], 72).

11. He quotes the following scholars with scripture references where they located *pluperfective wayyiqtol*: Kalisch in Gen 2:2; 26:18; Exod 11:1; Hitzig in Isa 8:3; 39:1; Jer 39:11; Jonah 2:4; Keil in Gen 2:19; Judg 2:6; 1 Kgs 7:13; 9:14. Driver also dismisses a number of examples proposed by Delitzsch and various Jewish scholars (Driver, *Treatise*, 84–88).

12. See pp. 62–63 for a discussion on 1 Kgs 9:10–14.

13. Ibid.

14. The אֲשֶׁר clause is a dependent relative clause.

to a time prior to verse 1. This is signaled by the phrase אַחַר שִׁלּוּחֶיהָ. Moses had sent away his wife before 18:1. The taking (receiving) of Moses' wife by Jethro is linked to the sending away by Moses, not to the time of hearing in 18:1. Exodus 18:2–4 as a whole is a parenthetical statement giving background to verse 5.

Driver claims that וַיִּקַּח in Exodus 18:2 has the same sense it bears in Genesis 12:5, arguing that in both cases the verb expresses the action of *taking* for the purpose of *bringing*.[15] However, Exodus 18:2 and Genesis 12:5 have two major differences: (1) Exodus 18:2 adds the phrase אַחַר שִׁלּוּחֶיהָ "after he [Moses] had sent her away." (2) Unlike Genesis 12:5, Exodus 18:2 repeats the names of individuals in verse 2 and verse 5. Genesis 12:5 only states it for לקח, not for בוא. Exodus 18:2 is a different text from Genesis 12:5. Here the use of *taking* is not for the purpose of the trip mentioned in verse 5; rather it is for *receiving* into Jethro's home after Moses sent his wife and children away. It should be seen as a background statement. Jethro, the father-in-law of Moses, had taken Zipporah, the wife of Moses, after Moses had sent her away.

W. J. Martin

Martin rightly notes, "the purpose of a verbal system is to distinguish, alone or with the help of the context, the various time-phases and the nature of the actions associated with them."[16] Therefore, he concludes that context should be given due place in analyzing the meaning and function of a verbal system. Acknowledging that "there is no specific form in Hebrew for a secondary tense such as the pluperfect," Martin points out that "a situation often demands that the form of the verb be taken in this sense."[17] He argues that "such situations are bound to occur in all experience, whether expressed by a special form or not."[18]

---

15. Ibid., 86.
16. Martin, "'Dischronologized' Narrative," 181.
17. Ibid., 181.
18. Ibid.

He makes the comment that even in languages which have one unique form for the *pluperfect*, this form is not the only form used for the *pluperfect*. The simple past or perfect can also be used to communicate a *pluperfect* sense.[19]

Martin then argues that "passages in which there is a discrepancy between the strict chronological order and the order of recital are probably to be found in all historical narrative, whatever the language." He supports his conclusion by providing instances from the Gospels along with Egyptian and Assyrian documents.[20] Among the examples he gives is 1 Kings 9:14 where a *wayyiqtol* clause is temporally overlaid with the preceding clause:[21]

10a וַיְהִי מִקְצֵה עֶשְׂרִים שָׁנָה אֲשֶׁר־בָּנָה שְׁלֹמֹה אֶת־שְׁנֵי הַבָּתִּים אֶת־בֵּית יְהוָה וְאֶת־בֵּית הַמֶּלֶךְ: (protasis a)

11a חִירָם מֶלֶךְ־צֹר נִשָּׂא אֶת־שְׁלֹמֹה בַּעֲצֵי אֲרָזִים וּבַעֲצֵי בְרוֹשִׁים וּבַזָּהָב לְכָל־חֶפְצוֹ (protasis b)

11b אָז יִתֵּן הַמֶּלֶךְ שְׁלֹמֹה לְחִירָם עֶשְׂרִים עִיר בְּאֶרֶץ הַגָּלִיל: (apodosis: background)

12a וַיֵּצֵא חִירָם מִצֹּר לִרְאוֹת אֶת־הֶעָרִים אֲשֶׁר נָתַן־לוֹ שְׁלֹמֹה (initiatory)

12b וְלֹא יָשְׁרוּ בְּעֵינָיו: (momentous negation)

---

19. Greek, for instance, has a special form for the *pluperfect* tense but it sometimes uses the imperfect for a *pluperfect* idea. Wallace calls this a "pluperfective" imperfect (Daniel B. Wallace, *Greek Grammar Beyond the Basics: An Exegetical Syntax of the New Testament with Scripture, Subject, and Greek Word Indexes* [Grand Rapids: Zondervan, 1996], 549). Wallace does not include a "pluperfective" function for the aorist. Robertson suggests that in Greek both the aorist indicative and the imperfect were used for a *pluperfect* idea: "[t]he Greek cared nothing for relative time, though that was not the only use for the past perfect, as just stated. Ordinarily the aorist ind. was sufficient for a narrative unless the durative idea was wanted when the imperfect was ready to hand" (A. T. Robertson, *A Grammar of the Greek New Testament in the Light of Historical Research* [Nashville, TN: Broadman, 1934], 903). Cf. F. Blass, A. Debrunner, and Robert W. Funk, *A Greek Grammar of the New Testament and Other Early Christian Literature* (Chicago and London: University of Chicago Press, 1961), 171. An example from Luke 2:20 does support the conclusion that the aorist, like the imperfect, has a *pluperfective* function: καὶ ὑπέστρεψαν οἱ ποιμένες δοξάζοντες καὶ αἰνοῦντες τὸν θεὸν ἐπὶ πᾶσιν οἷς ἤκουσαν καὶ εἶδον καθὼς ἐλαλήθη πρὸς αὐτούς, "The shepherds returned, glorifying and praising God for all they had heard and seen, as it had been told them" (NRSV). There are four aorist verbs in this verse. The first aorist verb continues the narrative from v. 19, the other three are flashbacks to events preceding the event of the first aorist verb. While the phrase "for all they had heard and seen" refers to their experience at the place where the child was, the phrase "as it had been told them" refers to an even earlier experience at the field when the angel spoke to them.

20. Martin, "'Dischronologized' Narrative," 183–184.

21. Ibid., 186.

13a וַיֹּאמֶר (sequential)
מָה הֶעָרִים הָאֵלֶּה אֲשֶׁר־נָתַתָּה לִּי אָחִי
13b וַיִּקְרָא לָהֶם אֶרֶץ כָּבוּל עַד הַיּוֹם הַזֶּה׃
14 וַיִּשְׁלַח חִירָם לַמֶּלֶךְ מֵאָה וְעֶשְׂרִים כִּכַּר זָהָב׃ (flashback)

1 Kings 9:10–14 is a narrative that introduces a flashback narrative that captures what happened during the twenty years of building.

A   Hiram: at the end of 20 years (ended with a flashback) (vv. 10–14)
   B   Labor: flashback before the end of the 20 years (הֶעֱלָה) (vv. 15–24)
   B' Worship: flashback of worship until the end the temple (וְהֶעֱלָה) (v. 25)
A' Hiram: gave sailors to Solomon to bring gold from Africa (vv. 26–28)

Verses 10–11 constitute background information. The temporal setting for Solomon's gift (v. 11a) is at the end of the twenty years of building (v. 10a). The foregrounded narrative begins in verse 12. Hiram's giving (v. 10b) is also a background to Solomon's gift (v. 11a). Verse 14 speaks of Hiram's giving of gold. This, however, is not a new gift but a flashback to a previous gift in order to (1) bring the gift into the foreground to emphasize its contrast with Hiram's unhappiness with Solomon's gift, and (2) to add information, that is, the quantity of his gift. If it were a continuation, then it means Hiram sent King Solomon gold twice even after his unhappiness with the gifts he received; this is unlikely. Even if verse 14 is taken as a continuation of 11a, the two are interrupted by another event in 11b–13. Therefore, verse 14 is still temporally overlaid in relation to the event of verses 11b–13.

David Baker

Baker argues that BH does not have a specific form for the *pluperfect*, unlike English, French, and other languages.[22] Though BH only has two basic verbal forms, each has more than one function.[23] He identifies three ways

---

22. David Weston Baker, "The Consecutive Non-perfective as Pluperfect in the Historical Books of the Hebrew Old Testament: Genesis–Kings" (Master of Christian Studies thesis, Regent College, 1971), 1.

23. Ibid., 2.

BH communicates a *pluperfect* sense and groups these into three categories. The first category deals with the perfective, that is, *qatal*. He argues that the *pluperfect* sense of the *qatal* form "is determined strictly from the context and situation in which it is found."[24] The second category deals with those situations where *wayyiqtol* (which he calls *consecutive non-perfective*) follows a *qatal* form. This form has a *pluperfect* sense which forces the *wayyiqtol* to have a *pluperfect* sense. The *wayyiqtol* assumes the same sense as the preceding verbal form.[25] In the third category, Baker deals with the *wayyiqtol* form that does not follow a *qatal* with *pluperfect* sense and yet the *wayyiqtol* has a *pluperfect* sense.[26] For all three categories, it is "strictly the context and the situation which will govern the sense of the verbal form."[27] Baker rightly emphasizes that context should guide the exegete in identifying the *wayyiqtol* clause as temporally overlaid. However, he has not given any specific ways the context guides the exegete. Baker gives many examples to illustrate the third category. Nevertheless, most of his examples can be explained some other way. One example that does illustrate temporal overlay is Joshua 2:16:[28]

8a וְהֵמָּה טֶרֶם יִשְׁכָּבוּן (protasis)
8b וְהִיא עָלְתָה עֲלֵיהֶם עַל־הַגָּג (apodosis)
9 וַתֹּאמֶר אֶל־הָאֲנָשִׁים (initiatory)
9b–13
14 וַיֹּאמְרוּ לָהּ הָאֲנָשִׁים (sequential)
נַפְשֵׁנוּ תַחְתֵּיכֶם לָמוּת אִם לֹא תַגִּידוּ אֶת־דְּבָרֵנוּ זֶה וְהָיָה בְּתֵת־יְהוָה לָנוּ אֶת־הָאָרֶץ וְעָשִׂינוּ עִמָּךְ חֶסֶד וֶאֱמֶת:
15 וַתּוֹרִדֵם בַּחֶבֶל בְּעַד הַחַלּוֹן כִּי בֵיתָהּ בְּקִיר הַחוֹמָה וּבַחוֹמָה הִיא יוֹשָׁבֶת: (sequential)
16 וַתֹּאמֶר לָהֶם (flashback)
הָהָרָה לֵּכוּ פֶּן־יִפְגְּעוּ בָכֶם הָרֹדְפִים וְנַחְבֵּתֶם שָׁמָּה שְׁלֹשֶׁת יָמִים עַד שׁוֹב הָרֹדְפִים וְאַחַר תֵּלְכוּ לְדַרְכְּכֶם:
17 וַיֹּאמְרוּ אֵלֶיהָ הָאֲנָשִׁים (sequential)
17b–20

---

24. Ibid., 4.
25. Ibid., 22, 54.
26. Ibid., 55.
27. Ibid., 54.
28. Ibid., 70.

21a וַתֹּאמֶר (sequential)
כְּדִבְרֵיכֶם כֶּן־הוּא
21b וַתְּשַׁלְּחֵם (sequential)
21c וַיֵּלֵכוּ (reiterative)
21d וַתִּקְשֹׁר אֶת־תִּקְוַת הַשָּׁנִי בַּחַלּוֹן: (concluding)

Verse 8 begins a new scene. Rahab asked for kindness (vv. 9–13). The men promised (v. 14). She let the men down by a rope through the window of her house. Then, as an afterthought, the author gives another dialogue between Rahab and the two spies. Martin rightly notes, "The situation, the sleeping city, the silence of the dead of night, makes it evident that Rahab's instructions must have preceded the descent from the wall."[29] Cook calls this coincidental, "the complex activity of lowering them (i.e. getting the rope, tying it off, etc.) overlaps with her giving them directions."[30] The author has already shown the need for caution by reporting the royal search for the two men. Therefore, the dialogue between Rahab and the two men must have occurred prior to her letting them down. Without verse 15 the dialogue consists of verses 9–21a. Verse 15 must have occurred after the dialogue (vv. 9–21a) but before she sent them (v. 21b).

Waltke and O'Connor

Waltke and O'Connor see *wayyiqtol* as having two distinct characteristics: subordination and perfective. They affirm that in the biblical text, as we have it, *wayyiqtol* "must be understood to represent the pluperfect."[31] They give three examples of a *wayyiqtol* clause whose event is chronologically prior to the preceding clause. These examples are Numbers 1:48, 1 Kings 13:12, and Exodus 4:11–12, 18.[32]

---

29. Martin, "'Dischronologized' Narrative."

30. John A. Cook, *Time and the Biblical Hebrew Verb: The Expression of Tense, Aspect, and Modality in Biblical Hebrew*, Linguistic Studies in Ancient West Semitic, vol. 7 (Winona Lake, IN: Eisenbrauns, 2012), 290.

31. Bruce K. Waltke and M. O'Connor, *An Introduction to Biblical Hebrew Syntax* (Winona Lake, IN: Eisenbrauns, 1990), 553.

32. Ibid., 552–553. See below for a defense of Num 1:48 as a case of *temporal overlay*. See appendix 2 for a defense of 1 Kgs 13:12.

Randall Buth

Buth uses the phrase "temporal overlay" to refer to the concept of flashbacks. This is made clear when he differentiates temporal overlay from semantic and temporal overlap: "Of course, various degrees of partial semantic and temporal overlap with a preceding sentence are possible, up to and including a hendiadys like וַיַּעַן וַיֹּאמֶר 'answered and said'. Problems begin to be felt when the *wayyiqtol* form refers to an event (or state) that took place before the previous verb or as a parallel but distinct event."[33]

Buth distinguishes between two types of temporal overlay. (1) The marked temporal overlay is one that is grammatically signaled by means of a *waw-X-qatal* structure. (2) With regard to unmarked temporal overlay he comments, "when the temporal development of the story pauses and retreats but a *wayyiqtol* structure is used for the verb, then the grammar is not signaling the temporal overlay."[34]

Buth argues that when the grammar does not signal the temporal overlay, there are "two different ways in which the temporal overlay can be signaled outside of the grammar."[35] The first is by way of a "lexical reference and/or repetition" that can be understood as pointing back specifically to a previous event. He offers examples from the Moabite Stone, Judges 20:31–47, and Leviticus 16:6–11 as fitting this way of marking the temporal overlay.[36] The second is by means of "culturally natural semantic relationships with the previous sentence." He concludes with a comment that acknowledging the existence of unmarked temporal overlay cannot be seen as one's attempt to harmonize texts of "different sources or corrupted texts."[37] One of the examples he gives as an example of unmarked temporal overlay is Judges 11:1c:

10:17a וַיִּצָּעֲקוּ בְּנֵי עַמּוֹן (initiatory)
17b וַיַּחֲנוּ בַּגִּלְעָד (sequential)
17c וַיֵּאָסְפוּ בְּנֵי יִשְׂרָאֵל (sequential)
17d וַיַּחֲנוּ בַּמִּצְפָּה: (sequential)

---

33. Buth, "Methodological Collision," 138–139.
34. Ibid., 142.
35. Ibid.
36. See below for a discussion on Judg 20:31–41.
37. Ibid., 151.

18 וַיֹּאמְרוּ הָעָם שָׂרֵי גִלְעָד אִישׁ אֶל־רֵעֵהוּ (sequential)
מִי הָאִישׁ אֲשֶׁר יָחֵל לְהִלָּחֵם בִּבְנֵי עַמּוֹן יִהְיֶה לְרֹאשׁ לְכֹל יֹשְׁבֵי גִלְעָד:
11:1a וְיִפְתָּח הַגִּלְעָדִי הָיָה גִּבּוֹר חַיִל (embedded paragraph–introductory)
1b וְהוּא בֶּן־אִשָּׁה זוֹנָה (supplemental)
1c וַיּוֹלֶד גִּלְעָד אֶת־יִפְתָּח: (foreground)
2a וַתֵּלֶד אֵשֶׁת־גִּלְעָד לוֹ בָּנִים (sequential)
2b וַיִּגְדְּלוּ בְנֵי־הָאִשָּׁה (sequential)
2c וַיְגָרְשׁוּ אֶת־יִפְתָּח (sequential)
2d וַיֹּאמְרוּ לוֹ (conincidental)
לֹא־תִנְחַל בְּבֵית־אָבִינוּ כִּי בֶן־אִשָּׁה אַחֶרֶת אָתָּה:
3a וַיִּבְרַח יִפְתָּח מִפְּנֵי אֶחָיו (consequential)
3b וַיֵּשֶׁב בְּאֶרֶץ טוֹב (sequential)
3c וַיִּתְלַקְּטוּ אֶל־יִפְתָּח אֲנָשִׁים רֵיקִים (sequential)
3d וַיֵּצְאוּ עִמּוֹ: (concluding)

Buth considers 11:1c as a flashback by comparing it with 11:1a and b only. However, not only is it a flashback compared to 11:1a and b, but also when compared with the previous narrative that ended the previous chapter (i.e. 10:18). In fact, 11:1–3 is a flashback story that explains how Jephthah became the solution for the problem introduced in the preceding chapter. The story that paused in 10:18 is picked up in verse 4 but the reader would not understand why the elders chose Jephthah without verses 1–3, which introduce him.

Cook takes 11:1a as simply introducing the discourse topic.[38] Though this is true, we still have to assume that the ongoing state described in 11:1a as well as the verbless clause in 1b are related to the time set by the preceding discourse. That is, at the time the people were asking who could fight the Ammonites for them, Jephthah was a mighty warrior as well as the son of a prostitute.

C. John Collins

Collins builds his study on the findings of others, especially that of Randall Buth. As such, he begins his article with a survey of scholarship. He considers

---

38. Cook, *Time and the Biblical Hebrew Verb*, 294.

Buth's criteria "too restrictive to cover all of the data."³⁹ Collins then makes some modification to the two criteria that Buth identified and adds one more criterion:

(1) Buth's first criterion, "lexical reference and/or repetition," is modified to a general statement. Collin restates this criterion as: "Some anaphoric references explicitly point back to a previous event."

(2) Buth's second criterion, "common cultural experience," is modified by Collins to "the logic of the referent." He states: "The logic of the referent could signal an event that happened prior to the event of the preceding *wayyiqtol*."

(3) The verb begins a section or paragraph. This last criterion was the only possible criterion identified by Driver, as mentioned above.

Collins concludes his article by applying the three criteria to 1 Samuel 14:24 and Genesis 2:19. He disagrees with a reading of the *pluperfect* in 1 Samuel 14:24, but agrees with the NIV's reading of the *pluperfect* in Genesis 2:19.⁴⁰ Collins asks if the *wayyiqtol* in 1 Samuel 14:24 is temporally overlaid on the basis of the three criteria but then concludes "surely the answer is 'no.'"⁴¹ He supports Long in rejecting a flashback reading here. However, Long rejects such a reading because he denies that a *wayyiqtol* clause could be temporally overlaid. He argues instead that the *wayyiqtol* is mainly sequential.⁴² Therefore, he considers the *wayyiqtol* in verse 24 as consequential.⁴³ Contrary to Collins and Long, the *wayyiqtol* is indeed temporally overlaid according to the second criterion. נגשׂ in 14:24a is indeed a back reference to 13:6. In 13:6, the author does not clarify what caused the people's distress (נגשׂ). The distress due to the Philistines is implied in 13:6a with the verb צרר. In 14:24 the author clarifies the cause of the people's נגשׂ by making it

---

39. C. John Collins, "The Wayyiqtol as 'Pluperfect': When and Why," *TynBul* 46, no. 1 (1995): 127.

40. Most translations take the *wayyiqtol* in 1 Sam 14:24 to be *pluperfective* (e.g. NIV, NRSV, NET).

41. Ibid., 135.

42. V. Philips Long, *The Reign and Rejection of King Saul: A Case for Literary and Theological Coherence*, Society of Biblical Literature: Dissertation Series, ed. David L. Petersen, vol. 118 (Atlanta, GA: Scholars Press, 1989), 114.

43. Ibid.

a new discourse topic in 14:24a. The *wayyiqtol* in 14:24b is then a parenthetical statement to clarify the cause of the people's נגשׁ.

Genesis 1–2 is a doublet. The doublets (1:1–2:4a; 2:4b–25) tell the creation account from two different perspectives. As such they are not meant to be chronological. Both begin with a temporal clause. The introduction for both deals with emptiness (1:1–2; 2:4b–6). The creation account is given in 1:3–31and 2:7–24. In the former, אלהים creates. He is distant from his creation as he creates just by his words. In the latter, the Lord makes. He is imminent as he makes his creations by his hands. The conclusion is given in 2:1–3 and 2:25. The best way to see Genesis 1–2 is as two ways of telling the same creation account. Just as the two ways God relates to his creation – he is distant from his creation but at the same time immanent – are complementary, so are the two creation accounts. They are not in chronological order to each other. They are not in contradiction; rather, they complement each other. Therefore, the *wayyiqtol* in Genesis 2:19 is best seen as sequential within the narrative of 2:4a–25.

Alexander Andrason

Andrason defines *wayyiqtol* as "a computation of the anterior and simultaneous trajectories in the three time frames [past, present and future] spread to narrative discourse and narration proper."[44] He argues that *wayyiqtol* may express logical and/or temporal consecutive actions, as well as resumption and summary. He also argues that, with respect to the concept of taxis, *wayyiqtol* expresses anterior actions that are *perfect* within the present time frame and *pluperfect* within the past time frame.[45] Andrason gives three examples for the *pluperfect* function. However, only one of them (Num 1:48–49) should be strictly considered an example of a *temporally overlaid wayyiqtol* clause.[46] The two other examples (Gen 39:13–14 and Gen 32:34) both follow a pluperfect *qatal*. In both cases, the *wayyiqtol* clause is sequential. Consider Genesis 31:34, which is his second example:[47]

---

44. Alexander Andrason, "Biblical Hebrew *Wayyiqtol*: A Dynamic Definition," *Journal of Hebrew Scriptures* 11, no. 8 (2011): 46.
45. Ibid., 25–27.
46. See below for a discussion on this verse.
47. Ibid., 26.

34a וְרָחֵל לָקְחָה אֶת־הַתְּרָפִים (pluperfect)
34b וַתְּשִׂמֵם בְּכַר הַגָּמָל (sequential)
34c וַתֵּשֶׁב עֲלֵיהֶם (sequential)
34d וַיְמַשֵּׁשׁ לָבָן אֶת־כָּל־הָאֹהֶל (sequential)
34e וְלֹא מָצָא[48]: (momentous negation)

Andrason considers both 34b and 34c as instances of temporally overlaid *wayyiqtol* clauses. However, both are sequential in relation to the preceding clause, that is, 34b to 34a and 34c to 34b.

John A. Cook

Cook argues "simply put, if temporal succession is determined by a number of semantic factors, including viewpoint and situation aspect and adverbial modification, then a single verbal gram – regardless of how it is identified semantically – cannot fully correlate with temporal situation."[49] Therefore, he concludes that *wayyiqtol* could be used to express events that are not temporally successive. He makes an observation that the *wayyiqtol* "appears in contexts with a variety of sorts of temporal overlay."[50] His use of temporal overlay includes what should be seen strictly as *temporal overlap* (e.g. his coincidental *wayyiqtol*).

Cook discusses a type of *temporal overlay* where the pluperfect meaning can be expressed with a *wayyiqtol*. He gives three cases in which this type of *temporal overlay* can be found. (1) The *wayyiqtol* follows a pluperfect *qatal*. (2) The *wayyiqtol* follows a temporal protasis. These two are examples of a sequential *wayyiqtol* clause. (3) The third case he gives is that of Buth's first criterion, where a "lexical reference and/or repetition" signals *temporal overlay*.[51]

---

48. Cf. Roy L. Heller, *Narrative Structure and Discourse Constellations: An Analysis of Clause Function in Biblical Hebrew Prose*, Harvard Semitic Studies, ed. Jo Ann Hackett and John Huehnergard, vol. 55 (Winona Lake, IN: Eisenbrauns, 2004), 24; Robert E. Longacre, *Joseph–A Story of Divine Providence: A Text Theoretical and Textlinguistic Analysis of Genesis 37 and 39–48,* 2nd ed. (Winona Lake, IN: Eisenbrauns, 2003), 79.

49. Cook, *Time and the Biblical Hebrew Verb*, 288.

50. Ibid., 289.

51. Ibid., 291–294.

Cook, however, concludes that "a past-perfect meaning cannot be associated with *wayyiqtol*."[52] He adds that in all of the above three cases "which signal a break in the default interpretation of the clauses as temporally successive – the *wayyiqtol* conveys continuity within that newly established deictic frame; any apparent past-perfect sense is a pragmatic implicature and not semantic."[53]

Cook dismisses several of the examples offered by Baker, Buth, and Collins. For example, he considers the *wayyiqtol* in Judges 20:36b as sequential and concludes that treating it as *temporally overlaid* is a "means of harmonizing redactional difficulties."[54] However, a detailed analysis of Judges 20:29–48 shows that the author of Judges is intentionally using a temporally overlaid *wayyiqtol* as a means of narration, not a means of the reader's harmonization of a difficult passage.

Judges 20:19–48 captures Israel's attempt to fight at Gibeah. Verses 19–21 capture the first failed attack; verses 22–25 capture the second failed attack; in verses 26–28 Israel sought the Lord. Verses 29–48 capture the third and successful attack. This last attack took place in four stages.

In verse 29 Israel placed men in ambush around Gibeah. Verses 30a–33b report how the rest of the army went to Gibeah and moved from their array in front of Gibeah (v. 30b) to their array at Baal Tamar (v. 33b). Benjamin thought this was victory. However, Israel had planned this defeat.

29 וַיָּשֶׂם יִשְׂרָאֵל אֹרְבִים אֶל־הַגִּבְעָה סָבִיב׃ (initiatory)

30a וַיַּעֲלוּ בְנֵי־יִשְׂרָאֵל אֶל־בְּנֵי בִנְיָמִן בַּיּוֹם הַשְּׁלִישִׁי (simultaneous)

30b וַיַּעַרְכוּ אֶל־הַגִּבְעָה כְּפַעַם בְּפָעַם׃ (sequential)

31a וַיֵּצְאוּ בְנֵי־בִנְיָמִן לִקְרַאת הָעָם (sequential)

31b הָנְתְּקוּ מִן־הָעִיר (dramatic)[55]

31c וַיָּחֵלּוּ לְהַכּוֹת מֵהָעָם חֲלָלִים כְּפַעַם בְּפַעַם בַּמְסִלּוֹת אֲשֶׁר אַחַת עֹלָה בֵית־אֵל וְאַחַת גִּבְעָתָה בַּשָּׂדֶה כִּשְׁלֹשִׁים אִישׁ בְּיִשְׂרָאֵל׃ (sequential)

32a וַיֹּאמְרוּ בְּנֵי בִנְיָמִן (sequential)

נִגָּפִים הֵם לְפָנֵינוּ כְּבָרִאשֹׁנָה

---

52. Ibid., 294.
53. Ibid.
54. Ibid.
55. This happened at the same time 31a was happening.

32b וּבְנֵי יִשְׂרָאֵל אָמְרוּ (flashback)
נָנוּסָה וּנְתַקְּנֻהוּ מִן־הָעִיר אֶל־הַמְסִלּוֹת:
33a וְכֹל אִישׁ יִשְׂרָאֵל קָמוּ מִמְּקוֹמוֹ (resumption of v. 31b?)
33b וַיַּעַרְכוּ בְּבַעַל תָּמָר (sequential)

While the rest of the army faked a defeat in 30a–33b, the men in ambush went to Gibeah and won a victory over Benjamin by the Lord's help. Then the sons of Benjamin saw their defeat. The "sons of Benjamin" could only mean the army in the wilderness. The reference to their seeing their defeat meant that they saw the defeat of the city by the men in ambush (vv. 33c–36a). אִישׁ יִשְׂרָאֵל is a phrase used for the army faking defeat (cf. v. 36b clearly differentiates אִישׁ יִשְׂרָאֵל from אֹרֵב "the men in ambush").

33c וְאֹרֵב יִשְׂרָאֵל מֵגִיחַ מִמְּקֹמוֹ מִמַּעֲרֵה־גָבַע: (meanwhile)
34a וַיָּבֹאוּ מִנֶּגֶד לַגִּבְעָה עֲשֶׂרֶת אֲלָפִים אִישׁ בָּחוּר מִכָּל־יִשְׂרָאֵל (sequential)
34b וְהַמִּלְחָמָה כָּבֵדָה (supplemental)
34c וְהֵם לֹא יָדְעוּ כִּי־נֹגַעַת עֲלֵיהֶם הָרָעָה: (parenthetical)
35a וַיִּגֹּף יְהוָה אֶת־בִּנְיָמִן לִפְנֵי יִשְׂרָאֵל (sequential)
35b וַיַּשְׁחִיתוּ בְנֵי יִשְׂרָאֵל בְּבִנְיָמִן בַּיּוֹם הַהוּא עֶשְׂרִים וַחֲמִשָּׁה אֶלֶף וּמֵאָה אִישׁ (epexegetical)
35c כָּל־אֵלֶּה שֹׁלֵף חָרֶב: (supplemental)
36a וַיִּרְאוּ בְנֵי־בִנְיָמִן כִּי נִגָּפוּ (sequential)

The two armies are now combined in 36b–41b. This section is a flashback explaining how the story moved from the defeat of Israel (v. 32a) to the defeat of Benjamin (v. 36a). Verse 36b[56] is a flashback that gives explanation. It speaks of how the army that faked defeat did so by trusting the men in ambush.

36b וַיִּתְּנוּ אִישׁ־יִשְׂרָאֵל מָקוֹם לְבִנְיָמִן כִּי בָטְחוּ אֶל־הָאֹרֵב אֲשֶׁר שָׂמוּ אֶל־הַגִּבְעָה: (foreground)
37a וְהָאֹרֵב הֵחִישׁוּ (but: at the same time with v. 36b)
37b וַיִּפְשְׁטוּ אֶל־הַגִּבְעָה (sequential)
37c וַיִּמְשֹׁךְ הָאֹרֵב (sequential)
37d וַיַּךְ אֶת־כָּל־הָעִיר לְפִי־חָרֶב: (sequential)
38a וְהַמּוֹעֵד הָיָה לְאִישׁ יִשְׂרָאֵל עִם־הָאֹרֵב הֶרֶב לְהַעֲלוֹתָם מַשְׂאַת הֶעָשָׁן

---

56. So Chisholm, *Judges and Ruth*, 479, n. 40.

מִן־הָעִיר: (parenthetical)

39a וַיַּהֲפֹךְ אִישׁ־יִשְׂרָאֵל בַּמִּלְחָמָה (sequential)[57]

39b וּבִנְיָמִן הֵחֵל לְהַכּוֹת חֲלָלִים בְּאִישׁ־יִשְׂרָאֵל כִּשְׁלֹשִׁים אִישׁ כִּי אָמְרוּ אַךְ נִגּוֹף נִגָּף הוּא לְפָנֵינוּ כַּמִּלְחָמָה הָרִאשֹׁנָה: (flashback)

40a וְהַמַּשְׂאֵת הֵחֵלָּה לַעֲלוֹת מִן־הָעִיר עַמּוּד עָשָׁן (sequential–highlight)

40b וַיִּפֶן בִּנְיָמִן אַחֲרָיו (sequential)

40c וְהִנֵּה עָלָה כְלִיל־הָעִיר הַשָּׁמָיְמָה: (dramatic)

41a וְאִישׁ יִשְׂרָאֵל הָפַךְ (flashback to 39a)

41b וַיִּבָּהֵל אִישׁ בִּנְיָמִן כִּי רָאָה כִּי־נָגְעָה עָלָיו הָרָעָה: (sequential)

Jan Joosten

Joosten uses the term "backtracking" to refer to temporal overlay.[58] Like Baker, Joosten acknowledges that one must infer from the context whether or not the *wayyiqtol* clause expresses an event that is chronologically prior to the event of the preceding clause.[59] He argues that *backtracking* could occur within the narrative or in a separate paragraph introduced with a ויהי temporal clause.[60] One of the examples he offers for *backtracking* within the narrative is 2 Samuel 11:18–19.[61]

18a וַיִּשְׁלַח יוֹאָב (sequential)

18b וַיַּגֵּד לְדָוִד אֶת־כָּל־דִּבְרֵי הַמִּלְחָמָה: (sequential)

19a וַיְצַו אֶת־הַמַּלְאָךְ לֵאמֹר (foreground)

כְּכַלּוֹתְךָ אֵת כָּל־דִּבְרֵי הַמִּלְחָמָה לְדַבֵּר אֶל־הַמֶּלֶךְ:

Verse 19a is a foreground *wayyiqtol* clause, which introduces a flashback to verse 18a. When verse 19a is compared with verse 18b, the event of verse 19a occurred chronologically prior to verse 18b. In the absence of verse 18b, verse 19a could be seen as a case of coincidental *wayyiqtol* assuming the sending (v. 18a) and giving message (v. 19a) occur simultaneously.[62] It is also

---

57. Their turning back to fight indicates that they had seen the smoke. In v. 40 Benjamin also looked back and saw the smoke.

58. Jan Joosten, *The Verbal System of Biblical Hebrew: A New Synthesis Elaborated on the Basis of Classical Prose*, Jerusalem Biblical Studies, vol. 10 (Jerusalem: Simor, 2012), 171.

59. Ibid.

60. Ibid., 172–173.

61. Ibid.

62. John A. Cook, "The Hebrew Verb: A Grammaticalization Approach," *ZAH* 14, no. 2 (2001): 259.

possible to see the event of verse 19a as chronologically prior to verse 18a, that is, the message (v. 19a) had been given before sending the messenger(s) (v. 18a). In summary, verse 19a is a temporally overlaid clause whose event is chronologically prior to the immediately preceding clause.

Joosten offers 1 Kings 11:15–17 as an example of *backtracking* that is introduced with ויהי and temporal clause:[63]

15a וַיְהִי בִּהְיוֹת דָּוִד אֶת־אֱדוֹם . . .
15b וַיַּךְ כָּל־זָכָר בֶּאֱדוֹם . . .
17a וַיִּבְרַח אֲדַד . . .

Joosten considers verse 17a as an instance of *backtracking*. It is true that in relation to verse 14, verse 17a is chronologically prior. However, the ויהי and temporal clause in verse 15a introduce a new scene. Within the new scene that began in verse 15a, verse 17a is simply sequential.

Robert B. Chisholm

In his recently published commentary on Judges and Ruth, Chisholm offers categories that he uses to analyze both mainline (*wayyiqtol*) and offline clauses of the narratives in these two biblical books. He lists flashback as one of the mainline categories. He argues that "sometimes the narrator interrupts the chronological sequence of events and uses a *wayyiqtol* clause to refer to a prior action that now becomes relevant."[64]

Chisholm notes that a *wayyiqtol* clause could (1) refer back to an action that preceded the episode or scene chronologically (e.g. 2:23; 3:16), and (2) recall an event that occurred within the time frame of the story being related (16:3; 20:36; 21:6). With regard to its location within the narrative, the *wayyiqtol* clause can open an episode or scene (e.g. 2:6; 12:1).[65]

One of the examples Chisholm offers as a case of *temporal overlay* is Judges 21:6. He argues that it "provides the reason why Israel assembled at Bethel to mourn. It flashes back chronologically to a time before the assembly was called (v. 2). Note how verses 6b–8a give a more detailed report of their words (cf. v. 5) and how verse 8a is very similar to verse 5a."[66] Indeed, the

---

63. Joosten, *Verbal System of Biblical Hebrew*, 172.
64. Chisholm, *Judges and Ruth*, 75.
65. Ibid.
66. Ibid., 482, n. 59.

assembly's desire to find wives for the Benjaminites might not have been the reason the Israelites assembled at Bethel. This may have been a development after the second day. On the first day (vv. 2–3) no such concern is evident. However, the *wayyiqtol* in verse 6a captures the Israelites' concern for the destruction of a tribe and so captures what happened before the Israelites assembled in verse 2.

Identifying Temporally Overlaid *Wayyiqtol* Clauses

All of the scholars in the survey agree that BH most often expresses temporal overlay through the grammatical form *pluperfect qatal*, a grammatically marked form.[67] An unmarked *temporal overlay* introduces a clause whose event is chronologically prior to the preceding clause.

Although Driver and sometimes Cook consider some of these instances as cases of "redactional difficulties," others, with the exception of Chisholm, interpreted the data to mean the *wayyiqtol* verb form itself sometimes can have a *pluperfect* sense. This dissertation prefers to take the conversation from the *wayyiqtol* verb form to the *wayyiqtol* clause as Chisholm does. The author works with the assumption that nothing in the semantics of the *wayyiqtol* verb form prevents it from introducing temporally overlaid clauses. As Andrason rightly notes, "[f]rom the functional-semantic perspective, the *wayyiqtol* is a quite complex formation – it displays uses that correspond to the concepts of tense, aspect, taxis, modal, and text type, as well as those accompanied by other nuances such as consecution."[68]

In looking for "hard evidence" for the existence of unmarked temporal overlay as part of the Hebrew language system, Buth gives the following guideline:

---

67. This is when *qatal* is preceded by a *waw* and/or some other "sentence element." (Collins, "The Wayyiqtol as 'Pluperfect,'" 118). This is also referred to as a *waw-X-qatal* construction (Randall Buth, "Methodological Collision between Source Criticism and Discourse Analysis: The Problem of 'Unmarked Temporal Overlay' and the Pluperfect/Nonsequential *Wayyiqtol*," in *Biblical Hebrew and Discourse Linguistics,* ed. Robert D. Bergen [Dallas: Summer Institute of Linguistics, 1994], 139).

68. Andrason, "Biblical Hebrew *Wayyiqtol*," 24. Cook also notes, "although a 'basic' or 'primary' meaning may be determined for a particular verb form, the form is not thereby impeded from expressing other temporal, aspectual, or modal nuances typical of verbal systems, in addition to discourse-pragmatic functions," (John A. Cook, "The Hebrew Verb: A Grammaticalization Approach," *ZAH* 14, no. 2 [2001]: 118).

Internally, we can examine the attestations in the Hebrew text for consistency, limitation, and motivation of such a strucure: *consistency* because that shows that the structure is part of the system of the language; *limitation* because "unmarked temporal overlay" is working against the common structures of the language (without some limitations the whole system would dissolve); *motivation* because Hebrew is a human language and there must be some communicative or psychological purpose for a structure to develop or be accepted beyond mere "static" or "background noise."[69]

In keeping with Buth's advice, this dissertation attempts to answer the following three questions at the clausal level: (1) with regard to *consistency*, are there instances in BH where a *wayyiqtol* introduced clause is chronologically prior to the preceding clause? (2) with regard to *limitation*, how can one know when the *wayyiqtol* clause is temporally overlaid if it is not grammatically marked? and (3) with regard to *motivation*, why would an author use a *wayyiqtol* when he could have grammatically marked the temporal overlay with a *pluperfect qatal*? All of the scholars in the above survey have helped answer part or all of these questions. This dissertation proposes a way forward by synthesizing their contributions, particularly those of Buth and Cook.

The *consistency* criterion is met by ample instances of unmarked temporal overlay in the Hebrew text. See the examples offered below.

With regard to the *limitation* criterion the "final decision largely depends on general contextual considerations."[70] As Baker noted it is "strictly the context and the situation which will govern the sense of the verbal form."[71] Form is not enough. Therefore, in agreement with Buth and Collins, the following two signals in the *wayyiqtol* clause itself can help the reader identify the clause as temporally overlaid.[72]

---

69. Buth, "Methodological Collision," 145.

70. Paul Joüon and T. Muraoka, *A Grammar of Biblical Hebrew*, 2nd ed., SubBi, vol. 27 (Rome: Editrice Pontificio Instituto Biblico, 2006), 118da.

71. Baker, *The Consecutive Non-perfective*, 54.

72. In some cases it may not be present within the *wayyiqtol* clause itself but within the scene or episode being related, as in Gen 12:1. See appendix 2 for a discussion on this verse.

Flashback in the Prologue

(1) Some anaphoric reference within the *wayyiqtol clause* must clearly indicate that the event or action being described by that clause took place prior to the event or action described by the preceding clause. However, resumption signaled with lexical repetition should be distinguished from such kind of temporal overlay. The temporal overlay that introduces flashback is different from resumption. A resumptive *wayyiqtol* clause picks up an interrupted story line in order to continue it or close it. A temporally overlaid *wayyiqtol* clause, on the other hand, "interrupts" the storyline with regard to temporal progression.

For example, 1 Samuel 22: 35–37:

35a וַתַּעֲלֶה הַמִּלְחָמָה בַּיּוֹם הַהוּא
35b וְהַמֶּלֶךְ הָיָה מָעֳמָד בַּמֶּרְכָּבָה נֹכַח אֲרָם
35c וַיָּמָת בָּעֶרֶב
35d וַיִּצֶק דַּם־הַמַּכָּה אֶל־חֵיק הָרָכֶב׃
36 וַיַּעֲבֹר הָרִנָּה בַּמַּחֲנֶה כְּבֹא הַשֶּׁמֶשׁ לֵאמֹר אִישׁ אֶל־עִירוֹ וְאִישׁ אֶל־אַרְצוֹ׃
37a וַיָּמָת הַמֶּלֶךְ וַיָּבוֹא שֹׁמְרוֹן
37b וַיִּקְבְּרוּ אֶת־הַמֶּלֶךְ בְּשֹׁמְרוֹן׃

35a The battle continued on that day.
35b Now the king was propped up in his chariot facing the Arameans
35c and he died at evening
35d and the blood from the wound flowed into the bottom of the chariot.
36 Then a cry went through the camp when the sun went down "Every man to his city, and every man to his country!"
37a The king died
37b and was brought to Samaria
37c and they buried the king in Samaria.[73]

In the example above, 37a is a lexical repetition of 35c. However, this is a case of resumption. The report on the king, which was interrupted in 35d–36, is resumed and concluded in 37.

---

73. Author's translation.

(2) The logic of the *wayyiqtol* clause must indicate that the event described in it took place prior to the preceding verb. Buth calls this "culturally natural semantic relationship with the previous sentence."[74] Since "logic" is a general term, one should take caution when applying this *criterion* to any text. For example, Baker suggests that Genesis 29:12 should be regarded as *pluperfect* because "it only seems fitting that in order to maintain the young lady's decorum and modesty, Jacob would have introduced himself to Rachel prior to kissing her."[75] As Wenham notes, "This unusual sequence of actions (surely it would have been expected for Jacob to introduce himself before kissing his cousin and weeping?) portray a man swept along by the joy of meeting his cousin."[76] Therefore, though in one sense it would have been logical for Jacob to introduce himself before kissing Rachel, considering his emotional state it would be understandable for him to express his emotion before introducing himself. So it is best to see the *wayyiqtol* (ויגד) as consecutive.

One form of "logic" that needs to be considered in the study of BH texts has to do with quoted material. When book "A" quotes material from book "B," the quoted material can be assumed to be a "flashback" only if the time-frame in book "B" precedes that of book "A" and the quoted material does not describe an event with a negation. Consider the following example: Book "B" contains the statement, "X did not finish his book." If book "A" quotes this material after any number of years and yet "X" still has not finished writing his book, book "A" would still use the simple past, not a *pluperfect* to describe the non-event.

Collins, building on Driver, suggests a third criterion: the *wayyiqtol* opens a new section or paragraph.[77] None of the texts that Driver and Collins used illustrate this third criterion. All the texts they offered as examples can be explained by using either of the prior two criteria. Collins seemed to see this when he noted that 2 Samuel 13:34, 2 Samuel 12:26, and Jonah 1:17 [2:1] can be explained using the first criterion. Regarding 2 Samuel 13:34 Collins says, "the anaphoric reference in v. 34 is a way of picking up one thread of

---

74. Buth, "Methodological Collision," 142.

75. Baker, *The Consecutive Non-perfective*, 70.

76. Gordon J. Wenham, *Genesis 16–50*, WBC, ed. David A. Hubbard, Gleen W. Baker, and John D. W. Watts, vol. 2 (Dallas, TX: Word, 1994), 231.

77. Collins, "The Wayyiqtol as 'Pluperfect,'" 128.

a plot, after another has been followed, without introducing anything like contrast or prominence."[78] What is true is that there could be some instances in which the *wayyiqtol* clause could be seen as temporally overlaid according to either of the first two criteria, and at the same time that clause could begin a new paragraph. There are several instances when the clause occurs in the middle of a scene or an episode. Therefore, this dissertation will not use this criterion in identifying unmarked temporal overlay.

When approaching the issue of *motivation*, that is, with regard to why a *wayyiqtol* clause is used instead of grammatically marking it with a *pluperfect qatal*, the author draws attention to Buth's proposal:

> In cases where lexical reference or repetition signals a back-reference, again we can hypothesize that the author is primarily portraying mainline events with the *wayyiqtol* structure. The constraint of adding details to a passage without also demoting them off the mainline gives rise to this nonsequential use of the *wayyiqtol*. Thus, for both lexically signaled temporal overlay as well as semantically natural temporal overlay the *wayyiqtol* structure lifts a clause to the mainline without making another relationship prominent.[79]

Wayyiqtol is the most common narrative verb that describes the foregrounded story. Even when it describes a flashback (which normally is background information), the *wayyiqtol* brings the flashback into the foreground. This would allow the author to make the flashback an important part of his story and at the same time avoid the risk of having the reader take the material as secondary information compared to the foregrounded story.[80]

Why the author chooses to foreground background information should be analyzed case by case.[81] Cook gives the following example to illustrate why an author foregrounds background information.[82]

---

78. Ibid., 134.
79. Buth, "Methodological Collision," 147–148.
80. John A. Cook, "The Semantics of Verbal Pragmatics: Clarifying the Roles of Wayyiqtol and Weqatal in Biblical Hebrew Prose," *JSS* 49, no. 2 (2004): 262.
81. Collins, "The Wayyiqtol as 'Pluperfect,'" 132.
82. The translation for both examples is Cook's.

23 וַיְהִי בָעֶרֶב וַיִּקַּח אֶת־לֵאָה בִתּוֹ וַיָּבֵא אֹתָהּ אֵלָיו וַיָּבֹא אֵלֶיהָ: 24 וַיִּתֵּן לָבָן לָהּ אֶת־זִלְפָּה שִׁפְחָתוֹ לְלֵאָה בִתּוֹ שִׁפְחָה: 52 וַיְהִי בַבֹּקֶר וְהִנֵּה־הִוא לֵאָה

And when it was evening he took Leah, his daughter and brought her to him and he went in to her. And Laban gave Zilpah, his maidservant, to her to be a maid for Leah his daughter. And when it was morning, behold, it was Leah. (Gen 29:23–25a)

28 וַיַּעַשׂ יַעֲקֹב כֵּן וַיְמַלֵּא שְׁבֻעַ זֹאת וַיִּתֶּן־לוֹ אֶת־רָחֵל בִּתּוֹ לוֹ לְאִשָּׁה: 29 וַיִּתֵּן לָבָן לְרָחֵל בִּתּוֹ אֶת־בִּלְהָה שִׁפְחָתוֹ לָהּ לְשִׁפְחָה: 30 וַיָּבֹא גַּם אֶל־רָחֵל וַיֶּאֱהַב גַּם־אֶת־רָחֵל מִלֵּאָה

And Jacob did so and he fulfilled this seven years and he gave to him Rachel, his daughter, for a wife. And Laban gave to Rachel, his daughter, Bilhah his maid to be a maid for her. And he came in to Rachel also and he loved Rachel more than Leah. (Gen 29:28–30a)

In 29:23, what took place on the wedding night is given. Then in verse 25, what took place in the morning is given. In between these two verses, the author gives a parenthetical note, which is clearly background information, using a *wayyiqtol* clause. Likewise, the giving of Bilhah, Rachel's maid, interrupts the narration since it occurs between Laban's giving of Rachel to Jacob and the marital consummation. When a *wayyiqtol* is used for background information, which could have been described using a *qatal* clause, it is "exegetically significant."[83] Cook comments on such significance in the above two passages: ". . . by using *wayyiqtol* forms, and intentionally interrupting the reports of the two sisters' marriages to Jacob, the narrator highlights and foreshadows the role of the maid-servants as surrogate mothers in the sororial feud between Leah and Rachel."[84]

In identifying unmarked temporal overlay, the key factor is not whether or not it can be translated into a *pluperfect* in the English language, but whether or not the action or event is present in the HB as having occurred prior to another past event. Rendering such instances with the simple past

---

83. Cook, "Semantics of Verbal Pragmatics," 262.
84. Ibid.

tense in English cannot be used to argue that the *wayyiqtol* clause is not expressing an event which is chronologically prior to the event of the preceding clause.

As argued above, since the *wayyiqtol* clause is used to bring the flashback into the foreground, in translating into English or any other language the tense of choice should be one that is used for foregrounding in that language. In keeping with the Hebrew, English translations should use the simple past because "the simple past tense ranks highest in English narrative (unless a story is told in the historical present)."[85] Therefore, the use of the simple past in English in the translation of unmarked temporal overlay would not necessarily create a problem, unless the logic is not "cultural" to the the modern reader. Instead of translating with the English pluperfect, it is preferable to use footnotes, teachings, and commentaries to make this feature of BH narrative understandable to the English reader lest the reader misunderstand the chronological relationship between the clauses.

Consider the following example from English that Zevit gives:[86]

(1a) John fell.

(1b) Max pushed him.

Zevit reasons that if one starts reading 1b followed by 1a, logic, that is, in his words "our experience of the world" would help the reader to know that the order of the two sentences is in conformity with the chronological sequence that actually happened. If, however, the reader were to read them in the order given above, the reader would still be able to recognize 1a as chronologically sequential to 1b. Though both are in simple past, 1b is clearly chronologically prior to 1a. Zevit argues though some English writers may use the *pluperfect*, those who are simply concerned with the pastness of two related events could choose to use the simple past and still be understood by their readers/listeners. He comments:

> . . . in English, people who wish to use the pluperfect "had pushed" do so. And therefore, when they do not use the pluperfect in utterances, they do not intend to do so; rather, they

---

85. Robert E. Longacre, *Joseph – A Story of Divine Providence: A Text Theoretical and Textlinguistic Analysis of Genesis 37 and 39–48* (Winona Lake, IN: Eisenbrauns, 1989), 61.

86. Zevit, *Anterior Construction*, 9.

employ the simple past to indicate two related events out of causal and chronological sequence because the pastness of the events, and that alone, is all that concerns them. They assume that competent listeners will comprehend the proper sequence. Hence, the "pluperfectness" of the second verb is actually a consequence of mental resequencing and interpretation, not of formal grammatical representation.[87]

Below is another example that can illustrate the use of the simple past in English to describe an event that is chronologically prior: "Whereas George W. Bush *pursued* a transformative, even revolutionary foreign policy, his father *worked* to insure that the post-Cold War world would not succumb to international lawlessness."[88] Here also, the author is not concerned with the chronological order of events. The author expects his readers to know the chronological order of the presidency of George W. Bush and his father. Here the pastness of the two events is what matters, not their chronological order. The author is simply interested in comparing the two presidents, not in clarifying the order of their presidency. This is true when the purpose of the author is to compare two individuals, group(s), or event(s) in the past.

Examples of Temporally Overlaid *Wayyiqtol* Clauses

This section gives some examples of temporally overlaid *wayyiqtol* clauses in BH. The examples come from such genres as genealogy (Gen 11:16, 18, 20, 24, 26), narrative prose (Josh 2:4; 8:12; Num 1:48; 9:1), and narrative discourse (Deut 1:9; 3:23).

Genesis 11:16, 18, 20, 24, 26

10a אֵלֶּה תּוֹלְדֹת שֵׁם (title)

10b שֵׁם בֶּן־מְאַת שָׁנָה (introductory)

10c וַיּוֹלֶד אֶת־אַרְפַּכְשָׁד שְׁנָתַיִם אַחַר הַמַּבּוּל׃ (initiatory)

11a וַיְחִי־שֵׁם אַחֲרֵי הוֹלִידוֹ אֶת־אַרְפַּכְשָׁד חֲמֵשׁ מֵאוֹת שָׁנָה (sequential)

11b וַיּוֹלֶד בָּנִים וּבָנוֹת׃ (simultaneous)

12a וְאַרְפַּכְשַׁד חַי חָמֵשׁ וּשְׁלֹשִׁים שָׁנָה (pluperfect)

---

87. Ibid., 9.

88. Marc J. O'Reilly and Wesley B. Renfro, "Like Father, Like Son? A Comparison of the Foreign Policies of George H. W. Bush and George W. Bush," *HAOL* 10 (2006): 30.

Flashback in the Prologue

12b וַיּוֹלֶד אֶת־שָׁלַח: (sequential)
13a וַיְחִי אַרְפַּכְשַׁד אַחֲרֵי הוֹלִידוֹ אֶת־שֶׁלַח שָׁלֹשׁ שָׁנִים וְאַרְבַּע מֵאוֹת שָׁנָה (sequential)
13b וַיּוֹלֶד בָּנִים וּבָנוֹת: (simultaneous)
14a וְשֶׁלַח חַי שְׁלֹשִׁים שָׁנָה (pluperfect)
14b וַיּוֹלֶד אֶת־עֵבֶר: (sequential)
15a וַיְחִי־שֶׁלַח אַחֲרֵי הוֹלִידוֹ אֶת־עֵבֶר שָׁלֹשׁ שָׁנִים וְאַרְבַּע מֵאוֹת שָׁנָה (sequential)
15b וַיּוֹלֶד בָּנִים וּבָנוֹת: (simultaneous)
16a וַיְחִי־עֵבֶר אַרְבַּע וּשְׁלֹשִׁים שָׁנָה (foreground)
16b וַיּוֹלֶד אֶת־פָּלֶג: (sequential)
17a וַיְחִי־עֵבֶר אַחֲרֵי הוֹלִידוֹ אֶת־פֶּלֶג שְׁלֹשִׁים שָׁנָה וְאַרְבַּע מֵאוֹת שָׁנָה (sequential)
17b וַיּוֹלֶד בָּנִים וּבָנוֹת: (simultaneous)
18a וַיְחִי־פֶלֶג שְׁלֹשִׁים שָׁנָה (foreground)
18b וַיּוֹלֶד אֶת־רְעוּ: (sequential)
19a וַיְחִי־פֶלֶג אַחֲרֵי הוֹלִידוֹ אֶת־רְעוּ תֵּשַׁע שָׁנִים וּמָאתַיִם שָׁנָה (sequential)
19b וַיּוֹלֶד בָּנִים וּבָנוֹת (simultaneous)

Genesis 11:10–32 is a genealogical list. Other than the verbless clauses in the title and the introductory clauses, *wayyiqtol* clauses predominate in the list. The *wayyiqtol* clauses in verses 16, 18, 20, 22, 24 and 26 are all temporally overlaid. This is signaled by a lexical phrase, that is, the ages of the individuals mentioned in these verses. Another clear indicator that the *wayyiqtols* in these verses are temporally overlaid is the use of *waw-X-qatal* in verse 12 and verse 14. The *waw-X-qatal* in these two verses parallels its function with the *wayyiqtol* clauses in verses 16, 18, 20, 22, 24 and 26. The author's choice to use the *wayyiqtol* instead of *waw-X-qatal* seems to be to avoid distraction that can be caused by the disjunctive construction *waw-X-qatal*.

Numbers 9:1

Num 1:1 וַיְדַבֵּר יְהוָה אֶל־מֹשֶׁה בְּמִדְבַּר סִינַי בְּאֹהֶל מוֹעֵד בְּאֶחָד לַחֹדֶשׁ הַשֵּׁנִי בַּשָּׁנָה הַשֵּׁנִית לְצֵאתָם מֵאֶרֶץ מִצְרָיִם

Num 9:1 וַיְדַבֵּר יְהוָה אֶל־מֹשֶׁה בְמִדְבַּר־סִינַי בַּשָּׁנָה הַשֵּׁנִית לְצֵאתָם מֵאֶרֶץ מִצְרַיִם בַּחֹדֶשׁ הָרִאשׁוֹן

The event of Numbers 1:1 occurred on the first day of the second month of the second year after the Exodus. The *wayyiqtol* clause opening Numbers 9:1 has a lexical reference, בַּחֹדֶשׁ הָרִאשׁוֹן, that explicitly marks the event of this verse as chronologically prior to that of Numbers 1:1. The narrative that precedes Numbers 9:1 is Numbers 8:5–26, which speaks of the consecration of the Levites who were chosen after Numbers 1:1, that is, after the first day of the second month. Numbers 1:1–6:27 happened within the second month. The narrative backtracked in Numbers 7:1–8:4 to the time prior to Numbers 1:1 by means of a וַיְהִי temporal clause, which can been seen as parallel in its function to a *waw-X-qatal*. Numbers 8:5–26 returns to the narrative trajectory of Numbers 1:1–6:27 by speaking about the ceremonial cleaning of the Levites who were chosen after Numbers 1:1.

Numbers is primarily thematic, not chronological. According to Numbers 9:1, the Lord commanded in the first month that the Passover could be observed on the fourteenth day of the second month of the second year. It is delayed until this chapter for the purpose of fitting the story to the chronology of the second month narrative that began in 1:1.

Numbers 1:48

1a יְדַבֵּר יְהוָה אֶל־מֹשֶׁה׃ . . . לֵאמֹר . . . (initiatory)
2–15 quotation: command regarding census
16 אֵלֶּה קְרִיאֵי הָעֵדָה נְשִׂיאֵי מַטּוֹת אֲבוֹתָם רָאשֵׁי אַלְפֵי יִשְׂרָאֵל הֵם׃ (summary)
17 וַיִּקַּח מֹשֶׁה וְאַהֲרֹן אֵת הָאֲנָשִׁים הָאֵלֶּה אֲשֶׁר נִקְּבוּ בְּשֵׁמוֹת׃ (sequential to 1a)
18a וְאֵת כָּל־הָעֵדָה הִקְהִילוּ בְּאֶחָד לַחֹדֶשׁ הַשֵּׁנִי (parenthetical)
18b וַיִּתְיַלְדוּ עַל־מִשְׁפְּחֹתָם לְבֵית אֲבֹתָם בְּמִסְפַּר שֵׁמוֹת מִבֶּן עֶשְׂרִים שָׁנָה וָמַעְלָה לְגֻלְגְּלֹתָם׃ 19 כַּאֲשֶׁר צִוָּה יְהוָה אֶת־מֹשֶׁה (sequential)
19b וַיִּפְקְדֵם בְּמִדְבַּר סִינָי׃ (summary)
List 20–43
44a אֵלֶּה הַפְּקֻדִים אֲשֶׁר פָּקַד מֹשֶׁה וְאַהֲרֹן וּנְשִׂיאֵי יִשְׂרָאֵל שְׁנֵים עָשָׂר אִישׁ (summary)
44b אִישׁ־אֶחָד לְבֵית־אֲבֹתָיו הָיוּ׃ (supplemental)
45 וַיִּהְיוּ כָּל־פְּקוּדֵי בְנֵי־יִשְׂרָאֵל לְבֵית אֲבֹתָם מִבֶּן עֶשְׂרִים שָׁנָה וָמַעְלָה כָּל־יֹצֵא צָבָא בְּיִשְׂרָאֵל׃ (supplemental)
46 וַיִּהְיוּ כָּל־הַפְּקֻדִים שֵׁשׁ־מֵאוֹת אֶלֶף וּשְׁלֹשֶׁת אֲלָפִים וַחֲמֵשׁ מֵאוֹת וַחֲמִשִּׁים׃ (supplemental)

Flashback in the Prologue

47 וְהַלְוִיִּם לְמַטֵּה אֲבֹתָם לֹא הָתְפָּקְדוּ בְּתוֹכָם: (contrastive)
48 וַיְדַבֵּר יְהוָה אֶל־מֹשֶׁה לֵּאמֹר: (flashback)
quote 49–53
54a וַיַּעֲשׂוּ בְּנֵי יִשְׂרָאֵל כְּכֹל אֲשֶׁר צִוָּה יְהוָה אֶת־מֹשֶׁה (concluding)
54b כֵּן עָשׂוּ: (reiterative)

The Lord spoke (v. 1) and gave a specific command (vv. 2–4) regarding a census that Moses and Aaron were to do with the help of tribal leaders (vv. 5–15). The obedience to the command is reported in verse 19b. The list in verses 20–43 and the paragraph in verses 44a–46 give static comment about characters involved in the census. The paragraph in verses 44a–46 is governed by participles and היה clauses, which give "inner-paragraph comments."[89] These clauses neither cause the narrative to progress nor break the narrative sequence.[90]

Numbers 1:47 introduces new characters within the discourse topic of the chapter. Contrary to Cook's proposal, 1:47 does not introduce a new discourse topic.[91] Numbers 1:47 still gives a static comment on the obedience of the census which was done in verse 19b. Numbers 1:47 employs a disjunctive clause to set up a contrast: But the Levites . . . Verses 48–49 then uses a flashback to 1:19 so the reader will understand why the Levites were not part of the census. The content of the command signals that the *wayyiqtol* clause in verse 48 is temporally overlaid with verse 47 and verse 19b. The narrative was progressing with some pauses but never backtracked until verse 48.

---

89. Heller, *Narrative Structure and Discourse Constellations*, 450–451.
90. Ibid., 441.
91. Cook, *Time and the Biblical Hebrew Verb*, 294.

Deuteronomy 1:9

6 יְהוָה אֱלֹהֵינוּ דִּבֶּר אֵלֵינוּ בְּחֹרֵב לֵאמֹר (initiatory)
רַב־לָכֶם שֶׁבֶת בָּהָר הַזֶּה:
7 פְּנוּ וּסְעוּ לָכֶם וּבֹאוּ הַר הָאֱמֹרִי וְאֶל־כָּל־שְׁכֵנָיו בָּעֲרָבָה בָהָר וּבַשְּׁפֵלָה וּבַנֶּגֶב וּבְחוֹף הַיָּם אֶרֶץ הַכְּנַעֲנִי וְהַלְּבָנוֹן עַד־הַנָּהָר הַגָּדֹל נְהַר־פְּרָת: 8 רְאֵה נָתַתִּי לִפְנֵיכֶם אֶת־הָאָרֶץ בֹּאוּ וּרְשׁוּ אֶת־הָאָרֶץ אֲשֶׁר נִשְׁבַּע יְהוָה לַאֲבֹתֵיכֶם לְאַבְרָהָם לְיִצְחָק וּלְיַעֲקֹב לָתֵת לָהֶם וּלְזַרְעָם אַחֲרֵיהֶם:
9 וָאֹמַר אֲלֵכֶם בָּעֵת הַהִוא לֵאמֹר (foreground)
לֹא־אוּכַל לְבַדִּי שְׂאֵת אֶתְכֶם: 10 יְהוָה אֱלֹהֵיכֶם הִרְבָּה אֶתְכֶם וְהִנְּכֶם הַיּוֹם כְּכוֹכְבֵי הַשָּׁמַיִם לָרֹב: 11 יְהוָה אֱלֹהֵי אֲבוֹתֵכֶם יֹסֵף עֲלֵיכֶם כָּכֶם אֶלֶף פְּעָמִים וִיבָרֵךְ אֶתְכֶם כַּאֲשֶׁר דִּבֶּר לָכֶם: 12 אֵיכָה אֶשָּׂא לְבַדִּי טָרְחֲכֶם וּמַשַּׂאֲכֶם וְרִיבְכֶם: 13 הָבוּ לָכֶם אֲנָשִׁים חֲכָמִים וּנְבֹנִים וִידֻעִים לְשִׁבְטֵיכֶם וַאֲשִׂימֵם בְּרָאשֵׁיכֶם:
14 וַתַּעֲנוּ אֹתִי וַתֹּאמְרוּ (sequential)
טוֹב־הַדָּבָר אֲשֶׁר־דִּבַּרְתָּ לַעֲשׂוֹת:
15 וָאֶקַּח אֶת־רָאשֵׁי שִׁבְטֵיכֶם אֲנָשִׁים חֲכָמִים וִידֻעִים (sequential)
וָאֶתֵּן אוֹתָם רָאשִׁים עֲלֵיכֶם שָׂרֵי אֲלָפִים וְשָׂרֵי מֵאוֹת וְשָׂרֵי חֲמִשִּׁים וְשָׂרֵי עֲשָׂרֹת וְשֹׁטְרִים לְשִׁבְטֵיכֶם:
16 וָאֲצַוֶּה אֶת־שֹׁפְטֵיכֶם בָּעֵת הַהִוא לֵאמֹר (sequential)
שָׁמֹעַ בֵּין־אֲחֵיכֶם וּשְׁפַטְתֶּם צֶדֶק בֵּין־אִישׁ וּבֵין־אָחִיו וּבֵין גֵּרוֹ: 17 לֹא־תַכִּירוּ פָנִים בַּמִּשְׁפָּט כַּקָּטֹן כַּגָּדֹל תִּשְׁמָעוּן לֹא תָגוּרוּ מִפְּנֵי־אִישׁ כִּי הַמִּשְׁפָּט לֵאלֹהִים הוּא וְהַדָּבָר אֲשֶׁר יִקְשֶׁה מִכֶּם תַּקְרִבוּן אֵלַי וּשְׁמַעְתִּיו:
18 וָאֲצַוֶּה אֶתְכֶם בָּעֵת הַהִוא אֵת כָּל־הַדְּבָרִים אֲשֶׁר תַּעֲשׂוּן: (sequential)
19a וַנִּסַּע מֵחֹרֵב (sequential)
19b וַנֵּלֶךְ אֵת כָּל־הַמִּדְבָּר הַגָּדוֹל וְהַנּוֹרָא הַהוּא אֲשֶׁר רְאִיתֶם דֶּרֶךְ הַר הָאֱמֹרִי כַּאֲשֶׁר צִוָּה יְהוָה אֱלֹהֵינוּ אֹתָנוּ (sequential)
19c וַנָּבֹא עַד קָדֵשׁ בַּרְנֵעַ: (concluding)

Deuteronomy 1:6–3:28 is a narrative discourse.[92] Moses began by reporting the Lord's command to leave Sinai in 1:6–8. Obedience to this command is reported in verse 19a followed by the journey report in verses 19b–c. Whereas verses 6–8 capture what happened at the end of their stay at Sinai, verses 9–17 takes the audience back to the time when they had just arrived at Sinai. It takes them to Exodus 18. Verse 18 summarized what

---

92. Heller, *Narrative Structure and Discourse Constellations*, 458–462.

happened during their stay at Sinai, namely, the giving of the Law (Exod 19–Num 10:10).

Deuteronomy 1:9, which takes the audience to the beginning of their stay at Sinai, is introduced with a *wayyiqtol* clause. The content of the speech in verses 9–17 signals that the *wayyiqtol* clause is chronologically prior to verse 6 where the narrative discourse began.

Deuteronomy 3:23

21 וְאֶת־יְהוֹשׁוּעַ צִוֵּיתִי בָּעֵת הַהִוא לֵאמֹר (initiatory)
עֵינֶיךָ הָרֹאֹת אֵת כָּל־אֲשֶׁר עָשָׂה יְהוָה אֱלֹהֵיכֶם לִשְׁנֵי הַמְּלָכִים הָאֵלֶּה
כֵּן־יַעֲשֶׂה יְהוָה לְכָל־הַמַּמְלָכוֹת אֲשֶׁר אַתָּה עֹבֵר שָׁמָּה: 22 לֹא תִּירָאוּם כִּי יְהוָה אֱלֹהֵיכֶם הוּא הַנִּלְחָם לָכֶם:

23 וָאֶתְחַנַּן אֶל־יְהוָה בָּעֵת הַהִוא לֵאמֹר: (foreground)
24 אֲדֹנָי יְהוִה אַתָּה הַחִלּוֹתָ לְהַרְאוֹת אֶת־עַבְדְּךָ אֶת־גָּדְלְךָ וְאֶת־יָדְךָ הַחֲזָקָה אֲשֶׁר מִי־אֵל בַּשָּׁמַיִם וּבָאָרֶץ אֲשֶׁר־יַעֲשֶׂה כְמַעֲשֶׂיךָ וְכִגְבוּרֹתֶךָ:
25 אֶעְבְּרָה־נָּא וְאֶרְאֶה אֶת־הָאָרֶץ הַטּוֹבָה אֲשֶׁר בְּעֵבֶר הַיַּרְדֵּן הָהָר הַטּוֹב הַזֶּה וְהַלְּבָנוֹן:

26a וַיִּתְעַבֵּר יְהוָה בִּי לְמַעַנְכֶם (sequential)
26b וְלֹא שָׁמַע אֵלָי (contrastive)
26c וַיֹּאמֶר יְהוָה אֵלַי (epexegetical)
רַב־לָךְ אַל־תּוֹסֶף דַּבֵּר אֵלַי עוֹד בַּדָּבָר הַזֶּה: 27 עֲלֵה רֹאשׁ הַפִּסְגָּה וְשָׂא עֵינֶיךָ יָמָּה וְצָפֹנָה וְתֵימָנָה וּמִזְרָחָה וּרְאֵה בְעֵינֶיךָ כִּי־לֹא תַעֲבֹר אֶת־הַיַּרְדֵּן הַזֶּה:
28 וְצַו אֶת־יְהוֹשֻׁעַ וְחַזְּקֵהוּ וְאַמְּצֵהוּ כִּי־הוּא יַעֲבֹר לִפְנֵי הָעָם הַזֶּה וְהוּא יַנְחִיל אוֹתָם אֶת־הָאָרֶץ אֲשֶׁר תִּרְאֶה:

29 וַנֵּשֶׁב בַּגַּיְא מוּל בֵּית פְּעוֹר: (summarizing)

Deuteronomy 3:21–29 is part of the narrative discourse that began in Deuteronomy 1:6. In verse 21 Moses commissioned Joshua. The use of the near demonstratives in "these kings" suggests that Moses' words to Joshua were spoken right after the defeat of the kings (Num 21:21–35), the defeat Moses had just narrated in Deuteronomy 2:24–3:11. Since he talked about the defeat of Sihon and Og (2:24–3:11), he decided to talk about the allocation of these lands (3:12–20). Then in verse 21 he continues the narrative from 3:11. Both the near demonstrative pronoun in לִשְׁנֵי הַמְּלָכִים הָאֵלֶּה and the temporal anaphor, בָּעֵת הַהִוא, resume the narrative that was paused by the report on land allocation.

In verses 23–28 Moses pleaded with the Lord to change his mind and allow him to enter Canaan. It seems that the defeat of the two kings might have prompted Moses to ask the Lord to change his mind by saying, "you have begun to show me your greatness and strength." This is probably a reference to the defeat of the two kings. The temporal anaphor, בָּעֵת הַהִוא, also supports seeing his prayer as happening right after the victory over these kings.

The Lord's response to Moses' plea included a command to commission Joshua (v. 28). Therefore, the lexical reference וְצַו אֶת־יְהוֹשֻׁעַ in verse 28, which was already accomplished in verse 21, explicitly marks the *wayyiqtol* clause at verse 23a as introducing a foregrounded flashback. The command to Joshua in verse 21 marked an obedience to verse 28. Moses narrates verses 23–29 as an explanation for why he had to commission Joshua.

Joshua 2:4

2:1a וַיִּשְׁלַח יְהוֹשֻׁעַ־בִּן־נוּן מִן־הַשִּׁטִּים שְׁנַיִם־אֲנָשִׁים מְרַגְּלִים
חֶרֶשׁ לֵאמֹר (initiatory)
לְכוּ רְאוּ אֶת־הָאָרֶץ וְאֶת־יְרִיחוֹ
1b וַיֵּלְכוּ (sequential)
1c וַיָּבֹאוּ בֵּית־אִשָּׁה זוֹנָה (sequential)
1d וּשְׁמָהּ רָחָב (supplemental)
1e וַיִּשְׁכְּבוּ־שָׁמָּה: (sequential)
2 וַיֵּאָמַר לְמֶלֶךְ יְרִיחוֹ לֵאמֹר (sequential)
הִנֵּה אֲנָשִׁים בָּאוּ הֵנָּה הַלַּיְלָה מִבְּנֵי יִשְׂרָאֵל לַחְפֹּר אֶת־הָאָרֶץ:
3 וַיִּשְׁלַח מֶלֶךְ יְרִיחוֹ אֶל־רָחָב לֵאמֹר (sequential)
הוֹצִיאִי הָאֲנָשִׁים הַבָּאִים אֵלַיִךְ אֲשֶׁר־בָּאוּ
לְבֵיתֵךְ כִּי לַחְפֹּר אֶת־כָּל־הָאָרֶץ בָּאוּ:
4a וַתִּקַּח הָאִשָּׁה אֶת־שְׁנֵי הָאֲנָשִׁים (flashback–parenthetical)
4b וַתִּצְפְּנוֹ (sequential–parenthetical)
4c וַתֹּאמֶר (sequential to v. 3)
כֵּן בָּאוּ אֵלַי הָאֲנָשִׁים וְלֹא יָדַעְתִּי מֵאַיִן הֵמָּה:

Verse 4a–b reports that Rahab hid the two spies. The narrative order is as follows: (1) the king sent messengers, (2) the messengers spoke to Rahab,[93]

---

93. Verse 3 should be read in light of v. 1. Both of them follow the structure: וַיִּשְׁלַח plus לֵאמֹר. In v. 1, the content of what Joshua said was fulfilled in v. 2. One can then assume

(3) Rahab hid the two men, (4) Rahab's response to the messengers. If the narrative order depicted the actual order of events, the implication would be that Rahab had hidden the men after the messengers had delivered the king's message and before she gave them her response (i.e. while they were at her house). This is very unlikely. The actual order of events must have been (1), (3), (2), and (4). The *wayyiqtol* of 4a is a *foreground wayyiqtol*, which meets the second criterion, that is, the logic of the event of verse 4a–b requires that hiding the spies must have taken place before the messengers arrived. Therefore, verse 4a–b should be read as a parenthetical note that describes what Rahab had done before the king's messengers spoke to her. Verse 6, which gives supplemental information that adds to verse 4a–b, also backtracks the narrative as did verse 4a–b but uses a *waw*-X-*qatal* construction. The author's use of a *foreground wayyiqtol* in verse 4a–b instead of a *background waw*-X-*qatal* as in verse 6 could be to make 4a–b, the parenthetical information, an important part of the narrative. It adds to the suspense of the narrative.

Joshua 8:12[94]

3a וַיָּקָם יְהוֹשֻׁעַ וְכָל־עַם הַמִּלְחָמָה לַעֲלוֹת הָעָי (initiatory)[95]
3b וַיִּבְחַר יְהוֹשֻׁעַ שְׁלֹשִׁים אֶלֶף אִישׁ גִּבּוֹרֵי הַחַיִל (expexegtical)
3c וַיִּשְׁלָחֵם לָיְלָה (sequential)
4 וַיְצַו אֹתָם לֵאמֹר . . . (simultaneous)
9a וַיִּשְׁלָחֵם יְהוֹשֻׁעַ (resumptive)
9b וַיֵּלְכוּ אֶל־הַמַּאְרָב (sequential)
9c וַיֵּשְׁבוּ בֵּין בֵּית־אֵל וּבֵין הָעַי מִיָּם לָעָי (sequential)
9d וַיָּלֶן יְהוֹשֻׁעַ בַּלַּיְלָה הַהוּא בְּתוֹךְ הָעָם (simultaneous)

---

that the content of the king's message in v. 3 was also fulfilled (i.e. his message has already been communicated to Rahab) even if the author does not report that. It should be assumed that the messengers must have spoken to her before she replied in 4c. The most likely place for the delivery of their message is v. 3 itself. In fact, the quoted speech itself is most likely what the messengers spoke to her rather than what the king said to them.

94. So Robert G. Boling, *Joshua: A New Translation with Notes and Commentary*, AB, ed. William Foxwell Albright and David Noel Freedman (Garden City, NY: Doubleday and Company, 1982), 239. He comments: "Without vv. 3–11, it would most naturally translate as simple past tense, 'He took,' following directly upon the order given him in v. 2! After incorporation of the parallel account in vv 3–11, the same verb would be understood as past perfect, referring back to the previous action."

95. וַיֹּאמֶר in v. 1 is introductory background.

10a וַיַּשְׁכֵּם יְהוֹשֻׁעַ בַּבֹּקֶר (sequential)
10b וַיִּפְקֹד אֶת־הָעָם (sequential)
10c וַיַּעַל הוּא וְזִקְנֵי יִשְׂרָאֵל לִפְנֵי הָעָם הָעָי: (sequential)
11a וְכָל־הָעָם הַמִּלְחָמָה אֲשֶׁר אִתּוֹ עָלוּ (pluperfect)
11b וַיִּגְּשׁוּ (sequential)
11c וַיָּבֹאוּ נֶגֶד הָעִיר (sequential)
11d וַיַּחֲנוּ מִצְּפוֹן לָעָי (sequential)
11e וְהַגַּי בֵּינוֹ וּבֵין־הָעָי: (supplemental)
12a וַיִּקַּח כַּחֲמֵשֶׁת אֲלָפִים אִישׁ (foreground)
12b וַיָּשֶׂם אוֹתָם אֹרֵב בֵּין בֵּית־אֵל וּבֵין הָעַי מִיָּם לָעִיר: (sequential)
13a וַיָּשִׂימוּ הָעָם אֶת־כָּל־הַמַּחֲנֶה אֲשֶׁר מִצְּפוֹן לָעִיר וְאֶת־עֲקֵבוֹ מִיָּם לָעִיר (reiterative)
13b וַיֵּלֶךְ יְהוֹשֻׁעַ בַּלַּיְלָה הַהוּא בְּתוֹךְ הָעֵמֶק: (foreground)

Joshua 8:3–13 captures the preparation for the battle against Ai, from choosing the army (v. 3) to their position north and west of Ai (v. 13). The thirty thousand mighty warriors of verse 3b refer to all the people of war of verse 3a. Joshua sent this army at night (v. 3c). As he sent them, he gave them instructions (vv. 4–8). The content of the instructions clearly indicates that the army is now divided into two: the ambush men (v. 4) and those who were with him (v. 5). Joshua sent the ambush men (v. 9a), and they positioned themselves at the place of ambush (v. 9b–c); but he stayed with the remaining army (v. 9d). Verses 10a–11e capture how Joshua and the rest of the army positioned themselves north of Ai. Verse 12a backtracks to the time when Joshua elected five thousand men (though their number was not specified earlier) and set them at the place of ambush (by his command, not by being physically present with them). Therefore, the *wayyiqtol* clause in verse 12a is temporally overlaid, signaled by verse 12b, which reports the action that has already taken place in verse 9a–c. Verse 13a reiterates the positioning of the two groups of army.

Summary

A clause whose event took place prior to the event in the preceding clause could be introduced via a *wayyiqtol* clause which is discourse-pragmatically marked. Though normally, BH uses pluperfect *qatal* to introduce chronolgically prior events, *foreground wayyiqtol* is used to bring such events into the foreground of the storyline. The use of contextual markers (i.e. lexical or anaphoric reference) signals that the event being narrated occurred chronologically prior to the preceding clause.

The *wayyiqtol* that follows a verb with a *pluperfect* sense (whether a pluperfect *qatal* or foreground *wayyiqtol*) is considered a *consecutive*. Such wayyiqtols are best translated with the English simple past tense, not with the *pluperfect / past perfect*.[96]

Flashbacks in Judges 1:1–3:6

To this point this dissertation has established a guideline for identifying temporally overlaid *wayyiqtol* clauses and has illustrated the existence of such instances in BH by giving some examples. The following section will identify four temporally overlaid *wayyiqtol* clauses in Judges 1:1–3:6 that meet the guidelines. As mentioned earlier, all of these *wayyiqtol* clauses introduce flashbacks that take the reader back to the time of Joshua, both to the time when he was still alive and to the time of the elders who outlived him.

Evaluation of Judah's Success (Judg 1:8–16, 20)

Judges 1:8–16 and 1:20 belong to the conquest report of Judah that is covered in 1:4–7 and 1:17–19. In 1:4–7, Judah engaged in a battle against a coalition at Bezek and won the battle bringing home a mutilated king who, very likely, was the leader of the coalition. In 1:17–19, Judah engaged in a conquest that ended with partial success.

As some have already pointed out,[97] editions of the HB such as *BHK*, *BHS*, and *BHQ*, insert פ (i.e. *petucha*) at the end of verse 7 signaling a paragraph break at that point.[98] These editions also consider verse 15 as the end of this new section and then take verse 16 as the beginning of another section.

Sasson agrees with these editions and takes verse 8 as opening a new section. He then argues that verses 8–11 could be taken as part of the preceding

---

96. Cf. Driver, *Treatise*, 84.

97. So Tammi J. Schneider, *Judges*, BO, ed. David W. Cotter (Collegeville, MN: Liturgical, 2000), 7.

98. Jack M. Sasson, *Judges 1–12: A New Translation with Introduction and Commentary*, AYB, ed. John J. Collins, vol. 6D (New Haven: Yale University Press, 2014), 138.

section that deals with the battle at Bezek.[99] He concludes that "adhering to the traditional division allows vv. 8–11 to play Janus, looking backward to Judah's continued assault on the Canaanites, but also looking forward to involving diverse groups that come to be part of Judah."[100]

Though one cannot be sure what the Masoretic division was based on, the division does not seem to structure the text with the intention of following the argument of the author of the book of Judges. One possible explanation for the Masoretic division of verses 8–15 as a separate paragraph is that these verses are based on the book of Joshua. Except for verse 8, the rest is more or less a direct quotation from Joshua (10:40; 15:13–19). It will be argued below that even verse 8 is implied in Joshua 10. Though Sasson and editions of the *HB* end this new section in verse 15, the structure of the text appears to point to verse 16 as the closing element. Verse 16 is more closely tied to verses 8–15 than to verses 17–20.

The topic of the narrative demonstrates that verse 16 belongs with verses 8–15. Although in verses 3–7 and 17–19 the subject is יהודה with שמעון, in verses 8–16 the subject is בני יהודה. Within verses 8–16 יהודה used twice, in verse 10 and in verse 16. The latter, מדבר יהודה, refers to part of the land, not the tribal people. In verse 10, יהודה refers to Caleb and so has specialized meaning, that is, a Judahite family, rather than the tribe of Judah.[101]

Webb explains the change of the subject from the singular יהודה to the plural בני יהודה differently. He argues that the distributive בני יהודה replaces יהודה after verse 8 and claims that it becomes the norm for the rest of the chapter.[102] He interprets this change as the author's attempt to show "the solidarity of the present Israelites with their ancestors and/or with one another."[103] Despite Webb's claim, the plural בני יהודה is used only in verses 8–16. The singular continues to be used in verses 17–19. Solidarity of the present Israelites with their ancestors is not what the author is communicating. In fact, he is doing exactly the opposite throughout the prologue.

---

99. Ibid.
100. Ibid.
101. See below for a discussion on the change from "Caleb" to "Judah."
102. Barry G. Webb, *The Book of Judges*, NICOT, ed. R. K. Harrison and Robert L. Hubbard (Grand Rapids: Eerdmans, 2012), 100.
103. Ibid.

Moreover, this change of tribal names does not occur for the other tribes as table 2 shows. The only tribe with two alternative titles in the prologue is Judah.

Table 2. Titles of the Tribes in Judges 1 and Joshua

Title 1	Title 2	Occurrences	Titles in Joshua
יְהוּדָה	בְּנֵי יְהוּדָה	1:2, 3, 4, **10**, **16**, 17, 18, 19 1:8, 9, 16	מטה יהודה; בני יהודה; שבט יהודה משפחת יהודה
שִׁמְעוֹן		1:3 (2x), 17	בני שמעון מטה בני שמעון
בְּנֵי בִנְיָמִן		1:21 (2x)	בני בנימן מטה בנימן
בֵּית־יוֹסֵף		1:22, 23, 35	בית יוסף; בני יוסף
מְנַשֶּׁה		1:27	בני מנשה שבט מנשה מטה מנשה
אֶפְרַיִם		1:29	בני אפרים מטה אפרים
זְבוּלֻן		1:30	בני זבולן מטה זבולן
אָשֵׁר		1:31, 32 (הָאָשֵׁרִי)	בני אשר מטה אשר
נַפְתָּלִי		1:33	בני נפתלי מטה נפתלי
בְּנֵי־דָן		1:34	בני דן מטה דן

Looking at table 2, one wonders why the author uses an alternate title for Judah and not the other tribes. A closer look at the distribution of Judah's title in Judges 1 and comparison to its distribution in the book of Joshua and the rest of the former prophets reveals that there is a rhetorical purpose for the change from יהודה to בני יהודה.[104]

The title יהודה occurs 230 times throughout the former prophets. In Joshua it occurs only twenty-four times. Every occurrence of the name יהודה, when it refers to the people instead of the land, is in construct with another word.[105] The author uses four words in construct with יהודה, all in the same sense: מטה occurs three times,[106] שבט[107] and משפחת[108] each occur one time, and בני יהודה occurs fourteen times. Therefore, it can be argued that when referring to the people of Judah who lived in the lifetime of Joshua, the phrase בני יהודה is the primary term used.

In Judges, יהודה occurs twenty-five times. Out of these, nine instances are used to refer to the territory. With the exception of the three occurrences of the construct בני יהודה, and the one occurrence of משפחת, in the remaining twelve occurrences of the name, יהודה is found by itself. Here also, it can be argued that when referring to the people of Judah who lived after the death of Joshua, the title used is יהודה, not בני יהודה.

Furthermore, when narrowing the distribution of בני יהודה, it can be seen that within the Former Prophets, בני יהודה is used only eighteen times. As mentioned above, fourteen of the eighteen occurrences are found in Joshua. The first occurrence is in Joshua 14:16, which introduces Judah's and Caleb's conquest that is also mentioned in Judges 1:8–16. The three other occurrences of the phrase are in Judges and all of these are in Judges 1:8, 9, 16. The last occurrence is found in 2 Samuel 1:18 where the usage

---

104. Philippe Guillaume, "An Anti-Judean Manifesto in Judges 1?" *BN* 95 (1998): 13. Guillaume sees a distinction between the two titles but takes it too far to claim without any evidence "one cannot exclude the possibility that the sons of Juda butchered the Juda which had brought Adoni-Bezeq back to Jerusalem." Frolov is right when he referred to Guillaume's claim as "far-fetched" (Serge Frolov, *Judges*, FOTL, ed. Rolf P. Knierim and Marvin A. Sweeney, vol. 18 [Grand Rapids: Eerdmans, 2013], 40).

105. Since the context of Josh 18:5 is allocation of land, it is best to see the term as referring to the allocated land, rather than to the people.

106. It does not occur again throughout the Former Prophets. It is used seven times in the Pentateuch (Exodus and Numbers only): Exod 31:2; 35:30; 38:22; Num 1:27; 7:12; 13:6; 34:19.

107. Other than in Josh 7:16, the phrase occurs only two times in the Former Prophets (1 Kgs 12:20; 2 Kgs 17:18).

108. The phrase occurs only once in Num 26:22 and Judg 17:7.

could be understood as being influenced by the reference to the Book of Yashar, which is mentioned earlier in Joshua 10:13.

Therefore, it can be concluded that the change to בני יהודה in Judges 1:8–16 is not arbitrary. The author of the book of Joshua uses the phrase בני יהודה to refer to the descendants of Judah who lived during the period covered by the book of Joshua (i.e. up until the death of Joshua). The author of Judges, on the other hand, uses the title יהודה to refer to the descendants of Judah who lived during the period covered by the book of Judges (i.e. after the death of Joshua). It can be concluded that by using בני יהודה, instead of יהודה, the author of Judges signals that he is referring to the people of Judah who were engaged in an earlier conquest before the death of Joshua, as can be confirmed by his quotation in the book of Joshua.

In the canonical form we have, Judges is a sequel to Joshua.[109] Judges narrates the history of Israel picking up where the book of Joshua ended. If Judges indeed is a sequel to Joshua, picking up where Joshua ended, then there must be a way to differentiate a tribe's action before Joshua's death from their's after his death. Using a different title for the tribe of Judah in the two books is consistent with the nature of the two books as sequential.

Since בני יהודה is a lexical reference that points to the time when Joshua was still alive, וילחמו (v. 8) – whose grammatical subject is בני יהודה – introduces a temporally overlaid *wayyiqtol* clause according to the first criterion. This *wayyiqtol* clause introduces a flashback to the conquest carried out by the ancestors of the present generation of the tribe of Judah.[110] Not just 1:8, but all of 1:8–16, which is structurally set apart as a unit by the use of בני יהודה both at the beginning and the end, is a flashback to a conquest that

---

109. See chapter 4 for a defense of this assumption.
110. So Robert H. O'Connell, *The Rhetoric of the Book of Judges*, VTSup, vol. 63 (Leiden: E. J. Brill, 1996), 72, n. 27; Eugene H. Merrill, *Kingdom of Priests: A History of Old Testament Israel*, 2nd ed. (Grand Rapids: Baker Academic, 2008), 162. KJV also takes v. 8 as a flashback and translates it as: "Now the children of Judah had fought against Jerusalem, and had taken it, and smitten it with the edge of the sword, and set the city on fire." Driver argues against a *pluperfect* reading for the *wayyiqtol* here but simply states "see the note in the Speaker's comm., where the Bishop of Bath and Wells remarks with truth, that 'there is nothing in the original to suggest or justify such a change of tense.'" And on the footnote 1 he says, "This verse is thought by some (Budde, *Richter u. Samuel*, 4) to be an incorrect gloss, due to a misunderstanding of v. 7 (as though the pronoun 'they' denoted the Israelites rather than the people of Adoni-bezek), and intended to explain how the Israelites were able to take Adonibezk to Jerusalem" (Driver, *Treatise*, 86).

took place during the time of Joshua.[111] It is a flashback not only because it is introduced with a temporally overlaid *wayyiqtol* clause in verse 8 but also because all of the events were implied or quoted from Joshua.[112] Judges 1:8–16 can be structured as below:

A Sons of Judah [had][113] **fought** Jerusalem (v. 8)
B Sons of Judah went down to **fight** . . . (v. 9)
   a He *went* to Hebron (v. 10)
   b He *went* from there to Debir (vv. 11–13)
     [Caleb gave Debir to Othniel and Acsah (vv. 14–15)][114]
   c He *went* and lived in Arad with the Kenites (v. 16b)[115]

As the above structure shows, the flashback first speaks of what the sons of Judah did in verses 8–9. In these verses the sons of Judah are the grammatical subject of the verbs. The verbs are also similar. In verse 8 it is לחם, and in verse 9 it is ירד להלחם. The root לחם is used in Joshua 10 to describe the battle against the coalition led by the king of Jerusalem. It is no longer used in the prologue until 3:1–2. The flashback then picks up a storyline that offers specific examples of the battle of verse 9. The storyline follows one Judahite family's devotion to the conquest in verses 10–16. Here the verb used to structure the text is הלך, and it is always third masculine singular. In all cases, it refers to Caleb.

---

111. Walter C. Kaiser, *A History of Israel: From Bronze Age through the Jewish Wars* (Nashville, TN: Broadman & Holman, 1998), 177.

112. If vv. 9–15 were not a flashback, the alternative would be to consider Josh 15:14–19 as taking place after Joshua's death (Jeffery S. Stevenson, "Judah's Successes and Failures in Holy War: An Exegesis of Judges 1:1–20," *ResQ* 44, no. 1 [2002]: 48). However, from reading Joshua, it is clear that the conquest took place in the life time of Joshua by Caleb. So Merrill, *Kingdom of Priests*, 138. See chapter 4 of this dissertation for discussion of this account.

113. The use of the pluperfect in English is only necessary to help the modern reader clearly understand that the event is chronologically prior to the preceding verses.

114. These verses constitute an embedded paragraph. Cf. Barnabas Lindars, *Judges 1–5: A New Translation and Commentary*, ed. A. D. H. Mayes (Edinburgh: T&T Clark, 1995), 31.

115. "Kenites had gone up with sons of Judah" (v. 16a) is a supplementary statement that does not move the story forward and so it is not part of the structure, which traces Caleb's movement.

The Battle of the Sons of Judah (vv. 8–9)

In Judges 1:7, the present generation of the tribe of Judah brought Adonibezek to Jerusalem. It was argued earlier that Judah must have been at home in Jerusalem.[116] Judges 1:8 refers to the attack on Jerusalem by the previous generation of Judah. Judah's burning of Jerusalem most probably took place during Joshua's fight against the coalition that was led by the Jebusite king of Jerusalem.[117] Though the city was burnt, the Jebusites were not totally destroyed. So the author of Joshua waited to include this until the section where he spoke of land yet to be conquered. Joshua 15:63 suggests that the sons of Judah had undertaken a battle against Jerusalem with partial victory. The construction יכל plus ירש suggests that they must have at least tried. Judges 1:8 is a reference to Joshua 15:63.

The collocation of שלח באש in 1:8 is used to refer to a raid, not total destruction. This is particularly clear in Judges 20:48. The Israelites raided the Benjaminite towns. The most common collocation to describe total destruction is שרף באש both in Joshua and Judges. This collocation is found six times in Joshua with the sense of total destruction.[118] An alternative collocation, נצת באש, is used in Joshua 8:8 and 8:19 with a clear indication from the context that it also referred to the total destruction of Ai. In Judges too, the common collocation is שרף באש. In Judges 18:27, the Danites attacked Laish, killed the inhabitants, and burnt the city. The collocation שרף באש is used there and refers to a total destruction. This is especially clear in the next verse which speaks of the Danites needing to rebuild the city in order to live in it.

Others have made a similar observation on different grounds. Block argues, "The fact that David had to reconquer Jerusalem suggests the Judahite hold on the city was weak and short-lived. It seems that shortly after they had sacked it the Jebusites moved in from the north and took control, which they then held for several centuries."[119] Sasson also argues that the vocabulary

---

116. See pp. 31–33 for a discussion on v. 7.
117. So Merrill, *Kingdom of Priests*, 162.
118. In Josh 6:24 it refers to Jericho's total destruction. In Josh 11:6, 9, and 11, it refers to the destruction of Hazor. In Josh 7:15, and 25, it refers to the destruction of a family.
119. Daniel I. Block, *Judges, Ruth*, NAC, ed. E. Ray Clendenen, vol. 6 (Nashville, TN: Broadman & Holman, 1999), 92.

used in 1:8 does not imply a total destruction.[120] Neither Block nor Sasson, however, takes 1:8 as a battle that took place in the lifetime of Joshua.

In light of Joshua 10, 15:63, and Judges 1:7–8, it is possible to reconstruct the battle against Jerusalem as follows: (1) the king of Jerusalem led a coalition against Joshua and Israel, (2) all of Israel led by Joshua fought against the coalition, (3) the sons of Judah went to the city of Jerusalem and attacked it with partial success. The Jebusites and the sons of Judah began to live together through a process that is not made clear anywhere in the OT. After the death of Joshua, Judah defeated another coalition (Judg 1:4–7), and brought Adoni-bezek, the coalition leader, to Jerusalem. There Judah humiliated and tortured the leader to terrify the Jebusites, who lived in Jerusalem with Judah.

The author's purpose in retelling this earlier attack on Jerusalem is to evaluate the seemingly positive success of the present generation of the tribe of Judah as seen in the victory at Bezek (vv. 4–7). Unlike the present generation, the previous generation had once tried to destroy the inhabitants of Jerusalem. Even if the previous generation ended up living with the Jebusites, as 1:8 implies, they had the intention to destroy the Jebusites. The present generation, however, was content to instill fear and live with the Jebusites, instead of attempting to destroy them. This difference of intention between the previous and the present generation will become more clear as the story progresses. What Judah did in 1:7 is not very different from what other tribes did in the rest of the chapter when they chose to force the Canaanites to do hard labor (1:28, 30, 33, and 35).

The author of the book of Judges also reminds the reader of another story from the time of Joshua by which they should evaluate the seemingly positive success of Judah. The second story found in verse 9 is a summary of another battle into which the sons of Judah had gone. The adverb אחר connects the battle in verse 8 and verse 9 chronologically as following one after the other.[121] This suggests that the battle described in verse 9 took place

---

120. "When construed with the verb *nākâ* (to a much lesser extent *hārag* and, rarely, *ḥālaš*), the phrase *lefî-ḥereb* (literally, 'at the mouth of the sword') occurs often in Scripture, implying slaughter, but not necessarily total. This is crucial to keep in mind, for fighting, capturing, sacking, or burning a city (no matter how brutal the slaughter of its citizens) does not necessarily imply permanent possession of it" (Sasson, *Judges 1–12*, 140).

121. Cf. Chisholm, *Judges and Ruth*, 111, n. 5.

right after the battle against Jerusalem. The three geographical locations used here are also used in Joshua 10:40, which summarized Joshua's battle against the coalition led by the king of Jerusalem. Verse 9 is referring to that. Though ascribed to Joshua in Joshua 10:40, it does not necessarily mean that he personally was responsible for the victories in all of these locations.

In Judges 1:8–9 the sons of Judah who lived before Joshua's death were engaging in battles one after the other. The present generation was content in only winning the battle on the battlefield (1:4–5). They did not follow up their victory but let the enemy leader live so that they could co-reside with the Jebusites by instilling fear in them (1:6–7).

The Conquest of a Judahite Family (vv. 10–16, 20)

The author gives the story of one Judahite family in verses 10–16 and verse 20 as part of the story of the battle that the sons of Judah went to fight in verse 9. A close look at verses 10–16 shows that Caleb is the subject of the report. The verb הלך begins and ends the section, as can be seen in the structure above. The significance of הלך as a structural marker is made clear when one observes the author's decision to delay using ירש to refer to Caleb's taking of Hebron in verse 10 to verse 20, and the change of עלה (Josh 15:14) to הלך (v. 12).

Caleb moved three times in these verses. He went to Hebron, then to Debir, and then to Arad. The move to Hebron is ascribed to Judah in verse 10. Later in verse 20 the author would clarify that it is specifically Caleb who took possession of Hebron. The change to Judah in verse 10 is to ascribe the achievement of Caleb to the tribe as a whole. The readers would know from the tradition in Joshua that it was actually Caleb who was personally responsible for victory over Hebron.[122] Stone rightly notes, "It is proper, in one account, to attribute an action or accomplishment to the overall commander (Joshua); in another, to name the tribe (Judah); and in still another, to name the person who apparently took the leading role in the action, and who received the place as his inheritance (Caleb)."[123]

---

122. Cf. Trent C. Butler, *Judges*, WBC, ed. Bruce M. Metzger et al., vol. 8 (Nashville, TN: Thomas Nelson, 2009), 23.

123. Joseph Coleson, Lawson G. Stone, and Jason Driesbach, *Joshua, Judges, Ruth*, Cornerstone Biblical Commentary, ed. Philip W. Comfort, vol. 3 (Carol Stream, IL: Tyndale House, 2012), 112.

What the author changes here is not just the subject. He also changes the verb from ירש (Josh 15:14 and Judg 1:20) to נכה (Judg 1:10). If the verb had not changed, it could very likely contribute to a dispute over who has the right to the land of Hebron. The change in the verb would prevent such possible implication. In agreement with the change of the verb and the subject – from Caleb to Judah – the author also changes both from singular to plural. In so doing, the author simply ascribes victory in battle to the tribe, but not the taking of the land. His purpose for ascribing Caleb's success to his tribe was so that he could compare the conquest of the present generation of the tribe of Judah (1:4–7) with the conquest of the earlier generation of the tribe whom Caleb represented.

Unlike the present generation of Judah, their ancestor was not content with victory at Hebron, so Caleb went to Debir. Instead of doing battle against it by himself, he offered an invitation to other Judahites. Caleb's invitation does not show his hesitation; rather, it shows his proactiveness in thinking of his daughter's future to have a worthy husband who shared his attitude towards the Canaanites.[124] Here both Othniel and Acsah are seen as proactive in getting land. It appears that Caleb gave Debir to Othniel and Acsah after Acsah had her husband ask for it.[125] Not content with what she had – like her father – she then requested springs of water "to complement her land holdings."[126]

The story about Caleb closes in verse 16. Here the author informs the reader of Caleb's move to Arad. However, he first gives a parenthetical statement in 16a that helps to clarify where and why Caleb moves. The disjunctive clause here is a pluperfect. This suggests that this move occurred prior to Caleb's change of venue in verses 10–15. Joined by the sons of Judah, the Kenites *had gone up* to the Negev of Arad. "The city of palm trees" is Jericho.[127] The reference to starting from Jericho suggests that it could have happened in the early days of the conquest.[128] The author would use a similar rhetori-

---

124. Cf. Chisholm, *Judges and Ruth*, 124.

125. See the translation in appendix 1.

126. Ibid.

127. Cf. Susan Niditch, *Judges: A Commentary*, OTL, ed. William P. Brown, Carol A. Newsom, and David L. Petersen (Louisville, KY: Westminster John Knox, 2008), 41; Lindars, *Judges 1–5*, 37.

128. O'Connell considers v. 16 as flashback (O'Connell, *Judges*, 72, n. 27).

cal strategy in 2:1 by mentioning the angel's travel from Gilgal to Bochim. Some from the sons of Judah could have joined the Kenites sometime after the battle at Jericho, the first conquest in the land.

After the parenthetical note that gives background to what follows, the author now gives the foregrounded story that reports Caleb's third move.[129] The subject of the verb הלך is third masculine singular and so refers to Caleb. The author has not indicated a change in subject. Caleb has been the subject since verse 10. He was the one who moved to Hebron. From there he moved to Debir. Caleb was the last subject mentioned before the parenthetical note. The author would have made it clear if there were a change of subject.

Sometime after the capture of the Negev of Arad, and after Caleb gave the land of Negev to Othniel and his daughter, Caleb moved to join the Kenites and lived with them. It is understandable for Caleb, "a Kenizzite, a member of a non-Israelite clan that had allied itself with Judah,"[130] to live with another non-Israelite group who allied itself with Judah.[131]

The author returns to present-day Judah in verse 17 and summarizes their attempt to take possession of their allotted land in verses 17–18. In verse 19, the author then gives a summary evaluation of Judah's partial success, which was reported in verses 17–18. Verse 19 summarizes Judah's victory in the hill country and partial success in the coastal plains. The cities of verse 18 are three of the five Philistine cities, which were yet to be conquered at the time of Joshua (cf. Josh 13:1–3).

Thematically, verse 20 belongs with verse 19. It also summarizes the success of the tribe's previous generation. Syntactically, verse 20 stands on its own. The subject of the plural verb at the beginning of verse 20 (ויתנו) is בני־יהודה. Verse 20 itself does not give the subject of the verb. One has to assume the subject was given before. So far, the plural verb is used when the subject of the verb is either: (1) the coalition of Judah and Simeon, or

---

129. V. 16 picks up vv. 11–13. Vv. 14–15 constitute an embedded paragraph.

130. Joseph Coleson, Lawson G. Stone, and Jason Driesbach, *Joshua, Judges, Ruth*, Cornerstone Biblical Commentary, ed. Philip W. Comfort, vol. 3 (Carol Stream, IL: Tyndale House, 2012), 112.

131. It seems this tradition was not available to or needed by the author of Joshua. This tradition suggests that Caleb did not dwell in either Hebron nor Debir. As for Debir he gave it to Othniel and Achsah. Though just speculation, it is possible that Caleb moved by his own choice to Arad, after the assignment of Hebron as a city of refuge in Josh 20.

(2) בני־יהודה. The coalition of Judah and Simeon cannot be the subject of the verb in verse 20, since Simeon was not involved in assigning inheritance to Caleb. בני־יהודה is the best alternative. And if, indeed, בני־יהודה is the subject of the verb, it signals that the *wayyiqtol* is a *pluperfective wayyiqtol*. The subject, בני־יהודה, and the object of the verb, לכלב, are both lexical references that shift the time frame back to when Joshua was still alive. The *wayyiqtol* also meets the second criterion because the assigning of the inheritance to Caleb had already taken place in the lifetime of Joshua (Josh 15:13–14).[132]

Using this flashback, the author evaluates the success of Judah in light of Caleb their ancestor. Although their ancestor took possession of the land that was assigned to him, they failed to take possession of all the territory that was allocated to them.

Comparison between Two Generations (Judg 2:6–10)

Judges 2:1–5 ended with a scene where the sons of Israel, after Joshua's death in 1:1, wept before the Lord, renamed the place "Bochim," and sacrificed to the Lord. Then in 2:6 Joshua dismissed the people. With regard to syntax, 2:6 begins with a *wayyiqtol*, which being understood by many as *consecutive*, has been a major problem in understanding the structure of the prologue as well as interpreting it. Joshua could not be alive to dismiss the people now at 2:6 if he had already died at 1:1. Scholars attempt to solve this problem either without explaining the syntax (those who understand *wayyiqtol* as consecutive) or by locating a flashback to the time of Joshua somewhere between 1:1 and 2:6.

Taking the *wayyiqtol* at 2:6 as *consecutive*, Sweeney proposes that "[a]lthough Judg. ii 6–10 may originally have had the assembly at Shechem as its referent, in the present form of the text Joshua dismisses the people from Bochim."[133] To allow Joshua to be alive again to dismiss the people from Bochim, Sweeney sees a major break at 2:1, despite the presence of a *wayyiqtol*, which to him is *consecutive*. He argues that the mention of the angel's movement from Gilgal to Bochim takes the reader to Joshua 5:13–15 where the angel had appeared to Joshua while the people camped at Gilgal.

---

132. See pp. 118–119 for a discussion of Josh 15:13–14.

133. M. A. Sweeney, "Davidic Polemics in the Book of Judges," *VT* 47, no. 4 (1997): 521. In so doing, Sweeney rejects the reading of Judg 2:6–10 in relation to the assembly at Shechem. He regards such an attempt as "a redaction-critical decision."

It is true that the reason for mentioning the angel's movement from Gilgal is rhetorical.[134] Though the mention of Gilgal reminds the reader of the previous conquest – Gilgal was the campsite during the previous conquest – it does not move the story's temporal clock back to that time. There is no syntactical or lexical marker that indicates that the events of 2:1–5 took place while Joshua was still alive. If he was not alive at that time, he could not have dismissed the people of 2:1–5. Frolov agrees with Sweeney that the major break that moves the story's temporal clock to the time of Joshua happened before 2:6, but he does not agree that it happened at 2:1. Rather, he suggests that the major break is found in 1:27–33. As argued in the introduction, none of Frolov's arguments supports his conclusion.[135]

Several other scholars take Judges 2:6–10 as a flashback. Block takes it as a flashback but not in a chronological sense. Rather, he considers it as a flashback in a rhetorical sense, which avoids the need to translate it with a pluperfect.[136] Webb, on the other hand, takes it as a flashback in a chronological sense despite the absence of "formal indicators of a flashback."[137] By "formal indicators of flashback" he refers to the disjunctive *qatal* as used in 1:16 and 11:1. He gives three proposals for the use of *wayyiqtol* here for what is clearly a narrative flashback.[138] First, he suggests that it could be "a case of defective syntax." Second, he proposes that these verses could have been part of Joshua 23 in their original context. Third, he suggests that the author quoted Joshua 24:28–29 failing to emend the syntax.

None of Webb's proposals seems to be necessary. First, using *wayyiqtol* for a pluperfect idea, as was argued above, is normal and should not be considered defective syntax. Second, 2:6–10 could not have been a continuation of Joshua 23 in another "original" text (which does not exist) since it would be repeated again in Joshua 24. Third, having seen the author make such deliberate lexical (cf. 1:12 and Josh 15:14) and syntactical changes (cf. 1:29 and 16:10; obtrusions in 2:22 and 3:2), it is unlikely that the author failed to emend the "defective syntax."

---

134. See pp. 35–39 for a discussion on 2:1–5.
135. See pp. 5–7 for a detailed interaction with Frolov's argument.
136. Block, *Judges, Ruth*, 119–120.
137. Webb, *Book of Judges*, 134.
138. Ibid., 134, n. 2.

Judges 2:6 begins with a temporally overlaid *wayyiqtol* clause that meets the first of the two criteria that signal such kind of clauses. As stated above, one of the criteria is "a lexical reference and/or repetition" that explicitly points back to a time prior to the preceding verb. Here the lexical reference is the name Joshua. Joshua has been explicitly mentioned as dead in 1:1, so the *wayyiqtol* in 2:6 is clearly a pluperfect. This *wayyiqtol* clause introduces a flashback to the time of Joshua that runs up to 2:10.

Taking Judges 2:6–10 as flashback, Butler calls it an "interpretative flashback."[139] Block, on the other hand, calls it "a rhetorical flashback," which is a key to interpret not 2:1–5 but 2:11–23: "just as the divine messenger had reminded the Israelites of Yahweh's past covenantal grace and Israel's failure to keep the covenant, so the narrator offers a retrospective look at Israel's past commitments in light of which the pattern of apostasy and infidelity described in this book are to be interpreted."[140]

However, a closer look at the text proves that it is an evaluative flashback, that is, one that evaluates the actions of the sons of Israel in 2:4–5. As the author has been doing several times throughout chapter 1, he now evaluates the *seemingly* positive response of the *weeping* and *sacrifice* of the sons of Israel. He compares the people who were at the meeting at Bochim with those at Shechem.

According to 2:6, the result of the meeting at Shechem was that the people went to their respective allotted land to take possession of it in obedience to the challenge from Joshua who was the "messenger of the Lord." The people at Bochim did not translate their *weeping* nor *covenant renewal*, which was implied through their *sacrifice* into obedience by taking possession of their allotted land, despite the messenger's direct confrontation. That the purpose of the messenger was to encourage Israel to break their covenant with the inhabitants of the land and even to dispossess them is clear from 2:1–3. The people at Shechem at least had the *intention* to take possession of the land. The people at Bochim did not show any such *intention*.

The flashback is not only intended to evaluate the actions of the sons of Israel in 2:1–5. It also allows the reader to understand why such a difference

---

139. Butler, *Judges*, 38.
140. Block, *Judges, Ruth*, 120.

exists between the two generations – the people at Bochim and the people at Shechem. Lindars, who considers Judges 2:6–10 to be an editorial insertion, proposes that the dismissal of 2:6 is "aimed at bringing back the narrative to the point reached at the *beginning* of the Prelude in 1.1."[141] At 1:1 the new generation of 2:10b has grown and is facing the period of testing. 2:6–10 looks at the previous generation until the death of its last survivors – the elders.

There are only two generations represented in these verses, as the summary verse (v. 10) indicates with הדור ההוא and דור אחר. The former includes Joshua, Caleb, Eleazar (cf. Josh 24:33). The reference to "the elders who outlived Joshua" might be a reference to Joshua 24:33, which mentions the death of Eleazar. Joshua was not the last person to die from his generation. The death of Eleazar in Joshua 24:29–33 marks the death of the elders who outlived Joshua. Therefore, the narrative of the prologue picked up from the time after the death of the elders, not just the death of Joshua. As argued above, Judges 1:1 mentioned the death of Joshua, but not that of the elders, due to the important role Joshua played in the history of Israel as the key leader. It is not possible to know when Caleb died. But, as mentioned above, the reference to him in Judges 1 cannot be used as a basis to argue that he was one of the elders who outlived Joshua.[142] Judges 2:6–10 takes the readers from Shechem to the setting in 1:1, not after 1:1.

Two key words unite verses 6–9 and reveal the author's intention for including these verses here:

    A   לנחלתו "The people's inheritance" (v. 6)
    B   עבד "The people served" (v. 7)
    B'   עבד "Joshua, servant of God" (v. 8)
    A'   נחלתו "Joshua's inheritance" (v. 9)

Using these two key words, the author portrays the previous generation in a positive manner. The people, as well as the leaders, served God, that is, in context, obediently took possession of the land.[143] The people were

---

141. Lindars, *Judges 1–5*, 94–95.
142. O'Connell puts Caleb in a different generation from both Joshua and Othniel, creating at least three distinct generations (O'Connell, *Judges*, 72–73).
143. Block, *Judges, Ruth*, 122.

intentional about taking possession of their inheritance. Joshua was an example to his generation by taking possession of the inheritance allotted to him.[144] The reference to the elders as those "who saw all the great deeds that the Lord had done to Israel" speaks of those who experienced the conquest. Therefore, verses 6–9 picture the generation as one who had the intention to take possession of the inheritance given to them. In verse 10, all of "that generation" passed away. The purpose of the reference to the passing of "that generation" is to emphasize the death of the generation who sought to take possession of their inheritance. It could also be the author's way of taking the reader back to the end of Joshua, that is, 24:32. Eleazar could represent, at least in a rhetorical sense, the passing of "that generation." If so, then Judges 2:10b refers to the new generation of 1:1.

Nothing in 2:10b portrays the new generation in a negative way. אחר could portray the generation either as "later, new," or "other" in the sense of "different." Even if one is to take the latter option, this is not a negative picture. This "new" or "different" generation refers to the children of the previous generation. The statement "they did not know" is best translated as "did not experience,"[145] not "acknowledge." ידע[146], as in Joshua 24:31, clearly means *to experience* or *to witness*. The point here is that the new generation represents the children who did not partake in the conquest and who now have grown and are ready for a battle lesson (2:21b–3:4). קום (come to the scene, appear)[147] is different from ילד. The new generation is not "the generation of people born after them" as in Sasson (cf. Ps 78:6, where both ילד and קום are used).[148] Webb notes, "the first intimations of the 'arising' of this 'other generation' are to be found, upon reflection, in the second half of chapter 1, but its full manifestation does not come until the outright apostasy of 2:11."[149] However, as the previous reflection informs, the "aris-

---

144. So Webb, *Book of Judges*, 138.
145. So Chisholm, *Judges and Ruth*, 148.
146. So Coleson, Stone, and Driesbach, *Joshua, Judges, Ruth*, 229.
147. *DCH* 228b.
148. Sasson, *Judges 1–12*, 184.
149. Barry G. Webb, *The Book of the Judges: An Integrated Reading*, JSOTSup Series, vol. 44 (Eugene, OR: Wipf & Stock, 2008), 107.

ing" of this new generation can be found not only in the second half but also in the beginning (1:1).

Therefore, by differentiating the present generation from the previous, the author clarifies to the readers that the generation in 1:1–2:5 is the generation of those who had not partaken in the previous conquest. In 1:1–2:5 they were given the chance[150] for another conquest, but all of them failed. Their failure is not described as *tried but could not* as in Joshua (Josh 15:63; 17:12). Rather, their failure is described as *they did not try*. They were not intentional about taking possession of the land. Instead, they lived in their inheritance with the foreigners.

Comment on the Period of Testing (Judg 2:23–3:4)

Before concluding the prologue with an *ending* (3:5–6), the author comments on the Lord's speech (2:20–21). His comment is found in 2:22–3:4. Polzin is right when noting that the Lord's direct speech is "fundamentally interpreted and semantically extended by the narrator's reporting words in 2:23."[151] However, this is not done just in 2:23 but throughout 2:22–3:4. Therefore, the primary function of 2:22–3:4 should be seen in reference to the words of the Lord in 2:20–21. It will be argued below that in addition to interpreting 2:20–21, the author's comment also sheds light on the prologue of Judges as a whole.

Verse 22 belongs to 2:23–3:4 both thematically and syntactically as shown in the structure below. With regard to subject matter, Webb comments that 2:23–3:4 "as a whole is about the *test* rather than the remaining nations as such."[152] This is even more evident when verse 22 is included. The information given includes (1) the time the test began (2) who the objects of the test were, (3) who the subjects of the test were, and (4) the purpose of the test.

The following structure captures the author's argument in 2:22–3:4.[153]

---

150. So 3:1–2.

151. Robert Polzin, *Moses and the Deuteronomist: A Literary Study of the Deuteronomic History, Part One: Deuteronomy, Joshua, Judges*, ISBL, ed. Herbert Marks and Robert Polzin (New York: Seabury, 1980), 153–156.

152. Webb, *Book of Judges*, 150.

153. Since Webb considers v. 22 as part of the Lord's speech, he does not include it in his structure of 2:23–3:4 and according to him, the intrusion in 3:1–3 begins with את כל אשר, not with לנסות. So, his structure of the parenthesis in 3:1b–2b does not include "to test Israel

A ... למען נסות בם את־ישראל השמרים "They were[154] for testing Israel by them [to know] whether they would keep . . ." (2:22)

    B ... וינח יהוה את־הגוים האלה "The Lord gave these nations rest . . ." (2:23)[155]

        B' ... ואלה הגוים אשר הניח יהוה "These are the nations the Lord gave rest . . ." (3:1–3)

A' ... ויהיו לנסות בם את־ישראל לדעת הישמעו "They were for testing Israel by them to know whether they would listen . . ." (3:4)

Both A and A' begin with a reference to the test which in turn is followed by an indirect question that clarifies the test. In verse 22, the death of Joshua inaugurated the test. By delaying the break-frame obtrusion until after וימת the author seems to suggest that the test did not begin until after Joshua died. This indicates that the period of testing began with the death of Joshua, not while he was still alive.

The content of 2:23 signals that the *wayyiqtol* clause in this verse is an instance of unmarked temporal overlay. The use of נוח in verse 23 parallels עזב in verse 21. Both of them are not used in their normal sense. Joshua's abandoning of the nations meant that he stopped pursuing them. Giving rest to Israel's enemies meant that the Lord stopped Israel from pursuing its enemies. The verb נוח is clarified in the same verse with the infinitive clause "by not dispossessing them quickly." When the enemy sought to fight Israel, as in the case of Joshua 10 and 11, then Israel was not at rest. This then, became the occasion for Israel to pursue the enemy and to take possession of their land. According to Joshua 23:1 no enemy came against Israel nor did Israel go after any enemy until after Joshua died (cf. Judg 1). Therefore, נוח in verse 23 is a lexical reference that signals a backtracking of the narrative to the time when Joshua was still alive. This is made more clear by the negative verbal clause that reiterates the point of the *wayyiqtol* clause: "he did not give them into the hand of Joshua."

---

by them" (Ibid., 149). These are the major differences between the present author's proposal and Webb's understanding of the text's structure.

154. For an argument that there could be a backwards ellipsis of וַיְהִי here, see pp. 52–53.

155. This verse reiterates 21b–22. So Butler, *Judges*, 49.

Before he names the nations that the Lord used to test Israel, the author comments on the subjects of the test and explains the test. The author's obtrusion in 3:1–3 can be structured as below:

  A לנסות בם את־ישראל "to test Israel by them"
      B את כל־אשר לא־ידעו את כל־מלחמות כנען "all those who did not know all the wars of Canaan"
  A רק למען דעת דרות בני־ישראל ללמדם מלחמה "only that later generations may experience the wars by teaching them warfare"
      B רק אשר־לפנים לא ידעום "only those who did not experience the wars before"

The subjects of the test are given in B and B'. These are the children of Israel who did not partake in the earlier conquest. The addition of רק in B' seems to clarify that the test is not meant for people like Othniel and Acsah who were part of this new generation. The nature of the test is clarified in A and A'. The comment on the test in 2:22 and 3:4 does not contradict what the author says about it in A and A'. In A and A', the author speaks of what the test actually was; whereas, in 2:22 and 3:4, the ultimate goal of the test is given.

The object of the infinitive דעת is missing in 3:2. However, the author has twice indicated that the object of דעת is כל־מלחמות כנען at the end of 3:1 and at the end of 3:2 by way of the object suffix attached to the verb (ידעום). This object suffix refers back to כל־מלחמות כנען. As in 2:10, דעת should mean "experience." Therefore, the test actually gave the new generation experience in war against the Canaanites. That the Lord would actively oversee the test is communicated in the phrase לְלַמְּדָם. This *piel* verb should be translated as "by teaching them." This is hinted at in the reference to the Lord's presence with Judah and the House of Joseph in 1:4, 19, and 1:22 respectively.

When the author's obtrusion is removed from 3:1–3, what remains is a reference to the objects of the test, the nations whom the Lord would use to test the new generation. As Butler notes, "the list ignores Judah's conquests of Philistine cities in Judg 1 as well as Israel's failures in chap. 1."[156] The reason for this, however, is because the author is speaking about the Lord's purpose at the time of Joshua's death which he referred to in 2:21b. Once

---

156. Ibid., 61.

again, Butler rightly notes, "the nations God allowed to coexist because of Joshua's old age (Josh 13:1) are now facing a generation too young to have participated with Joshua's conquering army."[157]

Here as well, the author takes the reader to a time preceding Judges 1:1. These verses then help the reader to reflect on the prologue beginning from 1:1. The Lord had intended for the sons of Israel to fight the Canaanites as their ancestors did. He gave them the same chance in Judges 1:1–2. Judah started to fight in 1:4–7, but it was short lived. The sons of Joseph also fought once but failed to continue. The rest of the tribes failed to proactively and reactively attempt to take possession of their inheritance. The Lord warned them that if they continued in their failure, the nations would not simply live with them but would be "thorns in their sides" and their gods would be a temptation. Not heeding the Lord's warning, they fell into the temptation of worshipping the gods of Canaan, of which the Lord had spoken. Having already warned them, the Lord's anger burned against Israel (2:14a), and announced his judgment (2:20b–21a) that he would not dispossess the nations any more. The Lord's words, that he would not dispossess the nations, signal the end of the testing period. He had planned to dispossess the nations by means of the test. Israel failed the test. So the Lord decided that he would no longer dispossess the nations before Israel; but that he would also use them to punish Israel (2:14b–19).

Summary

The prologue of Judges includes four flashbacks to the time of Joshua. These flashbacks are introduced with a temporally overlaid *wayyiqtol* clause that is marked by a lexical reference that clearly indicates that the time of the narrative has shifted to a time when Joshua was still alive. By using the *wayyiqtol*, instead of a pluperfect *qatal*, the author makes the flashbacks part of the foreground narrative. All of the flashbacks were used to evaluate or explain the preceding clause(s).

---

157. Ibid.

CHAPTER 4

Function of the Prologue – Part One

This chapter analyzes the function of the prologue by exploring the nature of its relationship with the book of Joshua. The decision to begin analyzing its function by first studying its relationship to the book of Joshua instead of its relationship to the rest of the material in the book of Judges itself is in agreement with Butler, who rightly argued that, "The first purpose of Judges 1 is not to serve as an introduction to what follows. Rather it serves as a contrast to what precedes. This means that we must first read Judg 1 in its relations to the book of Joshua before we too quickly rush ahead to see how it compares to the following narratives of Judges."[1]

Joshua as a Prequel to Judges

The וַיְהִי clause that begins the book of Judges marks it as a continuation of the book of Joshua.[2] In addition, Butler notes that the continuation is also made plain by the fact that Judges 1:1 takes up the heading of Joshua 24:29–32, "namely, the death of Joshua, as the point of temporal reference."[3] These facts suggest that in its canonical form, the book of Judges is a sequel

---

1. Trent C. Butler, *Judges*, WBC, ed. Bruce M. Metzger et al., vol. 8 (Nashville, TN: Thomas Nelson, 2009), 15–16.

2. Cf. Elizabeth Robar, *The Verb and the Paragraph in Biblical Hebrew: A Cognitive-Linguistic Approach*, Studies in Semitic Languages and Linguistics, vol. 78 (Leiden: Brill, 2015), 84–85, n. 21; Serge Frolov, *Judges*, FOTL, ed. Rolf P. Knierim and Marvin A. Sweeney, vol. 18 (Grand Rapids: Eerdmans, 2013), 24.

3. Trent C. Butler, *Joshua 13–24*, WBC, ed. deClaissé-Walford, 2nd ed., vol. 7B (Grand Rapids: Zondervan, 2014), 337.

to the book of Joshua.[4] A clear understanding of how the book of Joshua ended will help the reader understand in what ways the book of Judges as a whole, and the prologue in particular, continue from it.

Joshua 21:43–24:33

Seeing the close connection of Joshua 24 with the prologue of Judges, Engle claims that Joshua 24 was part of an original introduction to Judges that included Joshua 24:1–Judges 3:6.[5] Engle sees Joshua 24 as discontinuous from the rest of the book and thinks it fits better with Judges1:1–3:6.[6] Joshua 24 is part of the epilogue that covers Joshua 21:43–24:33 and is closely tied to this section.[7]

Joshua 21:43–24:33 has two functions which correspond to its two parts. The first part of the epilogue covers 21:43–22:6. O'Doherty rightly argues, "The account of the conquest seems to have been restricted to what is now Jos 1–12. Its immediate sequel and conclusion appears in Jos 21.43–22:6."[8] The function of 21:43–22:6 is to close the account of the conquest of the generation of Joshua and the elders who outlived him. It does so by informing the reader that what was promised by the Lord in 1:3–4 was fulfilled in 21:43–45. It also informs that the promise of the two and half tribes in 1:12–18 was also fulfilled in 22:1–6. Joshua's farewell to these tribes in 22:1–6 closes the account of the conquest.

The second part of the epilogue covers 22:7–24:33. The primary function of 22:7–24:33 is parallel to the function of the prologue of Joshua (Josh 1:1–11; 2:1–5:15); both sections prepare the people for what would come. Joshua 22:7–24:33 prepares the next generation for life in the land in the absence of Joshua and the elders.[9] It can be divided into four sections:

---

4. Klaas Spronk, "From Joshua to Samuel: Some Remarks on the Origin of the Book of Judges," in *The Land of Israel in Bible, History, and Theology: Studies in Honour of Ed Noort*, ed. Jacques van Ruiten and J. Cornelis de Vos, Supplements to Vetus Testamentum, vol. 124 (Leiden: Brill, 2009), 145.

5. John Michael Engle, "The Redactional Development of the Book of Judges" (PhD diss., Hebrew Union College–Jewish Institute of Religion, 2002), 3.

6. Ibid.

7. Consult appendix 3 for an outline of the structure of the book of Joshua.

8. Eamonn O'Doherty, "Literary Problem of Judges 1:1–3:6," *Catholic Biblical Quarterly* 18, no. 1 (1956): 5.

9. Cf. Butler, *Joshua 13–24*, 268.

A   22:7–34 Test for the people
   B   23:1–16 Commission of the people
   B' 24:1–28 Covenant for the people
A' 24:29–33 Evaluation of the people

B and B' are two events that can be seen as a unit.[10] The commissioning of the people in Joshua 23:1–16 prepares them for the covenant of Joshua 24:1–28. According to this structure, A' corresponds primarily with A. That is, the evaluation given for how the people did in A, and only secondarily for how they did in the rest of the book.

Chronologically, the events of 22:7–34 took place after 23:1–24:28. This has huge implications for understanding the meaning of 22:7–34. So chronology must be established first. Both 13:1 and 23:1 speak of Joshua's age with וִיהוֹשֻׁעַ זָקֵן בָּא בַּיָּמִים, which suggests that the allotment of land in 13:1–21:42 and the events of 23:1–24:28 happened within the same timeframe. The content of 23:1–16, especially the verb רְאוּ "see" in 23:4, further suggests that the events of 23:1–24:28 happened right after the distribution of the land. If so, we can safely assume that the events of 23:1–24:28 took place right after the allotment of land but before Joshua sent the two and half tribes home. It is unlikely that knowing his days were over (13:1; 23:1), Joshua would send the tribes home after the allocation of land in 22:6 only to call them back in 23:1–24:28.

Rather, it is better to assume that after the allocation of land, Joshua commissioned the people (23:1–16), renewed their covenant with the Lord (24:1–28), and finally sent all the tribes to their inheritances (24:18) with a special farewell to the two and half tribes (22:6). Then the events of 22:7–34 took place on their way to their homes.

In 22:7–34, if there is one thing that should stand out to the reader, it is the absence of Joshua and even of Eleazar who is replaced by his son Phinehas. It should stand out because Joshua was still alive, since this event took place right after Joshua sent the two and half tribes home in 22:6 and it happened before they reached their inheritance.[11] Assis claims that his

---

10. Ibid.
11. Cf. Elie Assis, "The Position and Function of Jos 22 in the Book of Joshua," *ZAW* 116, no. 4 (2004): 354–355.

absence, "is surely connected to the fact that Phinehas is the main figure in the story."[12] If, as Assis argues, the setting of the story was after the death of Joshua and Phinehas, then it would be understandable for Phinehas to be the main figure in the story. However, there is no reason to assume that either Joshua or Eleazar was dead at this time. The text does indicate that Joshua was alive because he was the one who sent the two and half tribes (22:7–8) and the event took place on their way to their inheritance, not some time after they had already returned home (22:9–10). Eleazar was also still alive. His death is not reported until after that of Joshua (24:33).

A better explanation for the absence of both Joshua and Eleazar can be found in recognizing that the events of 22:7–34 took place after Joshua commissioned the people (23:1–16) and renewed their covenant with the Lord (24:1–28). In 23:1–24:24 Joshua prepared the next generation for a time without his leadership.[13] There was no successor that Joshua was passing the leadership on to. The people were his successors. Just as the Lord commissioned him in 1:1–9, so also Joshua commissioned the people in 23:1–16 to assume responsibility for finishing the conquest on their own, under the leadership of the Lord. Joshua used almost identical phrases which the Lord had used when he commissioned him in 1:1–9. The following parallel can be observed in the two commissions:

Table 3: Commission of Joshua versus Commission of the People

Joshua by the Lord 1:1–9	The people by Joshua 23:1–16
Moses is dead v. 2	Joshua is dying vv. 2, 14
I am going to give you the land vv. 2–4	I have given you the nations v. 4
No one can stand against you vv. 5–6, 9	No one stood against you vv. 5, 9–10
be strong to keep the law vv. 7–8	be strong to keep the law vv. 6–8, 11–16

---

12. Ibid., 355.
13. Butler, *Joshua 13–24*, 268.

One of the major differences between the two commissions is that in the commissioning of the people there is emphasis on the need for keeping the law and the consequences for both breaking and keeping it. This emphasis is further translated into covenant renewal in 24:1–28. Making themselves witnesses, the people made a covenant to cling to the Lord and serve him even after Joshua's death. The covenant ceremony involved all the tribes of Israel (24:1).

Joshua 22

Having encouraged and warned the people and having renewed their covenant with the Lord, Joshua (and Eleazar) disappeared from the scene in 22:7–34 in order that they may give the next generation the chance to prove that they could indeed keep their covenant with the Lord, even after their death.[14] They were already preparing them to face such a challenge. As Bekkum rightly noted, "Joshua's tasks and duties as well as the promises made to him are passed on to a next generation, just as happened to Moses when YHWH passed his responsibilities and divine promises to Joshua."[15]

The problem that the people were left to deal with in the absence of Joshua and the elders was idolatry. The following narrative structure captures the plot of the story.

> *Exposition*: a potential for cultic violation (vv. 7–9)
> *Complication*: building of an altar (vv. 10–12)
> *Change*: a reminder of past cultic violations (vv. 13–20)
> *Resolution*: assurance that there is no cultic violation (vv. 21–33)
> *Ending*: loyalty to the Lord affirmed (v. 34)

The *exposition*, verses 7–9, gives background information. It prepares the reader for the building of the altar, telling the reader that the tribes had spoil from the conquest when they left which they used to build the altar. Though Joshua sent them home with spoil to divide among their brothers,

---

14. One could argue that it was because of their old age too. This could be true especially with reference to travel. However, this does not explain why they are not indicated as the ones who sent the messengers nor why the report was not given to them. And as argued above, the reason was not because either of them was dead.

15. Koert van Bekkum, *From Conquest to Coexistence: Ideology and Antiquarian Intent in the Historiography of Israel's Settlement in Canaan*, Culture and History of the Ancient Near East, vol. 45 (Leiden: Brill, 2011), 213–214.

they used it to build a huge altar. Using the spoil for building an altar could create an impression of idolatry in the mind of the reader as it did in the minds of Israelites (cf. v. 20). The problem Israel faced was potential idolatry.

The *complication* (vv. 10–12) captures, in a suspenseful manner, the building of the altar and allows the reader to pass judgment. Their stop at Geliloth and building of a sizable altar, when read in light of the exposition, suggests to the reader that the altar was a case of cultic violation. They used the spoil for idolatry as did Achan in Joshua 7. This was the conclusion of all Israel when they heard the news. Their decision to go to war further confirms to the reader that the altar was indeed a cultic violation.

The *change* (vv. 13–20) happens when Israel decides to speak with the two and half tribes. The message of Phinehas and the chief men clearly shows that in their mind the two and a half tribes had built the altar for idolatry. The sin at Peor and the sin of Achan were still fresh in Israel's mind.

The *resolution* (vv. 21–33) is found in the reply of the two and half tribes and the confirmation by Phinehas. In their reply they did not simply state that the purpose of the altar was to serve as a witness between them. Rather, they confirmed to Israel that they were faithful to the Lord and agreed that cultic violation deserves serious punishment.

The *ending* (v. 34) further confirms that even after the representatives of all Israel left, the two and half tribes kept their words. The altar they built was not for idolatry. Their commitment to the Lord had not changed.

The evaluation of the people is given by pointing to their unity against idolatry. "From a literary standpoint, this chapter highlights the unity of the twelve tribes. The reiteration of the 'whole assembly of the Lord' (v. 16), 'the whole community of Israel' (vv. 18, 20), 'each of the tribes of Israel' (v. 14) and 'the Israelites' (vv. 30–32) emphasizes the sense of community."[16] A united Israel was willing to go into a war against their brothers to protect themselves from Peor-like idolatry (cf. v. 17). The author tells this story to show how the Israelites handled a serious spiritual threat without the help of Joshua and the elders.

---

16. Hélène M. Dallaire, "Joshua," in *Numbers to Ruth*, ed. Tremper Longman III and David E. Garland, rev. ed., Expositor's Bible Commentary, vol. 2 (Grand Rapids: Zondervan, 2012), 1025.

The epilogue ends by evaluating the people in 24:29–33. This evaluation seems to focus on the people and how they did as long as Joshua and the elders were alive. Though this does not exclude evaluation of how they did in the entire book, it is likely that its function is primarily within the epilogue since 21:43–22:6 had closed the conquest narrative. Therefore, it is best to see 24:29–33 as an evaluation of how the people did in 22:7–34 when they handled a serious spiritual problem without the help of Joshua and the elders, though they were still alive. The evaluation is positive. The people did well. They served the Lord for as long as Joshua and the elders lived. As Butler rightly noted, "the final act of Joshua's generation is to cement their claim to the land by burying their heroes in the land, a land which a father could now give to his son (v 33)."[17] They lived up to what they were commissioned to do.

The evaluation covered the period up to the death of the last elder. As Howard noted, "the burials of these three men signified the ends of eras."[18] In Joshua 24:33 the period of the elders is over. The mention of the death of Eleazar marked the end of the period of the elders who outlived Joshua.

That the duration of their obedience was only during the period of the elders should prompt the reader to expect a different and negative story when turning the page to the prologue of Judges. There is no doubt that the author was aware of the failure of the next generation; that they did not serve the Lord after the death of Joshua and the elders. He hints at their failure in the pericope dealing with the allotment of land. However, he leaves the full assessment for the author of Judges.

Judges as Sequel to Joshua

Judges picks up where the book of Joshua left off. The book of Joshua ends by evaluating how the people did up till the death of the elders, that is, the death of Joshua and Eleazar. The book of Judges picks up the people's story after the death of their elders (Judg 1:1). The mention of the death of Joshua but not Eleazar in 1:1 is not an indication that Eleazar was alive.

---

17. Butler, *Joshua 13–24*, 343.
18. David M. Howard, *Joshua*, NAC, ed. E. Ray Clendenen, vol. 5 (Nashville, TN: Broadman & Holman, 1998), 442.

This simply is a literary style by which the author picks up the heading of the last paragraph of the book of Joshua.[19] It gives a general time-frame. It also emphasizes the important role Joshua played in the life of Israel.

In light of the end of Joshua, the primary purpose of the prologue of Judges, not just Judges 1, is to evaluate how the Israelites did after the death of the elders with respect to remaining in the land and their covenant with the Lord. In the process of evaluating how the people did after Joshua's death, the prologue uses material from the book of Joshua. This material comes primarily from the pericope dealing with land allotment (13:1–21:42). The material used covers what the book of Joshua stated as having been fulfilled in the lifetime of Joshua (i.e. the success of Caleb) as well as what the book implied as having transpired after his death (i.e. the failure of the tribes).

Success of a Judahite Family

It was argued in chapter 3 that the story of Caleb in Judges 1:9–16, 20 was a flashback to the book of Joshua. For the Caleb narrative to qualify as a flashback, it must do more than quote from the book of Joshua. The author must place the "flashback" in the lifetime of Joshua. Four texts in Joshua reveal that the account did indeed take place in the lifetime of Joshua.

According to Joshua 10:36–37, both Hebron and Debir were captured in the lifetime of Joshua, during the southern campaign. It is also made very clear that the campaign against these cities was a complete victory with all the inhabitants destroyed. These verses attribute the victory to Joshua. However, a close reading of the chapter clarifies that Joshua himself did not personally engage in the battle.

When Joshua was told that the five Amorite kings were hiding in the cave at Makkedah (10:17), Joshua told the army which brought him the message, "Roll large stones against the mouth of the cave, and set men by it to guard them; but do not stay there yourselves; pursue your enemies, and attack them from the rear. Do not let them enter their towns, for the Lord your God has given them into your hand" (vv. 18–19, NRSV). This suggests that Joshua himself was not joining them in their pursuit. This is confirmed in verse 21 when the author notes, "all the people returned safe

---

19. Butler, *Joshua 13–24*, 337.

to Joshua in the camp at Makkedah." The implication is that Joshua was part of the battle against some, but not all of the cities.

Joshua 11:21–23 is a summary of the conquest of Hebron and Debir. Here we are told again that Joshua was the one who conquered these lands. Both Joshua 10:36–37 and 11:21–23 are part of summary statements that capture the results of the conquest of Israel as a nation. The contribution of each tribe or family is attributed to the nation.

Joshua 13:1–21:42 deal with individual tribes and families, however, victory or failure of the tribes, not the nation, is given. In keeping with this, Joshua 14:6–15 and 15:13–19 ascribe the victory of Hebron to Caleb. Caleb's conquest of Hebron and Debir took place while Joshua was still alive. In Joshua 15:13–19 the use of the perfect for נתן "to give" indicates that Hebron was assigned to Caleb at an earlier time. With the *wayyiqtol* at verse 15, the author signals that Debir was taken right after Hebron's conquest. Therefore, even in Joshua, Caleb's conquest of Hebron and Debir are seen as past events.[20] This then should save one from wondering whether the same event in Judges 1:9–15 was after Joshua's death.

The mention of Gilgal in Joshua 14:6 also signals this event as having taken place when Israel was fighting the battle of Joshua 10–11. In Joshua, Gilgal was the location from which Israel set out to fight the Canaanites, whereas Shiloh was a location from which Joshua allocated the land. The last reference to Gilgal was at the end of the Southern campaign. It is likely that after the Northern campaign, Joshua moved to Shiloh where he allocated the land. Gilgal was later associated as "Joshua's victory headquarters" when the angel of the Lord is said to come from Gilgal in Judges 2:1.[21]

The closing references to the allotment of the land (Josh 19:51), whose wording echoes the opening (14:1), state that the allotment was done at Shiloh. Just as was true of the two and half tribes east of Jordan (Josh 13), Caleb's story took place before the allotment of land began.

---

20. Eugene H. Merrill, *Kingdom of Priests: A History of Old Testament Israel*, 2nd ed. (Grand Rapids: Baker Academic, 2008), 152.
21. Lee Roy Martin, "From Gilgal to Bochim: The Narrative Significance of the Angel of Yahweh in Judges 2:1," *Journal for Semitics* 18, no. 2 (2009): 339; Cf. Robert B. Chisholm, *A Commentary on Judges and Ruth*, Kregel Exegetical Library (Grand Rapids: Kregel, 2013), 138.

Failure of the Tribes

Besides the success of Caleb, the author of Judges also used material from Joshua 13:1–21:42 that captures the failure of the tribes. According to Judges the failure is that of the generation after Joshua's death. Though Joshua 13:1–21:42 does not clearly indicate when the failure of the tribes actually began, the impression a reader might get is that the failure was that of the generation before Joshua's death.

The People before Joshua's Death

Several clues in the book of Joshua indicate that the failure could not have occurred during Joshua's lifetime. The positive comments regarding the generation before Joshua's death in the books of Joshua and Judges support this conclusion.

Positive Comments

In Joshua 23:8–9, towards the end of his life, Joshua himself commended the people with the words, "hold fast to the Lord your God, *as you have done to this day*. For the Lord has driven out before you great and strong nations; and as for you, *no one has been able to withstand you to this day*," (NRSV, emphasis mine). These verses capture Joshua's positive comments with regard to both the people's commitment to the Lord and their victory over the inhabitants of the land. The repeated phrase "to this day" emphasizes that this generation was doing well up to the time of Joshua's address. Joshua 24:31 adds that this positive behavior went on until the death of the elders.

The author of Judges also views the people under Joshua positively with regard to dispossessing their land. In Judges 2:6, which uses Joshua 24:28, the author gives an additional phrase: לָרֶ֫שֶׁת אֶת־הָאָ֫רֶץ. A reader of Joshua 24:28 might think that "going to their inheritance" is a reference to the land of which they already had taken possession. The writer of Judges clarifies that this "land" included both the land already possessed and the land not yet controlled. Therefore, the author of Judges sees in this phrase the people's motivation to take possession of their allotted land right after their commission (Josh 23) and the covenant renewal (Josh 24). In the eyes of the author of Judges, the people took initiative to finish the conquest up to this point (i.e. just before Joshua and the elders died).

Complete versus Partial Conquest

These positive comments, however, do not mean that their conquest was complete. Some look at the partial conquest report in Joshua 13:1–21:42 and argue that there are two different and contradictory accounts of the conquest in Joshua itself.[22] Some propose different stages of composition to reconcile this "contradiction."[23] A closer look at the reports reveals that they have no contradiction with each other.

Conquest as Fulfillment of the Lord's Promise

The book of Joshua begins with the Lord's promise to Joshua and the people, "Every place that the sole of your foot will tread upon I have given to you, as I promised to Moses"(Josh 1:3, NRSV). Therefore, the conquest reports should be read in light of this introductory statement in Joshua 1.

The first two paragraphs dealing with complete conquest are both summaries of the immediately preceding conquests. Whereas Joshua 10:40–43 summarizes the southern campaign, Joshua 11:16–23 summarizes the northern and the southern campaigns. Joshua 10:43 speaks of the return of Joshua and the army to the camp at Gilgal. This suggests that 10:40–43 has in view only the southern campaign. The content of this summary focuses on Joshua's commitment to the command of the Lord. Every city to which he went, Joshua did not leave any survivors. He dispossessed the inhabitants of every city to which he went. The Lord's promise that he had given the land, which their foot would tread on, was fullfilled.

Joshua 21:43–45 clearly echoes 1:3–4. The promise given in 1:3–4 is fulfilled. The language is general, summarizing. The focus is on the fulfillment of the promise. He gave all that he promised as long as they did their part to fight for it. Joshua 12 made it specific to the lands east of Jordan.

---

22. Eero Junkkaala, *Three Conquests of Canaan: A Comparative Study of Two Egyptian Military Campaigns and Joshua 10–12 in the Light of Recent Archaeological Evidence* (Finland: Abo Akademi University Press, 2006), 227. There are others who argue that the contradiction is between Joshua and Judges (Antony F. Campbell and Mark A. O'Brien, *Unfolding the Deuteronomistic History: Origins, Upgrades, Present Text* [Minneapolis: Fortress, 2000], 171). Joshua is said to give a "complete conquest" report; whereas, Judges gives a partial conquest report.

23. Yigal Levin, "Conquered and Unconquered: Reality and Historiography in the Geography of Joshua," in *The Book of Joshua*, BETL, ed. Ed Noort, vol. 250 (Leuven: Peeters, 2012), 370.

Joshua 21 is a summary of the conquest in the book and for that reason it does not have to be specific.

Conquest as Israel's Responsibility

The victory reported was for all Israel. Victory for all Israel does not mean the victory of individual tribes. Joshua's target in the conquest in Joshua was to defeat the enemies of all Israel. Each individual tribe was supposed to fight and dispossess the inhabitants from their respective inheritance. Total victory in the battles they fought does not mean dispossessing the inhabitants. The list of kings in Joshua 12 "does not say that Israel actually controls all the land."[24] In the conquest narrative, that is, Joshua 6–12, the term ירש is used only in 12:1 to refer to the dispossession of the inhabitants of the cities east of Jordan. The conquest reports in Joshua 11 and 12 do not use ירש. The use of ירש in Joshua 21:43–45 should be read in accordance with the nature of these verses as summary reports that emphasize the fulfillment of the promise of the Lord. Therefore, Joshua defeated the enemy of all Israel in Joshua 6–12 and some part of the land was dispossessed. Everywhere they went and fought they succeeded, but they did not go to every city whose king Joshua had defeated.

Joshua 13:1 clearly indicates that there were also other nations that the Israelites did not dispossess. However, these were nations outside of the conquered cities.[25] They were not among the cities Israel had fought in the previous campaigns. The accusation in Joshua 18:3, "how long do you slack to enter and dispossess the land?" suggests that each tribe still needed to dispossess the inhabitants from their allotted land. What they were slack to do was "enter" their allotted land.

The choice of the word "to enter" seems to be influenced by the command in 1:11 "to go in to dispossess the land," as well as the Lord's promise to Joshua in 1:3–4 which emphasized the need for them to set their feet in

---

24. Koert van Bekkum, "Remembering and Claiming Ramesside Canaan: Historical-Topographical Problems and the Ideology of Geography in Joshua 13.1–7," in *The Book of Joshua*, BETL, ed. Ed Noort, vol. 250 (Leuven: Peeters, 2012), 353.

25. Bekkum, *Conquest to Coexistence*, 214.

their allotted land. The promise was not unconditional.[26] Israel needed to fight for it by entering the land.

Summary

During the conquest led by Joshua, Israel won every battle they were engaged in and dispossessed every city to which they went.[27] However, there were cities that they did not dispossess, both cities of kings Joshua defeated and those he had not fought in either of the campaigns before. As Judges 2:21–3:4 tell us, the Lord himself prevented Joshua from going after every Canaanite city. Though there remained some nations to be dispossessed, the author focused on the fulfillment of the Lord's promise. Focusing on the fulfillment of the Lord's promise enourages the new generation that the Lord would fight for them – even if Joshua and the elders are dead – and they could dispossess the remaining land if they obey the Lord as did the previous generation.

The People after Joshua's Death

Both Joshua 13–21 and Judges 1 speak of the failures of the tribes after the death of Joshua. After Joshua's death, they gradually let the inhabitants of some of the lands return to their land and live with them and others like Dan lost their portion altogether.

Joshua 13:1–21:42

Five failure reports are given in Joshua 13:1–21:42. These are found in 13:13, 15:63, 16:10, 17:12 and 19:47. Joshua 13:13 captures the first failure report. Though the land was assigned to the two and a half tribes east of the Jordan, the failure was ascribed to the Israelites as a whole. As Butler noted, "this verse introduces a series of statements in Joshua and in Judg 1:19–36 describing territories not conquered by Israel, thus reflecting a

---

26. For a different view, see Thomas B. Dozeman, "Joshua 1.1–9: The Beginning of a Book or a Literary Bridge?," in *The Book of Joshua*, BETL, ed. Ed Noort, vol. 250 (Leuven: Peeters, 2012), 168. Dozeman views 1:3–4, and 1:7–9 as a separate composition, though by a single author, from 1:1–2, and 1:5–6 (Ibid., 168). Dozeman takes 1:1b–2 and 4–5 as unconditional promise, which is reinterpreted as conditional by the addition of 1:3–4 (ibid., 176). V. 2 is clearly conditional to Joshua as a leader, vv. 3–5 to the people (but includes Joshua too).

27. Joshua did not win the first battle against Ai.

task still before the people."²⁸ In fact, when the rest of the failure reports are studied in comparison to this report, the reader can notice the author's implicit rhetoric. As Hauch argued, there is "a discernible progression of Israel's failure to dispossess the remaining nations suggested in the movement from *did not* to *could not* to *would not*."²⁹ Since these cities were left over from the campaign by Moses, this failure could be seen as having some kind of effect on the latter failures. The act of dispossessing was absent beginning from Moses' time up to the time of writing. The Israelites did not make any attempt to dispossess these two cities. Instead they let the people live with them.

The second failure report is about Judah and is found in Joshua 15:63. When compared to the report in 13:13, one can see two differences: (1) The report blames an individual tribe, not the Israelites in general. This is true of the other three failure reports in this book. (2) The author adds יכל and in so doing hints at Judah's attempt, though unsuccessful, to dispossess the inhabitants of Jerusalem. This statement should be seen in light of the pericope in which it is found. The pericope dealing with the allotment of the land was intended to summarize not just what happened during Joshua's lifetime, but most importantly the status of the inheritance by the time the author was writing the book. Judah did dispossess Jerusalem at the time of Joshua. The flashback in Judges 1:8 recapitulated this attempt. The city was destroyed but the Jebusites were gradually able to return and cohabit with the Judahites.

The third failure report, that of Ephraim, is found in Joshua 16:10. In Joshua 10:33 in the southern campaign, the king of Gezer tried to help Lachish but Joshua defeated him and his army, leaving no survivors. However, there was no report of a follow up battle by going to Gezer itself. Apparently this was left for the tribe of Ephraim to do. But Ephraim did not. This report is different from 13:13 in that the author adds that the Canaanites were doing forced labor. This statement indicates that Ephraim clearly had power over the Canaanites who lived in Gezer since Ephraim had them do forced labor. Therefore, their failure to dispossess was willful disobedience.

---

28. Butler, *Joshua 13–24*, 67.

29. Gerhard Hauch, "Text and Contexts: A Literary Reading of the Conquest Narrative (Jos 1–11)" (PhD diss., Princeton Theological Seminary, 1991), 144.

The fourth failure report, of Manasseh, is found in Joshua 17:12. There are several changes in this report. (1) The author adds יכל as he did in the case of Judah to show Manasseh's attempted . . . failure. (2) The reason for failure is given by the changed report of cohabitation from the simple וַיֵּשֶׁב to לָשֶׁבֶת . . . וַיּוֹאֶל. The hiphil of יאל suggests that the Canaanites were determined and persistent.[30] Manasseh gave in to their determination. At least three of the cities' kings were killed by Joshua according to Joshua 12:21 (Taanach and Meggido), 12:23 (Dor). Manasseh was not able to dispossess them. (3) As in Ephraim, the inhabitants were pressed into forced labor. Yet, here it is the Israelites, not Manasseh, who are blamed (v. 13a). Manasseh is blamed for not using this occasion to dispossess them (v. 13b: notice the change to third person singular verb). Though at first, it was "inability" due to the "determination" of the Canaanites, later Manasseh became "willfully disobedient" to dispossess the Canaanites even when he had the chance to.

The last failure report is that of Dan and is found in 19:47. This report is totally different from 13:13 or the other three reports preceding it. Dan lost its allotted territory but was able to dispossess a city and live in it, though the city was not assigned to it.

The phrase "to this day" is found in Joshua 13:13, 15:63, and 16:10. It is not used in the report of Manasseh or Dan. The use of "to this day" shows that the purpose of the pericope is etiological.[31] Though this phrase is absent in the case of Manasseh and Dan, Dan's renaming of the conquered city is suggestive of etiological motive. The author's intent is to describe the status of the allotted lands at the time of writing.

Therefore, the failures reported in Joshua 13–21 were later failures though they began before Joshua's death.[32] The mention of Dan's failure clearly suggests that the author is aware of the failure reports found in Judges 1. The absence of some of these failure reports in Joshua 13:1–21:42 was not because the author was unaware of their existence. Rather, the author of Joshua 13:1–21:42 chose the tribes – with the exception of Dan – for whom

---

30. "יאל I," in *DCH*, ed. David J. A. Clines, vol. 4 (Sheffield: Sheffield Academic Press, 1998), 71.

31. Brevard S. Childs, "A Study of the Formula, 'Until This Day,'" *JBL* 82, no. 3 (1963): 280; Butler, *Joshua 13–24*, 87.

32. Walter R. Roehrs, "Conquest of Canaan according to Joshua and Judges," *Concordia Theological Monthly* 31, no. 12 (1960): 752. Roehrs considers Caleb's story too as later.

Joshua had defeated the kings of the cities that were allotted to them. The kings of the cities allotted to Judah, Ephraim and Manasseh were defeated and the death of their kings listed in Joshua 12. However, none of the kings of the cities which were allotted to other tribes were listed in Joshua 12.[33]

Judges 1:1–36

Judges 1:1–36 also reports the failures of the tribes to take possession of their allotted land. As Polzin argued, Judges 1:1–36 "paints the same kind of picture of Israel's partial military victories *after* Joshua's death as Joshua 13–21 described *before* his death."[34] However, several differences can be observed. The first difference is in its purpose. The phrase "to this day" is absent in Judges 1 except for Benjamin (1:21). This suggests that the purpose of Judges 1:1–36 is not etiological. Its purpose is to summarize the failure of the tribes during the period of testing, that is, after Joshua's death and before the first judge was raised.

Another difference between Joshua 13–21 and Judges 1:1–36 is that whereas Joshua 13–21 reports the failure of only four tribes, Judges 1:1–36 reports the failure of all the tribes except one. As argued above, the reason Joshua 13–21 reported the failure of Judah, Ephraim and Manasseh was because they had an opportunity to completely destroy and dispossess the inhabitants since Joshua had destroyed the kings of the cities' allotted to them.

Spronk argues that Judges 1:1–36 "utilizes materials from the book of Joshua . . . with some expansions to explicitly reflect the general success of Judah and the increasing failure of the other Israelite tribes, especially Dan."[35] An example given by Spronk is the blame put on the Benjaminites in Judges 1:21 for failing to dispossess the Jebusites though in Joshua 15:63 the blame was on the Judahites. However, as argued before, 1:7 also blames Judahites, since Judah kept Adoni-bezek alive in Jerusalem where Judah was still living with the Jebusites. Judges 1:8 captures a flashback to Judah's attempt to

---

33. Butler notes that Shimron-meron of Josh 12:20 could be the same as Shimron of Josh 19:15 which is allotted to Zebulun (Butler, *Joshua 13–24*, 533).

34. Robert Polzin, *Moses and the Deuteronomist: A Literary Study of the Deuteronomic History, Part One: Deuteronomy, Joshua, Judges*, ISBL, ed. Herbert Marks and Robert Polzin (New York: Seabury, 1980), 147.

35. Spronk, "From Joshua to Samuel," 145; K. Lawson Younger, "The Configuring of Judicial Preliminaries: Judges 1.1–2.5 and Its Dependence on the Book of Joshua," *JSOT* 68 (1995): 76.

destroy Jerusalem but "conquering and burning a city is one thing, definitively driving away the inhabitants is something else."[36] Though successful at first, Judah did not keep the Jebusites from returning to Jerusalem.

Still another difference, according to Younger, is that "where Joshua 13–19 is subtle or implicit in its description, Judges 1 is explicit."[37] This difference is better summarized by Fishbane:

> . . . one must observe that the conquest list found in Judg. 1:1–36 indicates that in many cases the invading people "did not dispossess . . ." the local population (vv. 19, 21, 27–33). In only one case is the reason for failure to dispossess the Canaanites attributed to inferior Israelite armament (v. 19). The basic force of the other uses of the formula . . . is to state that this was an intentional failure to wipe out the population. And indeed, just this point is explicitly made in v. 28: "Later, when the Israelites became strong, they put the Canaanites into workforces, but did not dispossess them." Clearly the old editor of this conquest list is concerned to explain why the promised land was not completely conquered. He did so by attributing the failure to a deliberate violation of older injunctions which commanded the removal of the nations of Canaan. By contrast an entirely different explanation for the failure to conquer the land can be found in (the earlier) Josh. 14–18. Here the issue is not that the Israelites were unwilling to dispossess the Canaanites, but that "they were not able . . . to dispossess them" (cf. Josh. 15:63 with Judg. 1:21, and Josh. 17:12 with Judg. 1:27).[38]

Both Joshua 13–21 and Judges 1 agree that the tribes failed to dispossess the inhabitants. However, according to Joshua 13–21 the failure was "inability." According to Judges 1, it was a result of willful disobedience.

---

36. Spronk, "From Joshua to Samuel," 145.
37. Younger, "The Configuring of Judicial Preliminaries," 85.
38. Michael Fishbane, *Biblical Interpretation in Ancient Israel* (Oxford: Clarendon, 1985), 203.

Summary

Joshua ended by evaluating how the people did until the death of the elders. The prologue of Judges begins by evaluating how they did after their death. Its evaluation is that the people failed to live up to what they were commissioned to do and to keep their covenantal oath soon after the death of Joshua (and that of the elders). They did not serve the Lord by completing the conquest. Judges depends on Joshua in reporting this failure. The change in Judges (though using Joshua's language) is rhetorical. It was primarily to emphasize that Israel under Joshua (as a nation and as individual tribes) attempted and were motivated – though only partially successful – to dispossess the inhabitants; the next generation (those after Joshua's death), however, were lax and were not motivated to obey the command to finish the conquest.

CHAPTER 5

Function of the Prologue – Part Two

In the previous chapter, the prologue's function as a sequel to the book of Joshua was examined. This chapter discusses the function of the prologue within the book of Judges itself by considering how it relates with both the central section and the epilogue. This is basically an examination of both chronological and logical/rhetorical relationships that the prologue has with the central section as well as the epilogue.

The Prologue versus the Central Section

In order to have a clear understanding of the relationship between the prologue and the central section, one has to first establish the chronological relationship. Only then can one understand the logical relationship. Therefore, this section deals with the chronological relationship followed by the logical relationship.

Chronological Relationship

According to Webb, "the events narrated in 1:1–2:5 all take place prior to the onset of apostasy and the advent of the first judge . . . The developments described in 2:6–3:6, on the other hand, coincide (temporally) with those narrated in the bulk of the book."[1] Amit, with a slight modification, argues that 1:1–2:5 captures events that happened in the period preceding that of the Judges; whereas, 2:11–3:6 captures the events of the period of the

---

1. Barry G. Webb, *The Book of the Judges: An Integrated Reading*, JSOTSup Series, vol. 44 (Eugene, OR: Wipf & Stock, 2008), 119–120.

judges.² Amit also argues that 2:6–10, which she sees as a transitional unit, "summarizes the first period as one in which the people served God, and prepares the reader for the second period, that of the generation that did not know the Lord."³ For Butler the prologue is, "a summary of the history of Israel following the death of Joshua until the onset of kingship."⁴ O'Doherty, on the other hand, takes the prologue as describing "the political and religious condition of the nation at the beginning of the age of the Judges."⁵

Judges 1:1–3:6 captures events from three periods as can be seen from the discussions in chapters 2 and 3 of this dissertation. (1) The period of Conquest (before Joshua's death), Judges 1:8–6, 20; 2:6–10; 2:23–3:4; (2) The period of Testing (after Joshua's death before the first judge), Judges 1:1–7, 17–19; 1:21–2:5; 2:10–14a, 20–21; 3:5–6; and (3) The period of Judges, Judges 2:14b–19. The end of the period of Testing (2:10–14a, 20–21) overlaps with the beginning of the period of Judges. For O'Doherty only the latter is intimately connected with the central section.⁶

The above division of Judges 1:1–3:6 into three periods shows that only 2:10–21 is directly related to the central section by covering material from the same time frame. The first two periods precede the period covered by the central section. This difference in the periods has implications for how each group of verses dealing with the three periods relate with the central section.

Logical Relationship

Since 2:11–19, 20–21 directly cover material from the same period as the central section, 2:11–21 should be studied first. Then the function of the rest of the prologue will be examined.

---

2. Yairah Amit, *The Book of Judges: The Art of Editing*, trans. Jonathan Chipman, BIS, ed. R. Alan Culpepper and Rolf Rendtorff, vol. 38 (Leiden: Brill, 1999), 135.

3. Ibid.

4. Trent C. Butler, *Judges*, WBC, ed. Bruce M. Metzger et al., vol. 8 (Nashville, TN: Thomas Nelson, 2009), 9.

5. Eamonn O'Doherty, "Literary Problem of Judges 1:1–3:6," *Catholic Biblical Quarterly* 18, no. 1 (1956): 1.

6. Ibid., 2.

Judges 2:11–19

Commentators generally consider Judges 2:11–19 as the heart of Judges, used to frame the stories of the central section.[7] Three observations will support taking 3:7–11, not 2:11–19, the volume's center:

(1) The formulas in 3:7–11 are more comprehensive than those in 2:11–19.

(2) Several elements in 3:7–11 do not appear in 2:11–19. Several elements in 3:7–11 but absent in 2:11–19 appear in the central section. Amit summarizes this point:

> The chapter of Othniel son of Kenaz thus serves as a reservoir of formulae, some of which are known to the reader from the exposition, and others which he will encounter in further reading. Every formula which the reader is liable to encounter in the future episodes will return him to this reservoir of formulae, which is the concretization of the general characterization of the period of the judges. It therefore seems that the creation of a reservoir of formulae is not by chance, but serves a compositional function.[8]

(3) The individual judges were not evaluated by the criteria from 2:11–19. The only evaluation done in 2:11–19 was that of the people, not the judges. The central section on the other hand evaluates the judges: "Whereas the judge of the introduction has not been evaluated because he was presented as God's (neutral) tool, the individual stories portray the judge as individual people with virtues and flaws."[9]

---

7. Barnabas Lindars, *Judges 1–5: A New Translation and Commentary*, ed. A. D. H. Mayes (Edinburgh: T&T Clark, 1995), 91.

8. Yairah Amit, *The Book of Judges: The Art of Editing*, BIS, ed. R. Alan Culpepper and Rolf Rendtorff, vol. 38 (Leiden: Brill, 1999), 163; for detailed comparison of the phrases in 3:7–11 with that of 2:11–19 as well as the frameworks in the rest of the central section, see Lawson Grant Stone, "From Tribal Confederation to Monarchic State: The Editorial Perspective of the Book of Judges" (PhD diss., Yale University, 1988), 277–278.

9. Susanne Gillmayr-Bucher, "Framework and Discourse in the Book of Judges," *JBL* 128, no. 4 (2009): 693.

The judges in the central section were evaluated in comparison with Othniel's account in 3:7–11.[10] Othniel's account could serve this purpose. Othniel is a "transitional figure" between the conquest generation and those of the period of the Judges. His "double appearance makes him a figure who both connects and demarcates between the two periods . . . Othniel thus constitutes a transitional figure, bringing out the characteristic feature of all the heroes of the book of Judges: they all act first and foremost by strength of God and his will."[11]

According to Chisholm, Ehud and Othniel form "a paradigmatic tandem."[12] Chisholm rightly notes that "only of these two is it said, 'the Lord raised up a savior,' and only these two are designated by the title 'savior.'"[13] However, the difference in style – whereas Ehud's account is scenic narrative, Othniel's is more of a report than a story[14] – suggests that Ehud's account should be seen as the other judges' account. This is probably why "Othniel's account is so brief and stylized. Just as likely, the narrator could have made the Othniel account more like that of Ehud or Deborah and Barak; but he chose to present it in an abbreviated, schematic form, whose brief phrases could be used as 'frame-elements' in later narratives."[15] Ehud seems to be presented as the only one who lived up to the standard set by Othniel.

Some scholars acknowledge that not all the elements of 2:11–19 are found in the central section. They do not take this to mean that 3:7–11, instead of 2:11–19, is the paradigmatic introduction. They consider 2:11–19 as the paradigmatic introduction but allow for it to be changed within the different stories of the central section. Webb argues that it is part of "a narrative abstract, an outline of the plot but it does not necessarily hinder our ability to appreciate the detailed presentation of character, situation, and

---

10. Philip E. Satterthwaite and Gordon J. McConville, *A Guide to the Historical Books*, Exploring the Old Testament, vol. 2 (Downers Grove, IL: InterVarsity Press, 2007), 79.

11. Amit, *Book of Judges*, 164.

12. Robert B. Chisholm, *A Commentary on Judges and Ruth*, Kregel Exegetical Library (Grand Rapids: Kregel, 2013), 198.

13. Ibid.

14. Cf. Robert H. O'Connell, *The Rhetoric of the Book of Judges*, VTSup, vol. 63 (Leiden: E. J. Brill, 1996), 82.

15. Satterthwaite and McConville, *A Guide to the Historical Books*, 79–80.

theme in the fully presented narrative which follows."[16] It is simply "one voice that starts a discourse with the narratives, changing the stories and being changed itself."[17] Butler also argues that "the pattern of chap. 2 serves its own theological purpose in introducing the book and is then used selectively and creatively to introduce in various creative ways the framework of the narratives."[18]

As Butler rightly argued, 2:11–19 "serves its own theological purpose."[19] The emphasis of 2:11–19 is on Israel's consistent sin (vv. 11–13, 17, and 19). Israel continued to sin against the Lord in judgment or in mercy. This message summarizes some aspects of the central section. It also explains that the enemies that arose against Israel in the central section were all raised by the Lord because of the evil Israel committed in his eyes. However, this does not mean the message of the central section was to show Israel's sin. The central section focuses on the Lord's deliverance of Israel using the judges despite Israel's sin and despite the failure/weakness of even the judges. Whereas 2:11–19 emphasizes Israel's sin, the central section emphasizes the Lord's deliverance.

Judges 2:20–21

These verses capture Israel's and the Lord's disinterest in dispossessing the inhabitants of the land. The Lord's decision not to dispossess them was a response to Israel's unwillingness to do so. Throughout the central section both of these decisions did not change. The nations stayed as the Lord had warned. The Lord helped Israel in times of crises but never helped them drive out the nations. Both panel one and panel two of the central section began (A, B and A', B') with external forces and ended (C and C') with internal forces (Canaanites/Philistines).[20] External forces caused Israel to lose its hold of some of the places it had won in the conquest by the Joshua generation.

---

16. Barry G. Webb, *The Book of Judges*, NICOT, ed. R. K. Harrison and Robert L. Hubbard (Grand Rapids: Eerdmans, 2012), 120.
17. Gillmayr-Bucher, "Framework," 691.
18. Butler, *Judges*, 58.
19. Ibid.
20. See Chisholm's proposal for the structure of the central section as "two overlapping panels" (Chisholm, *Judges and Ruth*, 44–46). The central section can be structured in two panels as follows:

Israel also continued with its disinterest to dispossess the nations. No one was an exception here. All of Israel was in the wrong. Lack of enthusiasm for battle continued. This is particularly seen in the Samson story, which takes up a large space in the central section: Israel wanted to live under Philistine rule. God had to take the initiative to cause enmity between the two through Samson. Of course, God's actions did not seek to motivate Israel to dispossess the Philistines. The Lord had sworn not to dispossess them. God's acts represented divine judgment on Israel.

That the Lord did not change his mind is made very clear in the two instances in the central section where he speaks (6:8–10; 10:11–14). There was no warning as in 2:1–5. The judgment of 2:20–21 was final. There was simply a reminder of this judgment. This suggests that the author wants the reader to expect nothing positive when reading the central section. The reader should neither expect that Israel would change nor that Yahweh would change. The role of the judges would not change with regard to the dispossessing of the inhabitants. The judges were not raised to dispossess them but simply to save Israel from their power. Therefore, at the very beginning Israel's relationship with the Lord was "in a state of deadlock," not at the end of the period of judges as Webb argued.[21]

Judges 1:1–2:10; 2:22–3:6

These verses summarize the period of testing, a period which precedes that of the central section. They also contain flashbacks to an even earlier time, the period of the conquest under Joshua. The function of the flashbacks within the prologue is to highlight the failure of the people during the period of testing by comparing their response with the success and enthusiasm of the people under Joshua. Therefore, the flashbacks do not have a direct relation

---

Panel One:
A. The Israelites did evil . . . (3:7–11)
B. The Israelites AGAIN did evil . . . (3:12–30)
C. The Israelites AGAIN did evil . . . (4:1–5:31)
Panel Two:
A'. The Israelites did evil . . . (6:1–10:5)
B'. The Israelites AGAIN did evil (10:6–12:7)
C'. The Israelites AGAIN did evil (13:1–16:31)

21. Webb, *Judges: An Integrated Reading*, 113–114; so Gillmayr-Bucher, "Framework," 690.

with the central section. It might be possible to argue for an implied rhetorical function that these verses play in relation to the central section.

As for the material that covers the period of testing (1:1–7, 17–19; 1:21–2:5, 10–21; 3:5–6), it serves as a prelude to the central section.[22] It provides "a military and theological context" to the central section.[23] As such this material can be seen as an etiological introduction because it explains the origin of the failed condition that Israel endured throughout the central section. These verses summarize the story of the period of testing and show how the failure resulted in the status of Israel, which the central section elaborates.

Summary

The prologue, whose message is summarized in 3:5–6, functions as a prelude. It describes events which occurred during the period of testing leading up to the situation that is exposed in 3:7–16:31. This prologue introduces very tersely the cyclic nature of the central section (2:10–14a, 20–21), and briefly summarizes some aspects of the whole period in 2:14b–19. But it is not as a whole intended to be a description or a summary of the central section. It "offers a theological reflection on the cause of the events that are found in Judges, a short summary of those events, and an evaluation of the behavior of the Israelites during the period of Judges."[24]

The Prologue versus the Epilogue

Having established the relationship of the prologue with the central section, it is now time to explore how the prologue relates to the epilogue of Judges. By pointing to the similarity of Israel's inquiry of the Lord in 20:23 and 1:1–2, Webb rightly notes that such instances prompt "us to read the end of the book in the light of its beginning, bringing closure to the whole."[25] The prologue's relationship with the epilogue is best understood if explored

---

22. Webb, *Book of Judges*, 120.
23. Daniel I. Block, *Judges, Ruth*, NAC, ed. E. Ray Clendenen, vol. 6 (Nashville, TN: Broadman & Holman, 1999), 77.
24. Lee Roy Martin, *The Unheard Voice of God: A Pentecostal Hearing of the Book of Judges*, JPTSup, ed. John Christopher Thomas, Rickie Moore, and Steven J. Land, vol. 32 (Blandford Forum: Deo Publishing, 2008), 80–81.
25. Webb, *Book of Judges*, 420–421.

in the following three steps: (1) establishing the unity of the epilogue, (2) reading the epilogue in light of Joshua 22, and finally (3) exploring the epilogue's connection with the prologue.

The Epilogue as a Unit

It is often said that the epilogue is a two-part conclusion. The first part, Judges 17–18, focuses on the Danites; whereas, the second part, Judges 19–21, focuses on the Benjamites.[26] Though this is true, it can be argued that, in their present form, they should be read as a unified, single plot narrative.[27]

Amit points to the temporal and geographical setting as well as the repeated appearance of a Levite as means of integrating the two parts. With regard to temporal setting, both parts belong to the period of the third generation from Egypt, that is, the first generation after Joshua's death. The mention of Jonathan son of Gershom, son of Manasseh in 18:30 and Phinehas son of Eleazar son of Aaron in 20:27 signals the temporal setting. With regard to geographical setting, the stories in both parts focus on "the hill country of Ephraim and its environs."[28] The mention of Shiloh in both narratives at 18:31 and 21:12, 19, 21 is also another means of integration.[29]

Amit, however, concludes that what the two parts have in common is just an impression of unity by means of "sophisticated use of integral incorporation."[30] She illustrates her argument: "whereas in the story of the Danites the Levite is an inseparable part of a plot concerned with a shrine and its personnel, in that of the concubine the fact that the concubine's husband belongs to the tribe of Levi is irrelevant."[31] Despite her claim, the Levite does play an important role in the narrative. The Levite incited the whole nation into civil war.[32]

---

26. Block, *Judges, Ruth*, 473.
27. See below for the plot of this single narrative.
28. Amit, *Book of Judges*, 351–353.
29. Yairah Amit, "Hidden Polemic in the Conquest of Dan: Judges 17–18," *VT* 60, no. 1 (1990): 5, n. 2; Webb, *Book of Judges*, 421, n. 7.
30. Amit, *Book of Judges*, 315–316.
31. Ibid., 353.
32. So Block, *Judges, Ruth*, 474; Webb, *Book of Judges*, 420.

Another means of integrating the two parts is the repeated editorial refrain.[33] The refrain has two parts. It is repeated three more times, giving 17–21 a chiastic structure, as pointed out by Webb who concludes, "the two narratives linked by this structure have so much in common that the conjunction is a very natural one":[34]

> A (17:6) *In those days there was no king in Israel: everyone did what was right in their own eyes*
> > B (18:1) *In those days there was no king in Israel*
> > B' (19:1) *In those days there was no king in Israel*
>
> A' (21:25) *In those days there was no king in Israel: everyone did what was right in their own eyes*

The first half of the refrain is simply descriptive: it describes the period as one where there was no king. It indicates that all of the events in Judges 17–21 occurred at a time when there was no king. As indicated above, the temporal setting for Judges 17–21 was the first generation after Joshua's death when Israel had no leader. Though the author was aware that judgeship preceded kingship, he described the period as one when there was no king, not as one when there was no judge. His choice seems to be prompted by (1) the time of writing when Israel had a king, or (2) the literary considerations, the epilogue serving as a transition to the book of Samuel.

The need for repeating this first half of the refrain was to emphasize that this was a period when the people were responsible. Joshua had left no successor. Rather, he prepared the people to finish the conquest and be loyal to the Lord even when he would no longer be around (Josh 22:7–24:33). Rather than being pro- or anti-monarchic, the first half of the refrain simply describes the period as when there was no leader and a period when responsibility fell on the people's shoulders.

The second half of the refrain is evaluative or judgmental. The refrain is the only place where the writer explicitly makes evaluation and so it is important to understand its meaning. The only clear meaning of "everyone did what was right in their own eyes" can be obtained in reference to Deuteronomy 12:8, an evaluative statement claiming that everyone was

---

33. Butler, *Judges*, 385.
34. Webb, *Book of Judges*, 419.

engaged in cultic violation. With regard to the first appearance of the refrain, though only one family violated the cultic rule (17:1–5), the writer blames everyone (17:6). Blaming everyone does not mean that everyone was doing the same thing. Webb interprets the refrain to mean "Micah and his mother were typical."[35] How can one family's mistake be an explanation of the whole nation's mistake? The best, and probably the only, explanation is that under normal religious practice, the people would have spoken against or even brought judgment on the family. Their silence is treated as a sin. Everyone was judged, not necessarily because they also joined in cultic violations, but because they did nothing.[36]

Judges 21:25 repeats the second half of the refrain, creating an inclusio.[37] Block suggests that 21:25 evaluates 21:1–24.[38] His decision can be extended: 17:6 evaluates 17:1–5, and 21:25 evaluates 17:7–21:24. Amit argues that the refrain does not fit the narrative of 19–21. She views the refrain as pro-monarchic and thus argues that the presence of a king would not be needed in 20–21. She views the leadership in Judges 20–21 so highly that the negative comment of the refrain cannot fit it.[39] As Wong pointed out, despite Amit's high view of the leadership in Judges 20–21, everyone in the story should be viewed negatively.[40] Besides, one cannot be sure whether the refrain is pro or anti-monarchic. One can only be sure that the mention of the absence of a king indicates that the people were responsible for the judgmental statement of the second half. When there was no king, responsibility was on the people. Deuteronomy 12:8 does not presuppose kingship. A king is not necessary for the centralization of the cult.

Therefore, the second appearance of the full refrain should also be seen as an evaluation of the people with regard to cultic violation. Boda makes the

---

35. Ibid., 426.

36. See below for the connection between 17–21 with Joshua 22 and the author's implied judgment.

37. Butler, *Judges*, 471.

38. Block, *Judges, Ruth*, 581. It is also possible to see 17:7–18:31 as an illustration of why the author judged everyone at 17:6 when it was only one family who violated the cult in 17:1–5. If so, then 21:25 can be seen as evaluating 19–21.

39. Amit, *Book of Judges*, 345–51.

40. Gregory T. K. Wong, *Compositional Strategy of the Book of Judges: An Inductive, Rhetorical Study*, VTSup, vol. 111 (Leiden: Brill, 2006), 137, n. 174.

following observation to suggest how chapters 19–21 are similar to chapters 17–18 with regard to cultic violation:

> Just as chs. 17–18 exposed threats to centralized worship in Israel with the creation of a personal sanctuary by Micah that was coopted by the Danites to form a rival cult center in the far north of Israel, so also chs. 19–21 have revealed similar ambiguity over the centralized cultic location during this period, with references to Bethel, Mizpah, Shiloh, and even Gibeah as places where assemblies were held and inquiries of Yahweh were made during the war against the Benjamites.[41]

Though the refrain at 21:25 could be seen as an evaluation of the lack of centralized worship in 19–21, a better understanding can be obtained when one reads 17–21 in light of Joshua 22.

Allusion to Joshua 22

Both Judges 19–21 and 17–18 allude to Joshua 22. Judges 17–18 alludes to Joshua 22 thematically and lexically. Thematically, Judges 17–18 deal with cultic violation, whereas Joshua 22 deals with "potential cultic violation."[42] Lexically, both Judges 17–18 and Joshua 22 allude to Deuteronomy 12:8. When read in light of Joshua 22, the absence of the people's reaction against cultic violation in 17–18 is striking! A reaction in the manner of Joshua 22 is, however, present in Judges 19–21, which also alludes to Joshua 22.

Judges 19–21 alludes to Joshua 22 by means of lexical reference, common theme and similarity of plot structure. With regard to lexical referents, the mention of Shiloh and Phinehas bring Joshua 22 into the mind of the reader. As for Shiloh, Frolov notes, "in an mistakable echo of the place's last mention in Joshua (22:9) it is referred to as 'Shiloh, which is in the land of Canaan.'" As for the mention of Phinehas, Chisholm notes that it "may facilitate a literary association with" Joshua 22:10–34.[43] Unlike in Joshua 22, Chisholm notes two problems here: "in Judges 20 Phinehas plays no

---

41. Mark J. Boda, "Judges," in *Numbers to Ruth*, ed. Tremper Longman III and David E. Garland, rev. ed., Expositor's Bible Commentary, vol. 2 (Grand Rapids: Zondervan, 2012), 1287.

42. Wong, *Compositional Strategy*, 73.

43. Chisholm, *Judges and Ruth*, 503.

role; . . . the Benjaminites, unlike the Transjordanian tribes in the earlier story, elevate tribal loyalty above national unity, even when it means harboring criminals. Rather than being reconciled, the participants fight a bloody civil war."[44] Niditch sees the topic of holy war as a common theme between the two narratives.[45]

Wong sees the allusion to Joshua 22 "more on similarity of plot and attendant circumstances than on direct linguistic correspondence, even though such correspondences do exist."[46] He sees "similar sequences of events" in Joshua 22 and Judges 19–20 though "with very different outcome" in both stories.[47] Wong then proposes that the allusion to Joshua 22 draws attention to Israel's responsibility, without denying that of Benjamin, "for plunging the nation into civil war."[48] He then argues that "the allusion, once established, also serves to bring out other important contrasts."[49] In Joshua 22, in the absence of Joshua, the people gathered at Shiloh to handle "a potential cultic violation."[50] A similar gathering took place in 19–21 but not at Shiloh, rather at Mizpah (20:1). He then asks: "why was there no similar gathering to deal with the idolatry of Micah and Dan?"[51] Amit asks similar questions, though to argue how 17–18 and 19–21 are not a unity:

> If both stories took place during the third generation after the Exodus, that is, during the same period, it is difficult to understand why the united assembly that set out so virulently against the tribe of Benjamin did not help the Danites with their existential problems. It is also difficult to understand why Micah, like the Levite, did not turn in his troubles to the assembly of Israel. Moreover, it is difficult to understand how the united assembly of Israel, that sought the Lord by means

---

44. Ibid.
45. Susan Niditch, "The 'Sodomite' Theme in Judges 19–20: Family, Community, and Social Disintegration," *Catholic Biblical Quarterly* 44, no. 3 (1982): 374–375.
46. Wong, *Compositional Strategy*, 71.
47. Ibid.
48. Ibid., 73.
49. Ibid.
50. Ibid.
51. Ibid.

of inquiry and fasting, did not attempt to prevent the worship of graven and molten images.[52]

Wong answers his question with the conclusion that there is "a clear shift of priorities in the collective psyche of the new generation. Thus, if Shiloh had indeed stood for the safeguarding of cultic purity in the generation of Joshua, in Judg. 18:31, it is portrayed almost as helplessly looking on as idolatry took hold at Dan."[53] Frolov, who sees allusion to Joshua 22 by the mention of Shiloh, makes a similar conclusion: "despite its newly regained unity Israel remains worlds apart from the ideal condition that allegedly prevailed under Joshua."[54] This was an ideal they were able to live up to even without Joshua's help. Now after his death, they have abandoned the ideal.

The plot of Judges 17–21 becomes clearer when the reader realizes that the entire epilogue should be read in light of the account in Joshua 22. The single-plot narrative of 17–21 begins with an *exposition* in Judges 17:1–6. The *exposition* captures a cultic violation in a family in Ephraimite hill country (17:1–6). In light of Joshua, the reader would expect the whole nation to come against this cultic violation. However, the judgment in 17:6 clearly suggests the absence of the people's reaction to this cultic violation.

The *complication* of the narrative is found in 17:7–18:31. A Levite, who is later identified as Jonathan the grandson of Moses (18:31), enters the scene, reviving the reader's expectation, but he himself embraces the sin of Micah instead of speaking against it (17:7–13). So the author blames the priest too. Then a tribe enters the scene. The tribe, which should have objected to the cultic violation of Micah's family and the priest, also embraces the sin (18:1–31). Mention of the Danite shrine puts the blame on the whole nation. This does not necessarily suggest "the disintegration of Israel's cult during the tribal period."[55] What the stories of 17–18 suggest is that Israel was to blame because it did not put a stop to the cultic violation of Micah's family, the Levite and the tribe of Dan as it had done once. At one point in

---

52. Amit, *Book of Judges*, 352.

53. Wong, *Compositional Strategy*, 74.

54. Serge Frolov, *Judges*, FOTL, ed. Rolf P. Knierim and Marvin A. Sweeney, vol. 18 (Grand Rapids: Eerdmans, 2013), 318.

55. Gale A. Yee, "Ideological Criticism: Judges 17–21 and the Dismemebered Body," in *Judges and Method: New Approaches in Biblical Studies*, ed. Gale A. Yee (Minneapolis: Fortress, 1995), 158.

their history Israel was willing to risk civil war to put a stop to a potential cultic violation in Joshua 22.

Judges 19:1–30 captures the *change*. A Levite spoke against a violation of his pride. This same Levite did not speak against the cultic violation of Judges 17–18, though he was aware of it. Since he lived within the same time and geography of the events of Judges 17–18, he would be aware of the cultic violation. The geographical description should allow the reader to blame this Levite, too, and expect nothing much from him.

The author uses the Levite's own words to show how he wanted to be seen as a "holy" person. He refused to go to Jerusalem, saying that the city belonged to foreigners. The author had indicated in 1:21 that the Benjamites lived with the Jebusites up to the time of writing. The Levite's words suggest that this was unacceptable. He also told the old man who hosted him that he was going to "the house of the Lord" (19:18). The author referred to him as simply "the man" but only twice as the Levite (19:1; 20:4).

Not bothered by the cultic violation he witnessed in the hill country of Ephraim where he lived, the Levite was offended by the violation of his pride by the Benjamites. The narrative of Judges 19 clearly indicated that he was not concerned for his concubine: He waited four months to bring her back (v. 2); even when he was at her father's place, he enjoyed fellowship with her father rather than with her (vv. 4–8); he did not mention her in his dialogue with the old man who hosted him (vv. 18–19); he gave her up to the gang to save himself (v. 25); he was prepared to leave without her (v. 27) and when he saw her, he did not show any kind of sympathy but spoke down to her (v. 28). The author does not clearly indicate whether the Levite made sure his concubine was dead before he cut her up. Nothing he did, even cutting her up and sending her body parts to the whole nation was out of care for her. The whole nation was moved to act together, but what moved them is not clearly stated (v. 30).

The *resolution* of the narrative is reached in 20:1–48. Israel, who did not speak against the cultic violation, reacted against the violation of the Levite's pride. They were willing to seek the face of the Lord, and to risk civil war, but what got them into civil war is not clearly stated. The story's *ending* is found in 21:1–25. Here Israel as a nation violated Shiloh by violating the virgins who came to worship. Not only was Israel silent when there was cultic violation at Dan, but they evoked more violation here.

Connection with the Prologue

As was true of the relationship between the prologue and the central section, establishing the chronological relationship between the prologue and the epilogue is key for a clear understanding of their logical relationship. As argued above, the events of the epilogue all occurred in the period of the first generation after Joshua's death. This was the same period in which the events of the prologue also occurred.

More specifically, as shown above, the events of the epilogue occurred after 1:34 and before 2:11. In Judges 1:34–35 Dan is said to have been pushed out of his allotted territory by the Amorites. The epilogue (18:1–31) picks up from Judges 1:34–35 and reports Dan's newly conquered city. This suggests that the epilogue chronologically follows the time of Judges 1:34–35, which occurred after the death of Joshua. The absence of a clear reference to idolatry, that is, worship of foreign gods as stated in Judges 2:11–13, suggests that the events of the epilogue occurred before the beginning of the period of judges.

Therefore, it can be concluded that, like the prologue, the epilogue covers the period of testing. The epilogue, however, does not cover Israel's failure to dispossess the inhabitants from the land. This is because Israel has already failed to do this as can be seen in the state of Jerusalem, where the Jebusites lived (19:11–12), as well as the state of the tribe of Dan who had to search for a territory different from that which was allotted to them (18:1–31).

Judges' epilogue confirms what the prologue concluded: Israel failed to do what they were commissioned to do at the end of Joshua. The prologue blamed every single tribe for failing to dispossess the inhabitants from the Land; the epilogue blamed every single individual for choosing their own way rather than the Lord's way, for tolerating cultic violation, and for not using their unity to fight cultic violation rather than destroying their own tribe. As the prologue indicated, the Lord had given them the period of testing to see if they would walk in his ways, but the epilogue concluded that Israel failed to walk in his ways. They chose their ways, not his. They tried to worship the Lord wherever, whenever, and however they wanted.

The prologue did not inform the reader how Israel moved from failure to dispossess the inhabitants from the land (Judg 1) to worship of other gods (2:11–13). This information is given in the epilogue: Israel failed to be faithful to its cultic life. Though Joshua had prepared Israel by renewing their covenant with the Lord, and though Israel swore that it would be faithful to keep the ways of the Lord (Josh 23:1—24:28), and though Israel had been faithful up to the death of Joshua (Josh 22:7–34; 24:29–33), in the period of the epilogue Israel began to be lax in punishing individuals, families and tribes who committed cultic violation (even if it meant civil war), as Israel had once done in Joshua 22:7–34.

> Within Judges, chapters 17–21 function as a large-scale example of "delayed revelation." At the end of a book in which so many things have gone wrong for Israel, they take us back to the beginning of the judges period and show how the very first generation after Joshua went badly astray, as evidenced by the corrupt behaviour of both individual Israelites and whole tribes. In the light of these incidents it is no surprise that later generations also turned away from YHWH as they did.[56]

By providing information absent in the prologue, the epilogue serves "as a complement to the prologue even from its inception."[57] Webb rightly concludes that chapters 17–21 in their present position "form a most appropriate epilogue to Judges."[58] O'Connell rightly argues, "it is with the addition of chs. 17–21 that the overall purpose of Judges comes into focus."[59] However, my understanding of the purpose is different from his. For him the purpose is "endorsement of Israel's king as the agent of Judges' desired higher standards of cultic and social order in Israel."[60] Regarding chapters 19–21 Frolov concludes that the pericope "preemptively denigrates Saul, priming the audience for his failure as a king."[61] How can chapters 17–21 then endorse kingship when it clearly prepares the audience for the failure

---

56. Satterthwaite and McConville, *A Guide to the Historical Books*, 93.
57. Wong, *Compositional Strategy*, 31.
58. Webb, *Book of Judges*, 420–21.
59. O'Connell, *Judges*, 266.
60. Ibid.
61. Frolov, *Judges*, 323.

of the first king? I think the purpose is a defense of the Lord as Israel's king and deliverer and a critique of the people. What the people failed to do in the prologue, they were able to do in the epilogue. The epilogue informs the reader that Israel's failure in the prologue was a willing rebellion, not inability. Frolov notes: "the Israelites who were unwilling or unable (with the single exception of Judah) to dislodge the Canaanites from their allotments now nearly succeed – as a remote result of the failure – in wiping out one of their constituent populations."[62]

A reader may ask as to why the author delayed the stories of chapters 17–21 until the end even if they happened within the same time period as the prologue and even if they provide missing information from the prologue. In response two observations are in order: (1) The prologue focuses on failure to dispossess as the cause of the state in which Israel is found throughout the period of the Judges. Its purpose was to show that the central section was a consequence of the failure to dispossess the land, not idol worship or Canaanization. The epilogue itself was a result of the failure to dispossess the land. Though the epilogue restates the point of the prologue, it also has its own emphasis and so, to avoid distraction as one moves from the prologue to the central section, the epilogue was put towards the end.

(2) Judges 17–21 is also put towards the end because it serves as transitional to the period of kings/the books of Samuel: "The refrain that runs through the epilogue . . . brings down the curtain on one period and anticipates another. Kingship, like judgeship, will have its place in Israel's ongoing history and prove useful in its time. But it, too, will fail through human sinfulness."[63] The refrain, without necessarily being either pro or anti-monarchy, not only looks back (explains what came before) but also looks ahead (to the time when kings exist). In this way it parallels the epilogue of Joshua, which summarizes the conquest period of Joshua and looks to prepare for the period of testing. By evaluating the people up to the death of Joshua as doing good, the author expects the reader to read ahead and see if they did well after the death of Joshua. So the epilogue of Judges as

---

62. Ibid., 318.
63. Webb, *Book of Judges*, 35.

well, evaluates the people without the king and expects them to evaluate them in the presence of a king.

Summary

The epilogue was intended to be read as a single unit, as can be inferred from the use of the refrain in 17:6 and in 21:25. In both cases the meaning of the refrain is the same. In both it is a judgment on everyman's cultic violation. The explanation for the author's use of the refrain in 21:25 with the same sense as 17:6 can be found when one compares 17–21 with Joshua 22. The people were once willing and ready, without the help of Joshua, to punish cultic violation even at the risk of civil war. After the death of Joshua they became lax when individuals, families and tribes committed cultic violation.

In keeping with our understanding that the book of Judges is a sequel to the book of Joshua, the epilogue of Judges parallels in its function as the prologue. The prologue sets the tone for the epilogue. The epilogue, too, evaluates the generation after Joshua's death with those during his lifetime. Based on this evaluation, the generation after his death failed to live up to the standard of the generation before his death.

CHAPTER 6

Conclusion and Implication

This chapter will summarize and conclude this dissertation. It will also briefly mention one implication of this study.

In chapter 1, the scope and organization of the prologue was given. It was argued that the prologue is a single narrative that runs from 1:1 through 3:6, focusing on the Israelites as its subject. The narrative has the following plot structure: *exposition* 1:1–2, *complication* 1:3–36, *change* 2:1–10, *resolution* 2:11–3:4, and *ending* 3:5–6.

In chapter 2, a detailed analysis of the prologue following the above plot structure was presented. In the *exposition*, the Israelites asked the Lord who would lead the battle against the imminent enemy they were facing as a nation. This was an inauguration of the period of testing. Just as in the book of Joshua, where both the southern and northern campaigns started with a battle against a coalition – enemies of all Israel – and then were followed by battles to dispossess the inhabitants of the different cities, so here the Israelites were found in the same situation. But the *exposition* leaves the reader wondering: would the Israelites fight the imminent enemy and then follow that battle with battles of individual tribes to dispossess their inheritances?

In 1:3–36 the reader encounters the *complication* of the narrative. Indeed Judah, who was assigned to lead the battle against the common enemy, succeeded in defeating the enemy with the help of Simeon. The success, however, was followed by a failure when they let the leader of the coalition live. Instead, they mutilated this king and let him live in Jerusalem with Judah in order to put fear in the Jebusites. Having once led a coalition against Israel, the Jebusites see the power of God remains with his people when they see another coalition "picking up scraps" under Judah's table.

After this initial success, only Judah and the house of Joseph followed this success with a battle to dispossess their inheritance. Each of these proved to be only partially successful. Not a single one of the other tribes dispossessed its inheritance. The reason for this failure was not inability but willful disobedience. Israel was militarily strong enough to force the inhabitants of some of the land to do forced labor for them. The climax of the tribes' failure was reached in the report of Dan's loss of their inheritance to the Amorites.

In the *change* the Lord confronted Israel by reminding them of his earlier warning that he would not *help them* drive out the nations if they themselves remained unwilling to do so. The Israelites felt sorry but no longer showed enthusiasm to dispossess the nations.

The *resolution* built on the theme of lacking true repentance by reporting their disobedience in doing what was evil the eyes of the Lord. The Lord's warning came true as he announced that he would no longer dispossess the nations from their inheritance. Instead these nations and others from outside Canaan would be used to punish Israel. When, under enemy power, Israel cried to the Lord to be saved, the Lord answered by raising up judges whose main role was to deliver the people from the enemy. The story's *ending* in 3:5–6 showed a different Israel from the Israel portrayed in the *exposition*. They were reacting to an imminent enemy threat in the *exposition*, but even that reaction is gone when the nations from within and without come to fight them. Rather, the Israelites made covenants of marriage with the inhabitants, worshipped their gods, and became like the Canaanites.

In chapter 3, it was argued that the author of the prologue used four flashbacks at four different stages in the narrative. These flashbacks were introduced with temporally overlaid *wayyiqtol* clauses. It was argued that the *wayyiqtol* clause was used to make these flashbacks, which are normally background information, part of the foreground narrative. The first flashback was in 1:8–16. This flashback captured the success of the sons of Judah in the southern campaign during Joshua's time. By showing how enthusiastic their ancestors were, the author blames Judah for letting Adoni-bezek live and for not destroying the Jebusites who were still living in Jerusalem. In the second flashback, 1:20, the author again blames Judah for the partial dispossession of their inheritance, unlike their ancestor who completely dispossessed the territory that was allotted to him. The third flashback, 2:6–10, blames all

Israel for being lax to enter and dispossess their allotted land. The Israelites in the time of Joshua were determined to finish the conquest, but after his death became willfully disobedient. The fourth and final flashback, 2:23–3:4, explains why the Lord decided to no longer dispossess the nations. The nations were left, the author says, in order to give the Israelites after Joshua's death the same practice in holy war as an expression of obedience to the Lord. However, as can be seen in the prologue, the Israelites failed to obey the Lord by dispossessing the nations. Instead they lived with them. The author then tells the reader that the period of testing is officially closed by the Lord's announcement of judgment for Israel's failure.

In chapter 4, the first part of the function of the prologue was discussed. This first function was in relation to the book of Joshua. It was argued that the book of Joshua ended as a prequel to the book of Judges, that is, it covered the period until the death of Joshua and his contemporaries. The book of Judges then picked up where the book of Joshua ended, that is, after the death of Joshua and the elders. The end of Joshua summarized how Joshua prepared the people for life in Canaan in his absence. This life included the dispossessing of the allotted land and covenant loyalty to the Lord. The people renewed their covenant with the Lord vowing to be loyal to him. In Joshua 22:7–34, Joshua then gave the people a chance to prove themselves. When the people found out that there was a potential cultic violation in Israel, in the absence of Joshua and the elders, they took the initiative, chose representatives and handled the potential problem. They were willing to risk civil war to keep Israel clean from cultic violation. The book ended in 24:29–33 by evaluating how the people did up until the death of Joshua and the elders who outlived him. The prologue of Judges picked up this story and evaluated how they did after the death of Joshua and the elders. The evaluation stated that the people failed to do what they were able to do before the death of Joshua. After his death, they lost the same enthusiasm to obey the Lord and dispossess the nations.

In chapter 5, the function of the prologue within the book of Judges was discussed. It was argued that the prologue is an etiological introduction that explains how Israel came to be in the cyclical problem described in the central section. It was the result of the failure of the Israelites to fully dispossess the inhabitants. The prologue informs the reader not to expect any change in the central section by showing how, at the beginning of the period of Judges, Israel's relationship with the Lord was in the state of deadlock. The role of the judges was to give temporary relief from the oppression of the nations within and without, not to dispossess them. The Israelites themselves, even the judges, did not change: they never showed enthusiasm to dispossess the nations but simply to defend themselves.

The second part of chapter 5 was a discussion of the function of the prologue in relation to the epilogue. The prologue set the tone for the epilogue. The epilogue too, whose events occurred within the same period as the prologue, evaluated how the people did in the absence of any leader. Though they were able to handle any problem even at the risk of civil war, the people were willfully disobedient to cleanse Israel from cultic violation as they once did in Joshua 22. The epilogue restates the evaluation of the prologue. The prologue blamed all Israel by narrating the failure of each tribe, and the epilogue blamed all Israel by narrating the failure of individuals.

An implication of this guilt of all Israel is that Israel's main problem was not leadership. It is often said that the book of Judges deals with the problem of leadership crisis.[1] Indeed, the central section describes the failures of the judges. However, the prologue's and even the epilogue's problems were not a result of the absence of a leader. Nor did the central section blame the leaders or suggest that the problems seen in the book were the result of lacking a leader. Rather, it blames every Israelite. When read in light of the end of Joshua, particularly Joshua 22:7–34, the prologue and the epilogue show that the people were able but unwilling to dispossess the inhabitants, cleanse Israel from cultic violation, and prove their loyalty to the Lord. Their willful disobedience led Israel to the cyclical problem found in the central section. The weakness of the judges as described in the central section serves a purpose which emphasized that the Lord's willingness to save Israel from enemy oppression was not because of the goodness of the judges. Neither the people nor the judges gave the Lord reason to deliver Israel. It was all his mercy.

The epilogue does blame the priesthood (Jonathan, Phinehas, and the Levite of Judg 19). The priesthood did not speak against cultic violation;

---

1. Cf. Trent C. Butler, *Judges*, WBC, ed. Bruce M. Metzger et al., vol. 8 (Nashville, TN: Thomas Nelson, 2009), lxxvii.

rather, the priesthood embraced it. Though they had the power to mobilize all Israel to put an end to cultic violation, they did not. They, however, did mobilize all Israel to enter into civil war to protect the honor of one of the Levites. That seems to be the only reasonable motivation able to cause Israel to enter into civil war.

The book does defend the leadership of the Lord. Indeed, "the presupposition of Judges is that YHWH is Israel's true ruler."[2] Joshua was aware that when he died, there would not be a leader to replace him. Nevertheless he did not assign any leader. It seems that both Joshua and the Lord deliberately avoided selecting a leader to replace Joshua. It seems that the Lord wanted to be recognized as the one who fights for them as Joshua told the people just before he died (Josh 23:10). Joshua did not make a mistake when he did not assign a successor. He commissioned all the people to be his successors. The Lord, as their leader, was willing to dispossess the inhabitants if the people stayed faithful to the covenant with him. The Lord was faithful. He did dispossess the inhabitants when Israel sought to do so. And in the central section, he was faithful in delivering the people by raising judges.

The book is neither pro-Judah nor anti-Benjamin. It is anti-Israelites. All of the tribes failed to keep their loyalty to the Lord. Judah might be seen as doing better than other tribes but Judah too, failed. The standard was set high by the generation of Joshua and his contemporaries, for example, Caleb. Judah failed to live up to the standard set by their ancestors, especially Caleb. All Israel failed to live up to their ancestors' standard.

---

2. Philip E. Satterthwaite and Gordon J. McConville, *A Guide to the Historical Books*, Exploring the Old Testament, vol. 2 (Downers Grove, IL: InterVarsity Press, 2007), 94.

APPENDIX 1

A Translation and a Syntactical Analysis of Judges 1:1–3:6

Appendix 1 gives the present author's translation of Judges 1:1–3:6 based on *BHS*. The translation is organized here according to this author's analysis of the plot-structure of the text of Judges 1:1–3:6 given in chapters 2 and 3 of this dissertation. The author's translation will follow the Hebrew Text. Translation of each clause is followed by a syntactical category, which is given in brackets. Unless indicated otherwise, each syntactical category describes a clause in relation to the clause that immediately precedes or follows it. When a parenthetical statement is present, the category is used in relation to the clause before the parenthetical statement. The syntactical analysis identifies three main elements of BH narrative: (1) *wayyiqtol* clauses, (2) non-*wayyiqtol* clauses, and (3) quotations. Bold font types mark non-*wayyiqtol* clauses as well as *foreground wayyiqtol* clauses, whereas quotations are marked by indentation.

Wayyiqtol Clauses

Wayyiqtol clauses could have one of the following three types of temporal and logical relationships with the clause preceding or following them: (1) successive,[1] (2) overlap,[2] and (3) overlay.[3] The following categories fall in one of these three relationships.

---

1. Logical or chronological progression, e.g. sequential, consequential.
2. Resumptive, reiterative, epexegetical, focusing/specifying.
3. Flashback/foreground *wayyiqtol*.

(1) *Introductory* refers to the *wayyiqtol* clause that offers background information (such as temporal setting) at the beginning of an episode or a scene.[4]

(2) *Initiatory/Narratival* refers to the clause that actually sets the story in motion as opposed to the *introductory clause* which simply gives background information.[5] Sometimes an *introductory clause* can be dependent on an *initiatory clause*. In such cases the *introductory clause* will be referred to here as *protasis*, whereas the *initiatory clause* will be referred to as *apodosis*.[6] When the *initiatory clause* is a sub-event within an episode or an event, it is called *transitional*.

(3) *Consequential* refers to the clause that is logically sequential to the preceding clause.[7]

(4) *Sequential* is used when the event being described is chronologically sequential to the preceding clause.[8]

(5) *Epexegetical* "clarifies, expands, or paraphrases the clause that precedes it."[9]

(6) *Specifying* gives specific examples of the event described in the preceding clause.[10]

(7) *Complementary* complements the preceding clause to give a more full picture.[11]

(8) *Resumptive* resumes a previously told event using a similar root and verb form.[12]

(9) *Reiterative* restates the event of the preceding clause.[13]

(10) *Iterative* captures an event that took place repeatedly.

---

4. *Gesenius' Hebrew Grammar*, ed. E. Kautzsch, trans. A. E. Cowley, 2nd ed. (Oxford: Oxford University, 1910), 111f.

5. Robert B. Chisholm, *A Commentary on Judges and Ruth*, Kregel Exegetical Library (Grand Rapids: Kregel, 2013), 81.

6. Alviero Niccacci, "Basic Facts and Theory of the Biblical Hebrew Verb System in Prose," in *Narrative Syntax and the Hebrew Bible: Papers of the Tilburg Conference 1996*, BIS, ed. Ellen Van Wolde, vol. 29 (Leiden: Brill, 1997), 191.

7. Bill T. Arnold and John H. Choi, *A Guide to Biblical Hebrew Syntax* (Cambridge: Cambridge University Press, 2003), 85.

8. Ibid., 84.

9. Ibid., 86.

10. Ibid., 87.

11. Chisholm, *Judges and Ruth*, 83.

12. Ibid., 82.

13. Ibid., 83.

(11) *Summarizing* summarizes the event described in the clauses that either precede or follow it. *Introductory summary* summarizes what follows it; whereas *concluding summary* summarizes what precedes it.[14]

(12) *Coincidental* refers to the *wayyiqtol* clause whose event occurred chronologically at the same time as the preceding clause.[15]

(13) *Foregrounding*: A *wayyiqtol* clause may capture an event that took place chronologically prior to the event described in the preceding clause. It can initiate a new scene or could simply be parenthetical. Some kind of anaphoric reference within the clause or the logic of the clause signals that the event being described took place prior to the event of the preceding clause. Cook coined the phrase "foreground *wayyiqtol.*"[16]

(14) *Concluding*: A *wayyiqtol* clause may signal the end of an episode or a scene.[17]

(15) *Embedded paragraph:* A *wayyiqtol* clause may be embedded when "the subject is lexically or grammatically identical (person, number, gender) to an actor (object or complement) in the clause(s) of the preceding paragraph"[18]

Non-*Wayyiqtol* Clauses

Two types of non-*wayyiqtol* clauses can be identified: (1) Verbal clauses are governed by *qatal, yiqtol,* or *weqatal,* and (2) non-verbal clauses are those governed by *participle*s or could be *verbless,* or *incomplete.*[19] These non-*wayyiqtol* clauses could "provide either non-sequential, 'background' information or mark episode boundaries . . . the type of information expressed

---

14. Paul Joüon and T. Muraoka, *A Grammar of Biblical Hebrew,* 2nd ed., SubBi, vol. 27 (Rome: Editrice Pontificio Instituto Biblico, 2006), 364.

15. John A. Cook, "The Hebrew Verb: A Grammaticalization Approach," *ZAH* 14, no. 2 (2001): 259.

16. John A. Cook, *Time and the Biblical Hebrew Verb: the Expression of Tense, Aspect, and Modality in Biblical Hebrew,* Linguistic Studies in Ancient West Semitic, vol. 7 (Winona Lake, IN: Eisenbrauns, 2012), 296.

17. Joüon and Muraoka, *Grammar of Biblical Hebrew,* 363.

18. Eep Talstra, "A Hierarchy of Clauses in Biblical Hebrew Narrative," in *Narrative Syntax and the Hebrew Bible: Papers of the Tilburg Conference 1996,* ed. Ellen Van Wolde, BIS, vol. 29 (Leiden: Brill, 1997), 103.

19. Roy L. Heller, *Narrative Structure and Discourse Constellations: An Analysis of Clause Function in Biblical Hebrew Prose,* Harvard Semitic Studies, ed. Jo Ann Hackett and John Huehnergard, vol. 55 (Winona Lake, IN: Eisenbrauns, 2004), 26.

in nonsequential, background comments is not of a single sort but can be differentiated between information closely related to the story line and information more remotely related to the story line."[20]

This is particularly true in Judges 1:3–36 whose genre (i.e. list of conquest account) allows the use of offline clauses at the beginning of the account of some tribes (e.g. Judg 1:30, 31, 33). Quotations are not analyzed except when they have performative function. In such cases such categories as *request* and *announcement* are used depending on the kind of function the direct speech has. Sometimes, a clause will further be described by a category that captures the speech function of direct speeches and/or the literary functions of the clause. These two are separated from the syntactical category by a colon. Also, when it is necessary to describe the syntactical function of a clause, this secondary function is separated from the primary function by means of *en dash* (–).

Most of the categories used above for *wayyiqtol* clauses are also used to describe non-*wayyiqtol* clauses.[21] Non-*wayyiqtol* clauses could be *contrastive* and could *highlight* an event. They may pause the narrative to give a vivid picture of a scene.[22] "*Momentous negation*" is a negated clause that "furthers the narrative along in the same way that a *wayyiqtol* verbal form would."[23]

Exposition (1:1–2)

1a וַיְהִי אַחֲרֵי מוֹת יְהוֹשֻׁעַ
1b וַיִּשְׁאֲלוּ בְּנֵי יִשְׂרָאֵל בַּיהוָה לֵאמֹר
מִי יַעֲלֶה־לָּנוּ אֶל־הַכְּנַעֲנִי בַּתְּחִלָּה לְהִלָּחֶם בּוֹ:
2 וַיֹּאמֶר יְהוָה
יְהוּדָה יַעֲלֶה הִנֵּה נָתַתִּי אֶת־הָאָרֶץ בְּיָדוֹ:

---

20. Ibid.; So John A. Cook, "The Semantics of Verbal Pragmatics: Clarifying the Roles of Wayyiqtol and Weqatal in Biblical Hebrew Prose," *JSS* 49, no. 2 (2004): 263; Serge Frolov, *Judges*, FOTL, ed. Rolf P. Knierim and Marvin A. Sweeney, vol. 18 (Grand Rapids: Eerdmans, 2013), 6.

21. So Arnold and Choi, *A Guide to Biblical Hebrew Syntax*, 87; Joüon and Muraoka, *Grammar of Biblical Hebrew*, 119a.

22. Chisholm, *Judges and Ruth*, 86.

23. Heller, *Narrative Structure and Discourse Constellations*, 24. So Robert E. Longacre, *Joseph – A Story of Divine Providence: A Text Theoretical and Textlinguistic Analysis of Genesis 37 and 39–48*, 2nd ed. (Winona Lake, IN: Eisenbrauns, 2003), 79.

1:1a After the death of Joshua, (*introductory/protasis:* temporal setting of 1b)

1b the Israelites inquired of the Lord, (*initiatory/apodosis: request*)

"Who should go up ahead of us to the Canaanites to fight against them?"

2a The Lord replied, (*consequential: response*[24])

"Judah will go up. Behold, I have given the land in his hand."

Complication 1:3–36

The Tribe of Simeon (v. 3)

3a וַיֹּאמֶר יְהוּדָה לְשִׁמְעוֹן אָחִיו
עֲלֵה אִתִּי בְגוֹרָלִי וְנִלָּחֲמָה בַּכְּנַעֲנִי וְהָלַכְתִּי גַם־אֲנִי אִתְּךָ בְּגוֹרָלֶךָ

3b וַיֵּלֶךְ אִתּוֹ שִׁמְעוֹן׃

3a Judah said to Simeon his brother, (*sequential/transitional:*[25] *request*)

"Go with me in my lot[26] so that we may fight the Canaanites and I will go, even I, with you in your lot."[27]

3b Simeon went[28] with him. (*consequential–summary*[29])

---

24. The response has performative function. The Lord replied to Israel in words. These words then set Judah apart for the task.

25. Verse 3 begins the list of each tribe's participation in the war against the inhabitants of the land which vv. 1–2 hinted at.

26. גורל "lot" is not used here in the sense of inheritance but simply military allotment that would determine who would lead the battle. The only other time it is used in Judges is in 20:9 where the whole of Israel was going to fight Gibeah. They plotted the battle with a lot. The lot decided who would lead the fight. So here in 1:3 Judah asked Simeon to join him in his lot to be the first to fight and promised that when the lot would fall on Simeon to be first, he would join him. Both Joshua and Judges distinguish נחלה and גורל. The latter is never used for the inheritance itself but to the notion that the inheritance was allocated by lot. Whether already conquered or simply allotted נחלה is used both in Judges and in Joshua to refer to the inheritance.

27. Or "when the lot falls on you."

28. This verb, unless accompanied by other verbs, does not in itself indicate attack or dispossessing. In all its uses in the prologue, it is never used in the sense of attacking. Therefore, any tribe who is said to have "gone" (הלך) can not be seen as "going up" (עלה) unless some other word/phrase indicates the "going up."

29. 3b and 4a are similar statements. One of them would be unnecessary if the narrator's interest were not to list each tribe's participation in the battle against the Canaanites. Simeon's response is not a speech. This suggests that the narrator's interest in 3a was to give background

Judah (with Simeon) (vv. 4–7)

4a וַיַּעַל יְהוּדָה
4b וַיִּתֵּן יְהוָה אֶת־הַכְּנַעֲנִי וְהַפְּרִזִּי בְּיָדָם
4c וַיַּכּוּם בְּבֶזֶק עֲשֶׂרֶת אֲלָפִים אִישׁ׃
5a וַיִּמְצְאוּ אֶת־אֲדֹנִי בֶזֶק בְּבֶזֶק
5b וַיִּלָּחֲמוּ בּוֹ
5c וַיַּכּוּ אֶת־הַכְּנַעֲנִי וְאֶת־הַפְּרִזִּי׃
6a וַיָּנָס אֲדֹנִי בֶזֶק
6b וַיִּרְדְּפוּ אַחֲרָיו
6c וַיֹּאחֲזוּ אֹתוֹ
6d וַיְקַצְּצוּ אֶת־בְּהֹנוֹת יָדָיו וְרַגְלָיו׃
7a וַיֹּאמֶר אֲדֹנִי־בֶזֶק
שִׁבְעִים מְלָכִים בְּהֹנוֹת יְדֵיהֶם וְרַגְלֵיהֶם מְקֻצָּצִים הָיוּ מְלַקְּטִים תַּחַת שֻׁלְחָנִי כַּאֲשֶׁר עָשִׂיתִי כֵּן שִׁלַּם־לִי אֱלֹהִים
7b וַיְבִיאֻהוּ יְרוּשָׁלָ͏ִם
7c וַיָּמָת שָׁם׃

    4a Then Judah went up (*introductory summary*)
    4b and the Lord handed the Canaanites and Perizzites into their hands. (*consequential*)
    4c and they struck them at Bezek – ten thousand men. (*complementary*)
    5a They met Adoni-bezek at Bezek. (*focusing*)
    5b and fought against him (*sequential*)
    5c and struck the Canaanites and Perizzites. (*sequential*)
    6a Adoni-bezek fled (*sequential–embedded paragraph*[30])
    6b but they pursued after him (*sequential*)
    6c and seized him (*sequential*)
    6d and cut off thumbs of his hands and the big toes. (*sequential*)
    7a Adoni-bezek said, (*sequential: request*[31])

---

information regarding Simeon's participation (i.e. to tell the reader that Simeon went into the battle because Judah asked him).

30. The embedded paragraph ends at v. 7 with וימת שם. The paragraph begins and ends with Adoni-bezek.

31. In light of the fact that Judah brought Adoni-bezek to Jerusalem, it is best to see the words of Adoni-bezek as request (having performative function).

"Seventy were the kings whose thumbs of their hands and big toes were cut. They were gathering food under my table. Just as I had done thus God has repaid me."

7b They brought him to Jerusalem (*consequential: response*)
7c and he died there. (*concluding*[32])

Flashback (vv. 8–16)

8a וַיִּלָּחֲמוּ בְנֵי־יְהוּדָה בִּירוּשָׁלַםִ
8b וַיִּלְכְּדוּ אוֹתָהּ
8c וַיַּכּוּהָ לְפִי־חָרֶב
8d וְאֶת־הָעִיר שִׁלְּחוּ בָאֵשׁ:
9 וְאַחַר יָרְדוּ בְּנֵי יְהוּדָה לְהִלָּחֵם בַּכְּנַעֲנִי יוֹשֵׁב הָהָר וְהַנֶּגֶב וְהַשְּׁפֵלָה:
10a וַיֵּלֶךְ יְהוּדָה אֶל־הַכְּנַעֲנִי הַיּוֹשֵׁב בְּחֶבְרוֹן
10b וְשֵׁם־חֶבְרוֹן לְפָנִים קִרְיַת אַרְבַּע
10c וַיַּכּוּ אֶת־שֵׁשַׁי וְאֶת־אֲחִימַן וְאֶת־תַּלְמָי:
11a וַיֵּלֶךְ מִשָּׁם אֶל־יוֹשְׁבֵי דְּבִיר
11b וְשֵׁם־דְּבִיר לְפָנִים קִרְיַת־סֵפֶר:
12a וַיֹּאמֶר כָּלֵב
אֲשֶׁר־יַכֶּה אֶת־קִרְיַת־סֵפֶר וּלְכָדָהּ וְנָתַתִּי לוֹ אֶת־עַכְסָה בִתִּי לְאִשָּׁה:
13a וַיִּלְכְּדָהּ עָתְנִיאֵל בֶּן־קְנַז אֲחִי כָלֵב הַקָּטֹן מִמֶּנּוּ
13b וַיִּתֶּן־לוֹ אֶת־עַכְסָה בִּתּוֹ לְאִשָּׁה:
14a וַיְהִי בְּבוֹאָהּ
14b וַתְּסִיתֵהוּ לִשְׁאוֹל מֵאֵת־אָבִיהָ הַשָּׂדֶה
14c וַתִּצְנַח מֵעַל הַחֲמוֹר
14d וַיֹּאמֶר־לָהּ כָּלֵב
מַה־לָּךְ:
15a וַתֹּאמֶר לוֹ
הָבָה־לִּי בְרָכָה כִּי אֶרֶץ הַנֶּגֶב נְתַתָּנִי וְנָתַתָּה לִי גֻּלֹּת מָיִם
15b וַיִּתֶּן־לָהּ כָּלֵב אֵת גֻּלֹּת עִלִּית וְאֵת גֻּלֹּת תַּחְתִּית:
16a וּבְנֵי קֵינִי חֹתֵן מֹשֶׁה עָלוּ מֵעִיר הַתְּמָרִים אֶת־בְּנֵי יְהוּדָה מִדְבַּר יְהוּדָה אֲשֶׁר בְּנֶגֶב עֲרָד
16b וַיֵּלֶךְ
16c וַיֵּשֶׁב אֶת־הָעָם:

---

32. This concludes the embedded story on Adoni-bezek.

8a Now the sons of Judah[33] [had][34] fought Jerusalem, (*foreground*)
8b captured it, (*sequential*)
8c struck it by the sword (*sequential*)
8d **and the city – they set on fire.** (*concluding*[35])
9 **After that the sons of Judah went down to fight the Canaanites who were living in the hill country, the Negev and the Shephelah.** (*introductory summary*)
10a Judah[36] went to the Canaanites who were living in Hebron. (*focusing*)
10b **Now the name of Hebron before was Kiriath Arba.** (*parenthetical*)
10c They struck[37] Sheshai and Ahiman and Talmai. (*sequential*)
11a He went[38] from there to those who live in Debir. (*sequential*)
11b **Now the name of Debir before was Kiriath Sefer.** (*parenthetical*)
12 Caleb said, (*sequential*)
"*whoever smites Kiryat sefer and captures it, I will give to him Acsah my daughter as wife.*"
13a Othniel, son of Kenaz, Caleb's younger brother, captured it (*sequential*)

---

33. See pp. 92–95, for a discussion of how this title signals a flashback to the ancestors of Judah who lived during the life time of Joshua.

34. The use of the English pluperfect is simply to help the modern reader not miss that this clause is chronologically prior to the preceding clauses.

35. The syntactic change to *waw-X-qatal* structure is motivated by the author's interest on the city. He inserted v. 8 to explain why Judah was able to bring Adoni-bezek to Jerusalem. According to v. 8, it is because Judah had already defeated Jerusalem and started to live in it. According to Josh 15:63 Judah's success in dispossessing the Jebusites was partial.

36. According to Josh 15:13–14, Caleb is the one responsible for attacking Hebron. However, here the narrator's interest is to evaluate the present generation of the tribe of Judah in light of the preceding generation. Therefore, the author considers the action of one man as the action of the tribe. There is no need to emend the text to "Caleb" as suggested by BHS editor. The change from the plural that is used in vv. 8–16 to a singular is because it is referring to one Judahite.

37. The plural refers to the tribe of Judah with the leadership of Caleb. Again, even if Josh 15:14 ascribes the dispossessing to Caleb, here it is attributed to the whole tribe in accordance with the author's rhetoric.

38. The third masculine singular verb refers to Caleb. The fact that Caleb enters the scene at v. 12 without being properly introduced is another evidence that he was the leader in the battles and the subject of the verbs in vv. 10–11.

13b and he gave him Acsah his daughter as wife. (*consequential*)
14a Now when she was about to go[39] (*introductory–embedded paragraph*[40])
14b she persuaded[41] him to ask the field[42] from her father (*initiatory*)
14c Then she got down from the donkey (*sequential*)
14d then Caleb said to her (*consequential*)
"*what to you?*"[43]
15a She said to him, (*sequential: request*)
"*give me blessing. Since you have given me the land of the Negev, give me springs of water.*"
15b Caleb gave her the upper spring and the lower spring. (*consequential: response*)
16a **Now the sons of Kenite the father-in-law of Moses had gone up with the sons of Judah from the city of Date Palm tree into the wilderness of Judah which is in the Negev of Arad.** (*pluperfect–supplemental to 16b–c*)

---

39. Heb: *in her going/coming*. It is very likely that here the scene is Acsah's departure with Othniel. Stone translates it: "When Acsah married Othniel, she urged him to ask her father for a field" (Lawson G. Stone, "*Book of Judges*," in *Dictionary of the Old Testament: Historical Books*, ed. Bill T. Arnold and H. G. M. Williamson [Downers Grove, IL: InterVarsity Press, 2005], 211).

40. The embedded paragraph (a new scene) begins at 14a. The subject of v. 14a (Acsah) was the object of the verb in 13b. The embedded paragraph runs from 14a–15b.

41. This verb should not be understood as what she tried to do and failed, but what she tried and succeeded to do. She persuaded Othniel and he did ask for the field. Acsah's statement "since you have given me the land of the Negev" in v. 15 clearly indicates that Caleb had already given the land to the couple. Since this giving is not mentioned anywhere else, it is best to see it in the statement "she persuaded him to ask the field from her father." Block suggests translating "she induced him [her father] by asking" and cites 2 Sam 24:1 as a similar example (Daniel I. Block, *Judges, Ruth*, NAC, ed. E. Ray Clendenen, vol. 6 [Nashville, TN: Broadman & Holman, 1999], 95–96). However, there are two requests in this anecdote. Whereas Othniel asks for *the field* (v. 13), i.e. "the land of the Negev" (v. 15), Acsah asks for *springs of water*. She persuaded her husband to ask for the land that he conquered. His victory did not necessarily mean he owned the land.

42. Refers to land or "territory of a tribe or of people" (HALOT 3:1308. E.g. Land of Moab in Ruth 1:2, 6, 22). Here it probably refers to Debir.

43. Or *what happened to you?* This question suggests that Caleb has seen something strange. The strangeness could be that instead of leaving, she got down from the donkey. It is very unlikely that Caleb asked this question when his daughter came to visit him. It makes more sense to see his question as a reaction to his daughter's mounting down from her donkey, though she was about to leave with Othniel.

16b He[44] went (*sequential to 11a*)
16c and lived with the people.[45] (*concluding*)

Judah *with Simeon* (vv. 17–19)

17a וַיֵּלֶךְ יְהוּדָה אֶת־שִׁמְעוֹן אָחִיו
17b וַיַּכּוּ אֶת־הַכְּנַעֲנִי יוֹשֵׁב צְפַת
17c וַיַּחֲרִימוּ אוֹתָהּ
17d וַיִּקְרָא אֶת־שֵׁם־הָעִיר חָרְמָה׃
18 וַיִּלְכֹּד יְהוּדָה אֶת־עַזָּה וְאֶת־גְּבוּלָהּ וְאֶת־אַשְׁקְלוֹן וְאֶת־גְּבוּלָהּ וְאֶת־עֶקְרוֹן וְאֶת־גְּבוּלָהּ׃
19a וַיְהִי יְהוָה אֶת־יְהוּדָה
19b וַיֹּרֶשׁ אֶת־הָהָר כִּי לֹא לְהוֹרִישׁ אֶת־יֹשְׁבֵי הָעֵמֶק כִּי־רֶכֶב בַּרְזֶל לָהֶם׃

17a Judah went with Simeon his brother (*resumptive–sequential*[46])
17b and they struck the Canaanites who lived in Zephath (*sequential*)
17c and they destroyed it (*sequential*)
17d and he[47] called the name of the city Hormah. (*sequential*)
18 Judah captured Gaza and its territory, and Ashkelon and its territory, and Ekron and its territory. (*sequential*)
19a Yahweh was with Judah (*summary*)
19b and dispossessed the hill country (*consequential*)[48]

---

44. Based on the LXX, the editor of *BHS* suggests the plural reading. However, the singular does make sense in the context and so there is no need to emend the text. The singular still refers to Caleb. Caleb was the last person mentioned before the parenthetical note "Now the sons of Kenite the father-in-law of Moses had gone up with the sons of Judah from the city of Date Palm tree into the wilderness of Judah which is in the Negeb of Arad." He does not seem to have settled in any of the places from which he dispossessed the inhabitants. It seems that he joined the people (i.e. sons of Kenite) by going to the Negev of Arad.

45. "The people" refers to the sons of Kenite. Hebron became a levitical city of refuge (Josh 20:7; 21:11, 13) and Debir was given to Othniel/Acsah. It is possible that Caleb left for the Negev of Arad after Hebron became a levitical city though he was able to stay.

46. It resumes the campaign of Judah with Simeon in vv. 4–7 that was interrupted by the flashback in vv. 8–16. It is also sequential to that campaign.

47. The singular refers to Judah. If it was referring to Simeon, he would have been clearly indicated as the subject as the author has done so far whenever he introduces a new subject. The chiastic structure of the *wayyiqtols* of this verse shows that 'he' refers to Judah:
A Judah went . . . B they struck . . . B' they destroyed . . . A' he called . . .

48. For the list of cities of the hill country assigned for Judah see Josh 15:48–60. This suggests that, though not reported, Judah did subsequent battles to take possession of all of the hill country that was assigned to him.

19c but did not dispossess those living in the valley because they had chariots of iron. (*contrastive*)⁴⁹

Flashback (v. 20)

20a וַיִּתְּנוּ לְכָלֵב אֶת־חֶבְרוֹן כַּאֲשֶׁר דִּבֶּר מֹשֶׁה
20b וַיּוֹרֶשׁ מִשָּׁם אֶת־שְׁלֹשָׁה בְּנֵי הָעֲנָק:

20a They [had] given Hebron to Caleb just as Moses had spoken (*foreground*)
20b and he dispossessed from there the three sons of Anak. (*sequential*)

The Tribe of Benjamin (v. 21)

21a וְאֶת־הַיְבוּסִי יֹשֵׁב יְרוּשָׁלַם לֹא הוֹרִישׁוּ בְּנֵי בִנְיָמִן
21b וַיֵּשֶׁב הַיְבוּסִי אֶת־בְּנֵי בִנְיָמִן בִּירוּשָׁלַם עַד הַיּוֹם הַזֶּה:

21a **The Jebusites who were living in Jerusalem – the sons of Benjamin did not dispossess.** (*summarizing*)
21b The Jebusites live with the sons of Benjamin in Jerusalem to this day. (*consequential*)

The Tribes of Joseph (vv. 22–29)

22a וַיַּעֲלוּ בֵית־יוֹסֵף גַּם־הֵם בֵּית־אֵל
22b וַיהוָה עִמָּם:
23a וַיָּתִירוּ בֵית־יוֹסֵף בְּבֵית־אֵל
23b וְשֵׁם־הָעִיר לְפָנִים לוּז:
24a וַיִּרְאוּ הַשֹּׁמְרִים אִישׁ יוֹצֵא מִן־הָעִיר
24b וַיֹּאמְרוּ לוֹ
הַרְאֵנוּ נָא אֶת־מְבוֹא הָעִיר וְעָשִׂינוּ עִמְּךָ חָסֶד:
25a וַיַּרְאֵם אֶת־מְבוֹא הָעִיר
25b וַיַּכּוּ אֶת־הָעִיר לְפִי־חָרֶב
25c וְאֶת־הָאִישׁ וְאֶת־כָּל־מִשְׁפַּחְתּוֹ שִׁלֵּחוּ:
26a וַיֵּלֶךְ הָאִישׁ אֶרֶץ הַחִתִּים
26b וַיִּבֶן עִיר
26c וַיִּקְרָא שְׁמָהּ לוּז

---

49. This clause could be understood as elliptical. Arnold and Choi note that ellipsis frequently occurs with negatives, as is the case in this verse (Bill T. Arnold and John H. Choi, *A Guide to Biblical Hebrew Syntax* [Cambridge: Cambridge University Press, 2003], 192).

26d הוּא שְׁמָהּ עַד הַיּוֹם הַזֶּה:
27a וְלֹא־הוֹרִישׁ מְנַשֶּׁה אֶת־בֵּית־שְׁאָן וְאֶת־בְּנוֹתֶיהָ וְאֶת־תַּעְנַךְ וְאֶת־בְּנֹתֶיהָ וְאֶת־יֹשֵׁב [יֹשְׁבֵי] דוֹר וְאֶת־בְּנוֹתֶיהָ וְאֶת־יוֹשְׁבֵי יִבְלְעָם וְאֶת־בְּנֹתֶיהָ וְאֶת־יוֹשְׁבֵי מְגִדּוֹ וְאֶת־בְּנוֹתֶיהָ
27b וַיּוֹאֶל הַכְּנַעֲנִי לָשֶׁבֶת בָּאָרֶץ הַזֹּאת:
28a וַיְהִי כִּי־חָזַק יִשְׂרָאֵל
28b וַיָּשֶׂם אֶת־הַכְּנַעֲנִי לָמַס
28c וְהוֹרֵישׁ לֹא הוֹרִישׁוֹ:
29a וְאֶפְרַיִם לֹא הוֹרִישׁ אֶת־הַכְּנַעֲנִי הַיּוֹשֵׁב בְּגָזֶר
29b וַיֵּשֶׁב הַכְּנַעֲנִי בְּקִרְבּוֹ בְּגָזֶר:

22a The house of Joseph,[50] too, went up against Bethel (*summarizing*)

22b *and Yahweh was with them.* (*circumstantial*)[51]

23a The house of Joseph spied Bethel. (*focusing*)

23b **Now the name of the city previously was Luz.** (*parenthetical*)

24a The spies saw a man going out from the city (*sequential*)

24b and they said to him, (*sequential: request*)

"*Show us an entrance to the city and we will do with you faithfully.*"

25a He showed them an entrance to the city (*consequential: response*)

25b and they struck the city with the sword (*sequential*)

25c but the man and his family – they sent away. (*contrastive*)[52]

26a The man went to the land of the Hittite (*consequential–embedded paragraph*)

26b and built a city. (*consequential*)

26c He called its name Luz. (*concluding*)

26d **That is its name up to this day.** (*supplemental*)

27a **Manasseh did not take possession of Beth Shan, and its surroundings, Taanach and its surroundings. Nor did they dispossess those living in Dor and its surroundings, nor**

---

50. Refers to the tribe of Ephraim and Manasseh together as in Josh 17:17.
51. The disjunctive clause highlights the Lord's presence with the house of Joseph.
52. The disjunctive could be to highlight the contrast.

those who live in Ibleam and its surroundings, nor those
living in Megiddo and its surroundings. (*summarizing*)

27b The Canaanites managed to remain in this land. (*consequential*)

28a Whenever Israel was strong, (*protasis: circumstantial*)[53]

28b They put the Canaanites to forced
labor. (*apodosis–consequential*)

28c **but certainly did not dispossess them.** (*contrastive*)

29a **Neither did Ephraim dispossess the Canaanites who were
living in Gezer.** (*summarizing*)[54]

29b The Canaanites lived in their midst in Gezer. (*consequential*)

The Tribe of Zebulun (v. 30)

30a זְבוּלֻן לֹא הוֹרִישׁ אֶת־יוֹשְׁבֵי קִטְרוֹן וְאֶת־יוֹשְׁבֵי נַהֲלֹל

30b וַיֵּשֶׁב הַכְּנַעֲנִי בְּקִרְבּוֹ

30c וַיִּהְיוּ לָמַס: ס

30a **Zebulun did not dispossess those who were living in Kitron
and those who were living in Nahalol.** (*summarizing*)

30b The Canaanites lived in their midst (*consequential*)

30c and they became forced labor. (*sequential*)

The Tribe of Asher (vv. 31–32)

31a אָשֵׁר לֹא הוֹרִישׁ אֶת־יֹשְׁבֵי עַכּוֹ וְאֶת־יוֹשְׁבֵי צִידוֹן וְאֶת־אַחְלָב וְאֶת־אַכְזִיב
וְאֶת־חֶלְבָּה וְאֶת־אֲפִיק וְאֶת־רְחֹב:

32 וַיֵּשֶׁב הָאָשֵׁרִי בְּקֶרֶב הַכְּנַעֲנִי יֹשְׁבֵי הָאָרֶץ כִּי לֹא הוֹרִישׁוֹ:

31 **Asher did not dispossess those who were living in Acco
nor those who were living in Sidon. Nor did they take
possession of**[55] **Ahlab, Achzib, Helbah, Aphek, or
Rehob.** (*summarizing*)

---

53. Verse 28 is an embedded – introduced with a ויהי clause – parenthetical statement, which informs the reader that not just Manasseh, but all of Israel failed to dispossess the Canaanites in these regions even when Israel gained military strength.

54. Verse 29 is parallel to v. 27. Both of them are contrasting statements. Despite their success at Bethel (vv. 22–26), they both failed to dispossess their respective allotted land.

55. The sign of accusative that is attached to all of the cities in the remaining half of the verse indicate that the missing phrase is לֹא הוֹרִישׁ, not אֶת־יֹשְׁבֵי.

32 Asher lived in the midst of the Canaanites who were living in the land because he did not dispossess them. (*consequential*)

The Tribe of Naphtali (v. 33)

33a נַפְתָּלִי לֹא־הוֹרִישׁ אֶת־יֹשְׁבֵי בֵית־שֶׁמֶשׁ וְאֶת־יֹשְׁבֵי בֵית־עֲנָת
33b וַיֵּשֶׁב בְּקֶרֶב הַכְּנַעֲנִי יֹשְׁבֵי הָאָרֶץ וְיֹשְׁבֵי בֵית־שֶׁמֶשׁ וּבֵית עֲנָת
33c הָיוּ לָהֶם לָמַס׃

33a **Naphtali did not dispossess the inhabitants of Beth Shemesh nor the inhabitants of Beth Anath** (*summarizing*)
33b and they lived among the Canaanites who were living in the land (*consequential*)
33c Now the inhabitants of Beth-shemesh and Beth-anath were forced labor for them. (*disjunctive-supplemental*)

The Tribe of Dan (vv. 34–36)

34 וַיִּלְחֲצוּ הָאֱמֹרִי אֶת־בְּנֵי־דָן הָהָרָה כִּי־לֹא נְתָנוֹ לָרֶדֶת לָעֵמֶק׃
35a וַיּוֹאֶל הָאֱמֹרִי לָשֶׁבֶת בְּהַר־חֶרֶס בְּאַיָּלוֹן וּבְשַׁעַלְבִים
35b וַתִּכְבַּד יַד בֵּית־יוֹסֵף
35c וַיִּהְיוּ לָמַס׃
36 וּגְבוּל הָאֱמֹרִי מִמַּעֲלֵה עַקְרַבִּים מֵהַסֶּלַע וָמָעְלָה׃ פ

34 The Amorites forced the sons of Dan to go to the hill country, for they had not allowed them to go to the plain. (*summarizing*)
35a The Amorites managed to remain in Har Heres, Aijalon, and Shaalbim (*consequential*)
35b Then the hand of the sons of Joseph became strong (*sequential*)
35c and the Amorites became forced labor. (*consequential*)
36 **The border of the Amorites was from the ascent of Akrabbim, from Sela and on up.** (*supplemental*)

Change (2:1–5)

2:1 וַיַּעַל מַלְאַךְ־יְהוָה מִן־הַגִּלְגָּל אֶל־הַבֹּכִים
1b וַיֹּאמֶר
אַעֲלֶה אֶתְכֶם מִמִּצְרַיִם וָאָבִיא אֶתְכֶם אֶל־הָאָרֶץ אֲשֶׁר נִשְׁבַּעְתִּי לַאֲבֹתֵיכֶם
וָאֹמַר לֹא־אָפֵר בְּרִיתִי אִתְּכֶם לְעוֹלָם׃ 2 וְאַתֶּם לֹא־תִכְרְתוּ בְרִית לְיוֹשְׁבֵי

A Translation and a Syntactical Analysis of Judges 1:1–3:6

הָאָרֶץ הַזֹּאת מִזְבְּחוֹתֵיהֶם תִּתֹּצוּן וְלֹא־שְׁמַעְתֶּם בְּקֹלִי מַה־זֹּאת עֲשִׂיתֶם:
3 וְגַם אָמַרְתִּי לֹא־אֲגָרֵשׁ אוֹתָם מִפְּנֵיכֶם וְהָיוּ לָכֶם לְצִדִּים וֵאלֹהֵיהֶם יִהְיוּ לָכֶם לְמוֹקֵשׁ:

4a וַיְהִי כְּדַבֵּר מַלְאַךְ יְהוָה אֶת־הַדְּבָרִים הָאֵלֶּה אֶל־כָּל־בְּנֵי יִשְׂרָאֵל
4b וַיִּשְׂאוּ הָעָם אֶת־קוֹלָם
4c וַיִּבְכּוּ:
5a וַיִּקְרְאוּ שֵׁם־הַמָּקוֹם הַהוּא בֹּכִים
5b וַיִּזְבְּחוּ־שָׁם לַיהוָה:

2:1a The messenger of the Lord went up from Gilgal to Bochim (*initiatory*)
1b and said, (*sequential*)
"I brought you up from Egypt and then brought you into the land which I had sworn to your fathers and then said,[56] 'I will not break my covenant with you forever. ²But you must not make a covenant with the inhabitants of this land. You must break their altars.' But you did not listen to my voice. What is this you have done? ³I also had said, 'I will not dispossess them from before you. Instead they will be with you at your sides[57] and their gods will be snare to you.'"
4a And as the messenger of the Lord spoke these words to all of the Israelites, (*protasis: circumstantial*)
4b the people raised up their voice (*apodosis*)
4c and wept. (*complementary*)
5a They called the name of that place Bochim (*sequential*)
5b and they sacrificed there to the Yahweh. (*concluding*)

Flashback (2:6–10)

6a וַיְשַׁלַּח יְהוֹשֻׁעַ אֶת־הָעָם
6a וַיֵּלְכוּ בְנֵי־יִשְׂרָאֵל אִישׁ לְנַחֲלָתוֹ לָרֶשֶׁת אֶת־הָאָרֶץ:
7a וַיַּעַבְדוּ הָעָם אֶת־יְהוָה כֹּל יְמֵי יְהוֹשֻׁעַ וְכֹל יְמֵי הַזְּקֵנִים אֲשֶׁר הֶאֱרִיכוּ יָמִים אַחֲרֵי יְהוֹשֻׁעַ אֲשֶׁר רָאוּ אֵת כָּל־מַעֲשֵׂה יְהוָה הַגָּדוֹל אֲשֶׁר עָשָׂה לְיִשְׂרָאֵל:

---

56. The *wayyiqtol* suggests that the speech was given after they entered the land.
57. So Trent C. Butler, *Judges*, WBC, ed. Bruce M. Metzger et al., vol. 8 (Nashville, TN: Thomas Nelson, 2009), 5.

8 וַיָּמָת יְהוֹשֻׁעַ בִּן־נוּן עֶבֶד יְהוָה בֶּן־מֵאָה וָעֶשֶׂר שָׁנִים׃
9 וַיִּקְבְּרוּ אוֹתוֹ בִּגְבוּל נַחֲלָתוֹ בְּתִמְנַת־חֶרֶס בְּהַר אֶפְרָיִם מִצְּפוֹן לְהַר־גָּעַשׁ׃
10a וְגַם כָּל־הַדּוֹר הַהוּא נֶאֶסְפוּ אֶל־אֲבוֹתָיו
10b וַיָּקָם דּוֹר אַחֵר אַחֲרֵיהֶם אֲשֶׁר לֹא־יָדְעוּ אֶת־יְהוָה וְגַם אֶת־הַמַּעֲשֶׂה אֲשֶׁר עָשָׂה לְיִשְׂרָאֵל׃

6a When Joshua [had] dismissed the people, (*foreground*)

6b the Israelites went each one to his inheritance to take possession of the land. (*sequential*)

7 The people served the Lord all the days of Joshua, and all the days of the elders who outlived Joshua, who had seen of all the great work of the Lord that he had done for Israel. (*consequential*[58])

8 Joshua, son of Nun, servant of Yahweh, died at the age of 110. (*supplemental*[59])

9 They buried him in the boundary of his inheritance, in Timnath-heres in Mount Ephraim, to the north of Mount Gaash. (*complementary*)

10a **All of that generation too were gathered to their fathers.** (*supplemental*)[60]

10b A different generation grew up[61] after them that did not know the Lord nor the work that he had done for Israel. (*concluding*)

Unraveling (2:11–21)

11a וַיַּעֲשׂוּ בְנֵי־יִשְׂרָאֵל אֶת־הָרַע בְּעֵינֵי יְהוָה
11b וַיַּעַבְדוּ אֶת־הַבְּעָלִים׃
12a וַיַּעַזְבוּ אֶת־יְהוָה אֱלֹהֵי אֲבוֹתָם הַמּוֹצִיא אוֹתָם מֵאֶרֶץ מִצְרַיִם
12b וַיֵּלְכוּ אַחֲרֵי אֱלֹהִים אֲחֵרִים מֵאֱלֹהֵי הָעַמִּים אֲשֶׁר סְבִיבוֹתֵיהֶם
12c וַיִּשְׁתַּחֲווּ לָהֶם

---

58. It is consequential, not sequential, because the author connects serving Yahweh with the people's intention to take possession of the land when they went to their inheritance. The rhetorical message is that dispossessing the inhabitants would lead to worshiping Yahweh, whereas failure to dispossess them would lead to worshipping other gods.

59. The death of Joshua (and even of those who outlived him) is implied in v. 7. Verses 8–10a give supplemental information about Joshua and those who outlived him.

60. The change from *wayyiqtol* to *qatal* in this verse is due to the presence of גַּם. גַּם highlights that the older generation has disappeared from the scene.

61. Cf. NET, NRSV, NIV.

A Translation and a Syntactical Analysis of Judges 1:1–3:6   169

12d וַיַּכְעִסוּ אֶת־יְהוָה:
13a וַיַּעַזְבוּ אֶת־יְהוָה
13b וַיַּעַבְדוּ לַבַּעַל וְלָעַשְׁתָּרוֹת:
14a וַיִּחַר־אַף יְהוָה בְּיִשְׂרָאֵל
14b וַיִּתְּנֵם בְּיַד־שֹׁסִים
14c וַיָּשֹׁסּוּ אוֹתָם
14d וַיִּמְכְּרֵם בְּיַד אוֹיְבֵיהֶם מִסָּבִיב
14e וְלֹא־יָכְלוּ עוֹד לַעֲמֹד לִפְנֵי אוֹיְבֵיהֶם:
15a בְּכֹל אֲשֶׁר יָצְאוּ יַד־יְהוָה הָיְתָה־בָּם לְרָעָה כַּאֲשֶׁר דִּבֶּר יְהוָה וְכַאֲשֶׁר נִשְׁבַּע יְהוָה לָהֶם
15b וַיֵּצֶר לָהֶם מְאֹד:
16a וַיָּקֶם יְהוָה שֹׁפְטִים
16b וַיּוֹשִׁיעוּם מִיַּד שֹׁסֵיהֶם:
17a וְגַם אֶל־שֹׁפְטֵיהֶם לֹא שָׁמֵעוּ
17b כִּי זָנוּ אַחֲרֵי אֱלֹהִים אֲחֵרִים
17c וַיִּשְׁתַּחֲווּ לָהֶם
17d סָרוּ מַהֵר מִן־הַדֶּרֶךְ אֲשֶׁר הָלְכוּ אֲבוֹתָם לִשְׁמֹעַ מִצְוֹת־יְהוָה
17e לֹא־עָשׂוּ כֵן:
18a וְכִי־הֵקִים יְהוָה לָהֶם שֹׁפְטִים
18b וְהָיָה יְהוָה עִם־הַשֹּׁפֵט
18c וְהוֹשִׁיעָם מִיַּד אֹיְבֵיהֶם כֹּל יְמֵי הַשּׁוֹפֵט כִּי־יִנָּחֵם יְהוָה מִנַּאֲקָתָם מִפְּנֵי לֹחֲצֵיהֶם וְדֹחֲקֵיהֶם:
19a וְהָיָה בְּמוֹת הַשּׁוֹפֵט
19b יָשֻׁבוּ
19c וְהִשְׁחִיתוּ מֵאֲבוֹתָם לָלֶכֶת אַחֲרֵי אֱלֹהִים אֲחֵרִים לְעָבְדָם וּלְהִשְׁתַּחֲוֹת לָהֶם
19d לֹא הִפִּילוּ מִמַּעַלְלֵיהֶם וּמִדַּרְכָּם הַקָּשָׁה:
20a וַיִּחַר־אַף יְהוָה בְּיִשְׂרָאֵל
20b וַיֹּאמֶר
יַעַן אֲשֶׁר עָבְרוּ הַגּוֹי הַזֶּה אֶת־בְּרִיתִי אֲשֶׁר צִוִּיתִי אֶת־אֲבוֹתָם וְלֹא שָׁמְעוּ לְקוֹלִי: 21 גַּם־אֲנִי לֹא אוֹסִיף לְהוֹרִישׁ אִישׁ מִפְּנֵיהֶם מִן־הַגּוֹיִם אֲשֶׁר־עָזַב יְהוֹשֻׁעַ וַיָּמֹת:

    11a The Israelites did what was evil in the eyes of the
        Lord (*initiatory*)

11b and served the Baals.⁶² (*epexegetical*)
12a They abandoned the Lord, the God of their fathers, who brought them from the land of Egypt (*complementary*)
12b and went after other gods from among the gods of the people who surrounded them (*complementary*)
12c and bowed down to them (*reiterative*)
12d and made the Lord angry. (*consequential*)
13a They abandoned the Lord (*resumptive of 12a*)
13b and served Baal and the Ashtaroths. (*complementary*)
14a And so the Lord's anger burned against Israel. (*consequential*)
14b He would give them into the hands of plunderers (*consequential–iterative*)
14c and they would plunder them. (*consequential–iterative*)
14d He would sell them into the hand of their enemies all around (*reiterative–iterative*)
14e **and they would not again be able to stand before their enemies.** (*consequential–iterative*)
15a Every time that they went out to fight,⁶³ the hand of the Lord would be against them for evil just as the Lord had spoken and just as the Lord had sworn to them. (*complementary–iterative*)
15b and it would distress them greatly. (*consequential–iterative*)
16a The Lord would then raise judges (*consequential–iterative*)
16b and they would deliver them from their plunderers (*consequential–iterative*)
17a **But even to the judges – they would not listen.**⁶⁴ (*contrasting–iterative*)
17b **Instead, they would become a harlot after other gods** (*complementary–iterative*)
17c and they would bow down to them. (*reiterative–iterative*)

---

62. The messenger of the Lord had warned the Israelites in 2:3 that the gods of the Canaanites would be a snare to them. That warning is fulfilled here.

63. Heb. "in all that they went out." The phrase clearly refers to the going out for war to fight back the enemy of v. 14e.

64. The disjunctive is due to the presence of גַּם and is used to highlight their disobedience.

17d **They would quickly turn aside from the ways[65] which their fathers had walked on by obeying the commandments of the Lord.** (*Epexegetical–iterative*)

17e **They would not do so.** (*reiterative-iterative*)

18a **Whenever the Lord would raise up judges for them, the Lord would be with each judge** (*transitional–iterative*)

18b **and would deliver them from the hand of their enemies all the days of each judge because the Lord was compassionate on account of their groaning before those who were oppressing and harassing them.** (*complementary–iterative*)

19a **After the death of each judge, they would turn back** (*Transitional–iterative*)

19b **and would act more corruptly than their predecessors by walking after other gods, by serving them and by bowing down to them.** (*complementary–iterative*)

19b **They would not drop any of their deeds or their stubborn ways.** (*reiterative–iterative*)

20a **The anger of the Lord burned against Israel** (*resumptive–reiterative[66] of v. 14a*)

20b **and he announced,** (*consequential*)

> "Because this nation has broken my covenant, which I had commanded their fathers, and did not listen to my voice. [21] I also will not continue to dispossess a single person before them from among the nations which Joshua had left unconquered and died."

---

65. In agreement with "commandments" in 3:4.

66. The anger of the Lord here is the same as that mentioned in v. 14a. Therefore, the words that the Lord speaks here in v. 20 describe God's decision that brought about the events narrated in vv. 14b–19. It also concludes the story of the events of the prologue. What would follow is a flashback (vv. 21b–3:4) and a conclusion (3:5–6).

Comment on the Period of Testing (2:22–3:4)

Author's Intrusion (2:22)

22 לְמַעַן נַסּוֹת בָּם אֶת־יִשְׂרָאֵל הֲשֹׁמְרִים הֵם אֶת־דֶּרֶךְ יְהוָה לָלֶכֶת בָּם כַּאֲשֶׁר — —
שָׁמְרוּ אֲבוֹתָם אִם־לֹא: — —

> 22 – *They were*[67] for testing[68] Israel by the nations[69] to see if they are going to keep the ways[70] of the Lord by walking in them just as their fathers kept? – (*intrusion*)

Flashback (2:23–3:4)

23a וַיַּנַּח יְהוָה אֶת־הַגּוֹיִם הָאֵלֶּה לְבִלְתִּי הוֹרִישָׁם מַהֵר
23b וְלֹא נְתָנָם בְּיַד־יְהוֹשֻׁעַ:
3:1a וְאֵלֶּה הַגּוֹיִם אֲשֶׁר הִנִּיחַ יְהוָה — — לְנַסּוֹת בָּם אֶת־יִשְׂרָאֵל אֵת כָּל־אֲשֶׁר
לֹא־יָדְעוּ אֵת כָּל־מִלְחֲמוֹת כְּנָעַן: 2 רַק לְמַעַן דַּעַת דֹּרוֹת בְּנֵי־יִשְׂרָאֵל לְלַמְּדָם
מִלְחָמָה רַק אֲשֶׁר־לְפָנִים לֹא יְדָעוּם: — — 3 חֲמֵשֶׁת סַרְנֵי פְלִשְׁתִּים וְכָל־הַכְּנַעֲנִי
וְהַצִּידֹנִי וְהַחִוִּי יֹשֵׁב הַר הַלְּבָנוֹן מֵהַר בַּעַל חֶרְמוֹן עַד לְבוֹא חֲמָת:
4 וַיִּהְיוּ לְנַסּוֹת בָּם אֶת־יִשְׂרָאֵל לָדַעַת הֲיִשְׁמְעוּ אֶת־מִצְוֺת יְהוָה אֲשֶׁר־צִוָּה אֶת־אֲבוֹ
תָם בְּיַד־מֹשֶׁה:

> 23a The Lord gave these nations rest not wanting to dispossess them quickly (*foreground*)
>
> **23b and so he did not give them into the hand of Joshua.** (*reiterative*)
>
> **3:1 These are the nations which the Lord had given rest – in order to test, by them, Israel, that is, all who did not know all the wars of Canaan, ²only that the generations of the Israelites may know by teaching them warfare, only those**

---

67. For an argument that there could be a backwards ellipsis of וַיְהִי here, see pp. 52–53.

68. Heb. ". . . in order to test Israel by them." The infinitive clause (i.e. v. 22 as a whole) is a break-frame intrusion that the author inserted here and it could be seen as dependent on the verb וַיָּמָת. The author inserted it to explain why Joshua left the nations unconquered. The purpose is in the mind of the test giver (i.e. the Lord), not Joshua. Joshua died so that the Lord may be able to test Israel in the absence of their military leader.

69. Heb. by them.

70. The noun דרך is probably plural and the י of the plural דרכי might have been accidentally dropped because of the following י on יהוה. The plural is preferable because it agrees in number with מצות found in 3:4 which has a similar construction.

who did not know the wars of Canaan[71] – ³the five lords of the Philistines, and all the Canaanites, the Sidonians and the Hivites living in Mount Lebanon, from Mount Baal Hermon to Lebo-Hamath. (*supplemental*)

4 They stayed in order to test Israel by them to know if they would listen to the commandments of Yahweh which he had commanded their fathers in the hand of Moses. (*reiterates 2:22*)

Ending (3:5–6)

5 וּבְנֵי יִשְׂרָאֵל יָשְׁבוּ בְּקֶרֶב הַכְּנַעֲנִי הַחִתִּי וְהָאֱמֹרִי וְהַפְּרִזִּי וְהַחִוִּי וְהַיְבוּסִי׃
6a וַיִּקְחוּ אֶת־בְּנוֹתֵיהֶם לָהֶם לְנָשִׁים
6b וְאֶת־בְּנוֹתֵיהֶם נָתְנוּ לִבְנֵיהֶם
6c וַיַּעַבְדוּ אֶת־אֱלֹהֵיהֶם׃

5 The Israelites lived in the midst of the Canaanites, Hittites, Amorites, Perizzites, Hivites and Jebusites.[72] (*summarizing*)
6a They took their daughters for themselves as wives (*sequential*)
6b and their own daughters they gave for their sons (*complementary*)
6c and they served their gods. (*consequential*)

---

71. The normal continuation of the clause is "These are the nations which the Lord had given rest" (v. 3). What comes in between these two statements is the author's break-frame obtrusion.

72. The disjunctive signals that the topic shifts from the nations/the test to the Israelites.

APPENDIX 2
Examples of Temporally Overlaid *wayyiqtol* Clauses

This section gives some more examples of *wayyiqtol* clauses that are temporally overlaid. Here too, the examples come from different genres within narrative prose.

Genesis 12:1

27a וְאֵלֶּה תּוֹלְדֹת תֶּרַח (title)
27b תֶּרַח הוֹלִיד אֶת־אַבְרָם אֶת־נָחוֹר וְאֶת־הָרָן (introductory)
27c וְהָרָן הוֹלִיד אֶת־לוֹט: (supplemental 1)
28 וַיָּמָת הָרָן עַל־פְּנֵי תֶּרַח אָבִיו בְּאֶרֶץ מוֹלַדְתּוֹ בְּאוּר כַּשְׂדִּים: (sequential)
29a וַיִּקַּח אַבְרָם וְנָחוֹר לָהֶם נָשִׁים (supplemental 2)
29b שֵׁם אֵשֶׁת־אַבְרָם שָׂרָי (supplemental 2:1a)
29c וְשֵׁם אֵשֶׁת־נָחוֹר מִלְכָּה בַּת־הָרָן אֲבִי־מִלְכָּה וַאֲבִי יִסְכָּה: (supplemental 2:2)
30a וַתְּהִי שָׂרַי עֲקָרָה (supplemental 2:1b)
30b אֵין לָהּ וָלָד: (reiterative)
31a וַיִּקַּח תֶּרַח אֶת־אַבְרָם בְּנוֹ וְאֶת־לוֹט בֶּן־הָרָן בֶּן־בְּנוֹ וְאֵת שָׂרַי כַּלָּתוֹ אֵשֶׁת אַבְרָם בְּנוֹ (initiatory)
31b וַיֵּצְאוּ אִתָּם מֵאוּר כַּשְׂדִּים לָלֶכֶת אַרְצָה כְּנַעַן (sequential)
31c וַיָּבֹאוּ עַד־חָרָן (sequential)
31d וַיֵּשְׁבוּ שָׁם: (sequential–durative)
32a וַיִּהְיוּ יְמֵי־תֶרַח חָמֵשׁ שָׁנִים וּמָאתַיִם שָׁנָה (supplemental)
32b וַיָּמָת תֶּרַח בְּחָרָן: (sequential)

12:1 וַיֹּאמֶר יְהוָה אֶל־אַבְרָם (foreground)
לֶךְ־לְךָ מֵאַרְצְךָ וּמִמּוֹלַדְתְּךָ וּמִבֵּית אָבִיךָ אֶל־הָאָרֶץ אֲשֶׁר אַרְאֶךָּ: 2 וְאֶעֶשְׂךָ לְגוֹי גָּדוֹל וַאֲבָרֶכְךָ וַאֲגַדְּלָה שְׁמֶךָ וֶהְיֵה בְּרָכָה: 3 וַאֲבָרֲכָה מְבָרְכֶיךָ וּמְקַלֶּלְךָ אָאֹר וְנִבְרְכוּ בְךָ כֹּל מִשְׁפְּחֹת הָאֲדָמָה:
4a וַיֵּלֶךְ אַבְרָם כַּאֲשֶׁר דִּבֶּר אֵלָיו יְהוָה (sequential summary)
4b וַיֵּלֶךְ אִתּוֹ לוֹט (expexegetical)
4c וְאַבְרָם בֶּן־חָמֵשׁ שָׁנִים וְשִׁבְעִים שָׁנָה בְּצֵאתוֹ מֵחָרָן: (supplemental)
5a וַיִּקַּח אַבְרָם אֶת־שָׂרַי אִשְׁתּוֹ וְאֶת־לוֹט בֶּן־אָחִיו וְאֶת־כָּל־רְכוּשָׁם אֲשֶׁר רָכָשׁוּ וְאֶת־הַנֶּפֶשׁ אֲשֶׁר־עָשׂוּ בְחָרָן (resumptive reiterative)
5b וַיֵּצְאוּ לָלֶכֶת אַרְצָה כְּנַעַן (sequential)
5c וַיָּבֹאוּ אַרְצָה כְּנָעַן: (sequential)
6a וַיַּעֲבֹר אַבְרָם בָּאָרֶץ עַד מְקוֹם שְׁכֶם עַד אֵלוֹן מוֹרֶה (sequential)
6b וְהַכְּנַעֲנִי אָז בָּאָרֶץ: (supplemental)
7a וַיֵּרָא יְהוָה אֶל־אַבְרָם (sequential)
7b וַיֹּאמֶר (coincidental)
לְזַרְעֲךָ אֶתֵּן אֶת־הָאָרֶץ הַזֹּאת
7c וַיִּבֶן שָׁם מִזְבֵּחַ לַיהוָה הַנִּרְאֶה אֵלָיו: (consequential)
8a וַיַּעְתֵּק מִשָּׁם הָהָרָה מִקֶּדֶם לְבֵית־אֵל (sequential)
8b וַיֵּט אָהֳלֹה בֵּית־אֵל מִיָּם וְהָעַי מִקֶּדֶם (sequential)
8c וַיִּבֶן־שָׁם מִזְבֵּחַ לַיהוָה (sequential)
8d וַיִּקְרָא בְּשֵׁם יְהוָה: (coincidental)
9 וַיִּסַּע אַבְרָם הָלוֹךְ וְנָסוֹעַ הַנֶּגְבָּה: (concluding)

The narrative section is 11:27–12:9, however, the author seems to tell it as a doublet (11:27–12:4; 12:5–9). The mainline story in both of these subsections starts the same way: וַיָּבֹאוּ . . . וַיֵּצְאוּ . . . וַיִּקַּח. In the first subsection (11:27–12:4), 11:27a–30b serve as background information for the mainline narrative that begins in 11:31a. The mainline narrative then continues through 12:4b until it is interrupted in 12:4c with the nominal clause that describes the age of Abram when he left Haran.

In 12:4a Abram left Haran according to the command of the Lord which is given in 12:1. Chronologically speaking, it may seem as though the Lord spoke to Abram in 12:1 after the death of his father (11:32). However, 12:4c clearly informs the reader that Abram left Haran at the age of seventy-five, about sixty years before his father died. His father was seventy when he had Abram, his first born, and when we add Abram's age at the time of departure to Haran, we get 145 for the age of his father. Therefore, the text in its present form clearly indicates that the Lord spoke to Abram and Abram left before his father's death. This signals that the *wayyiqtol* clause in 12:1 is temporally overlaid.

Sailhamer takes the speech event even further back into the past arguing that the reference to מֵאַרְצְךָ could only be Ur, "When the command is given to Abraham to leave the place of his birth (12:1; NIV, 'your country'), only Ur of the Chaldeans would be understood, despite the fact that the narrative of ch. 12 makes no mention of 'Ur.'"[1] Sailhamer points to Genesis 15:7, Nehemiah 9:7 and Acts 7:2–3 as external proofs that the call took place in Ur. Internally, the statement in 11:31 לָלֶכֶת אַרְצָה כְּנַעַן indicates that Terah and the family had Canaan in mind when they left Ur. It is possible that they left Ur as an obedience to God's call to Abram.

Joshua 4:12[2]

10a וְהַכֹּהֲנִים נֹשְׂאֵי הָאָרוֹן עֹמְדִים בְּתוֹךְ הַיַּרְדֵּן עַד תֹּם כָּל־הַדָּבָר אֲשֶׁר־צִוָּה יְהוָה אֶת־יְהוֹשֻׁעַ לְדַבֵּר אֶל־הָעָם כְּכֹל אֲשֶׁר־צִוָּה מֹשֶׁה אֶת־יְהוֹשֻׁעַ (introductory)

10b וַיְמַהֲרוּ הָעָם (initiatory)

10c וַיַּעֲבֹרוּ: (coincidental)

11a וַיְהִי כַּאֲשֶׁר־תַּם כָּל־הָעָם לַעֲבוֹר (protasis)

11b וַיַּעֲבֹר אֲרוֹן־יְהוָה וְהַכֹּהֲנִים לִפְנֵי הָעָם: (apodosis-sequential)

12 וַיַּעַבְרוּ בְּנֵי־רְאוּבֵן וּבְנֵי־גָד וַחֲצִי שֵׁבֶט הַמְנַשֶּׁה חֲמֻשִׁים לִפְנֵי בְּנֵי יִשְׂרָאֵל כַּאֲשֶׁר דִּבֶּר אֲלֵיהֶם מֹשֶׁה: (foreground)

13 כְּאַרְבָּעִים אֶלֶף חֲלוּצֵי הַצָּבָא עָבְרוּ לִפְנֵי יְהוָה לַמִּלְחָמָה אֶל עַרְבוֹת יְרִיחוֹ: (concluding)

Joshua 4:10a–13 captures the crossing of the Jordan. The narrative differentiates the crossing of the people (v. 10b) from the crossing of the ark/the priests (v. 11b) and the two and half tribes (v. 12). The crossing of the two and half tribes did not occur after the end of v. 11b, i.e., before the crossing

---

1. John H. Sailhamer, Walter C. Kaiser, and Richard S. Hess, *Genesis–Leviticus*, ed. Tremper Longman III and David E. Garland, Expositor's Bible Commentary (Grand Rapids: Zondervan, 2008), 148.

2. Noticed in K. Lawson Younger, "Joshua," in *Eerdmans Commentary on the Bible*, ed. James D. G. Dunn and John W. Rogerson (Grand Rapids: Eerdmans, 2003), 177.

of the ark and the priest. It could be seen as simultaneous crossing with the people/the Israelites in 11a or after they crossed. Therefore, the *wayyiqtol* clause in verse 12 is temporally overlaid meeting the second criterion, the logic of the clause.

A similar example is found in Joshua 8:11 which uses the *waw-x-qatal* to describe a parallel event that happened with the previous *wayyiqtol*.

10a וַיַּשְׁכֵּם יְהוֹשֻׁעַ בַּבֹּקֶר (sequential)³
10b וַיִּפְקֹד אֶת־הָעָם (sequential)
10c וַיַּעַל הוּא וְזִקְנֵי יִשְׂרָאֵל לִפְנֵי הָעָם הָעָי: (sequential)
11 וְכָל־הָעָם הַמִּלְחָמָה אֲשֶׁר אִתּוֹ עָלוּ (pluperfect)

Verse 11, "Now all the fighting people who were with him had gone up" refers to an action that probably refers to 10b. The text states that people of war had gone up before Joshua and the elders went up in 10c. The *wayyiqtol* of 4:12 functions in a similar way but as part of the foregrounded narrative.

1 Samuel 17:13⁴

4a וַיֵּצֵא אִישׁ־הַבֵּנַיִם מִמַּחֲנוֹת פְּלִשְׁתִּים (initiatory)
4b–7 (parenthetical)
8a וַיַּעֲמֹד (sequential)
8b וַיִּקְרָא אֶל־מַעַרְכֹת יִשְׂרָאֵל (sequential)
8c וַיֹּאמֶר לָהֶם (sequential)
8d–9 quotation
10 וַיֹּאמֶר הַפְּלִשְׁתִּי (sequential)
אֲנִי חֵרַפְתִּי אֶת־מַעַרְכוֹת יִשְׂרָאֵל הַיּוֹם הַזֶּה תְּנוּ־לִי אִישׁ וְנִלָּחֲמָה יָחַד:
11a וַיִּשְׁמַע שָׁאוּל וְכָל־יִשְׂרָאֵל אֶת־דִּבְרֵי הַפְּלִשְׁתִּי הָאֵלֶּה (coincidental)
11b וַיֵּחַתּוּ (sequential)
11c וַיִּרְאוּ מְאֹד: (sequential)

---

3. See chapter 3 for a discussion of Josh 8:3–13.

4. Noticed in David Weston Baker, "The Consecutive Non-perfective as Pluperfect in the Historical Books of the Hebrew Old Testament: Genesis–Kings" (Master of Christian Studies thesis, Regent College, 1971), 60.

12a וְדָוִד בֶּן־אִישׁ אֶפְרָתִי הַזֶּה מִבֵּית לֶחֶם יְהוּדָה (parenthetical)
וּשְׁמוֹ יִשַׁי (supplemental)
וְלוֹ שְׁמֹנָה בָנִים (supplemental)
וְהָאִישׁ בִּימֵי שָׁאוּל זָקֵן (supplemental)
בָּא בַאֲנָשִׁים: (supplemental)
13a וַיֵּלְכוּ שְׁלֹשֶׁת בְּנֵי־יִשַׁי הַגְּדֹלִים (foreground)
13b הָלְכוּ אַחֲרֵי־שָׁאוּל לַמִּלְחָמָה (reiterative)
13c וְשֵׁם שְׁלֹשֶׁת בָּנָיו אֲשֶׁר הָלְכוּ בַּמִּלְחָמָה אֱלִיאָב הַבְּכוֹר וּמִשְׁנֵהוּ אֲבִינָדָב
וְהַשְּׁלִשִׁי שַׁמָּה: (supplemental)
14a וְדָוִד הוּא הַקָּטָן (contrastive supplemental)
14b וּשְׁלֹשָׁה הַגְּדֹלִים הָלְכוּ אַחֲרֵי שָׁאוּל: (reiterative)
15 וְדָוִד הֹלֵךְ וָשָׁב מֵעַל שָׁאוּל לִרְעוֹת אֶת־צֹאן אָבִיו בֵּית־לָחֶם: (iterative)
16a וַיִּגַּשׁ הַפְּלִשְׁתִּי הַשְׁכֵּם וְהַעֲרֵב (iterative)
16b וַיִּתְיַצֵּב אַרְבָּעִים יוֹם: (iterative)

First Samuel 17:1–11 narrates the scene of the battlefield where the Philistines and Israel had gathered their armies. Verse 11 informs the reader that all of Israel was afraid because of the words of Goliath. Verse 16 then adds that Goliath continued to terrorize Israel for forty days. Verse 17 continues the foregrounded narrative by describing how David entered the scene of the battlefield. Verses 12 and 14 give background information about David. Verse 12 does pause the narrative sequence. It does not move the narrative forward nor does it backtrack it. It is a static comment. Such comments should be seen as states within the timeframe of the preceding clause. Therefore, verse 13, which is part of the foreground narrative, should be read in reference to the timeframe of verse 11. When compared to verse 11, the event of verse 13 is chronologically prior making verse 13 a temporally overlaid clause. Ewald agrees regarding verse 13: "A most remarkable construction is וילכו־הלכו . . . where the verb, first placed in sequence, is afterwards more definitely explained as the pluperfect by its own perfect."[5]

---

5. Heinrich Ewald, *Syntax of the Hebrew Language of the Old Testament*, trans. James Kennedy, first Gorgias Press ed. (Edinburgh: T&T Clark, 1881; repr., Piscataway, NJ: Gorgias Press, 2005), 254, n. 3.

1 Kings 13:12[6]

11a וְנָבִיא אֶחָד זָקֵן יֹשֵׁב בְּבֵית־אֵל (introductory)
11b וַיָּבוֹא בְנוֹ (initatory)
11c וַיְסַפֶּר־לוֹ אֶת־כָּל־הַמַּעֲשֶׂה אֲשֶׁר־עָשָׂה
אִישׁ־הָאֱלֹהִים הַיּוֹם בְּבֵית־אֵל אֶת־הַדְּבָרִים אֲשֶׁר דִּבֶּר
אֶל־הַמֶּלֶךְ (sequential)
11d וַיְסַפְּרוּם לַאֲבִיהֶם: (reiterative)
12a וַיְדַבֵּר אֲלֵהֶם אֲבִיהֶם (sequential)
אֵי־זֶה הַדֶּרֶךְ הָלָךְ
12b וַיִּרְאוּ בָנָיו אֶת־הַדֶּרֶךְ אֲשֶׁר הָלַךְ אִישׁ הָאֱלֹהִים אֲשֶׁר־בָּא
מִיהוּדָה: (foreground)
13a וַיֹּאמֶר אֶל־בָּנָיו (sequential)
חִבְשׁוּ־לִי הַחֲמוֹר
13b וַיַּחְבְּשׁוּ־לוֹ הַחֲמוֹר (sequential)
13c וַיִּרְכַּב עָלָיו: (sequential)

In 1 Kings 12:33–10 Jeroboam II was sacrificing an offering in the presence of all Israel. The old prophet, who is introduced in verse 11, apparently did not go. This portrays him positively. In verse 11c only one of his sons told him what happened and in verse 11d "his other sons" confirmed what he already heard from his son. Verse 12b clearly tells us that he had more than one son but they were not properly introduced in verse 11d. Apparently it was not enough for the father to be told by one son only. He needed the confirmation of the other(s) in order to take the matter seriously.

He then asked his sons by what road the man of God went (v. 12a). The text does not give the sons' response to their father. Instead, what we have in 12b literally reads, "his sons saw the way by which the man of God, who came from Judah, had gone." Emending the text (וַיִּרְאוּ) from *qal* to *hiphil* "they showed him" is not necessary. In fact, it would not make much sense to assume that they would show him (which entails taking him to the road or somewhere close) and then in verse 13a their father would ask them to saddle the donkey only after he saw the road. Rather, it is better to simply assume that he asked them in 13a after they told him (not showed him) in

---

6. Bruce K. Waltke and M. O'Connor, *An Introduction to Biblical Hebrew Syntax* (Winona Lake, IN: Eisenbrauns, 1990), 553.

12b. Verse 12b should be seen as implying their response. If the sons saw the way, they would tell their father. His sons must have clearly told him where the man of God went before he told his sons in verse 13 to saddle the donkey. Though there is clearly an ellipsis between 12a and 12b or 12b and 13a, this should not create a problem because the author has done the same thing between 11c and 11d. The reader can fill the gap from the information in verse 13 that the sons had told him which way the man of God had gone. Instead of just telling what they said, the author informs the reader how the sons were able to tell their father. The reader would have asked how they were able to tell their father if the author had simply informed the reader that the sons told their father where the man of God had gone. Verse 12b is then a temporally overlaid clause which captures what was true of the sons before their father's question in verse 12a.

Jonah 4:5 (JPS)

4a וַיָּחֶל יוֹנָה לָבוֹא בָעִיר מַהֲלַךְ יוֹם אֶחָד (initiatory)

4b וַיִּקְרָא (sequential)

4c וַיֹּאמַר (coincidental)

עוֹד אַרְבָּעִים יוֹם וְנִינְוֵה נֶהְפָּכֶת

5–9 repentance of Nineveah (sequential)

10a וַיַּרְא הָאֱלֹהִים אֶת־מַעֲשֵׂיהֶם כִּי־שָׁבוּ מִדַּרְכָּם הָרָעָה (sequential)

10b וַיִּנָּחֶם הָאֱלֹהִים עַל־הָרָעָה אֲשֶׁר־דִּבֶּר לַעֲשׂוֹת־לָהֶם (sequential)

10c וְלֹא עָשָׂה: (momentus negation)

4:1a וַיֵּרַע אֶל־יוֹנָה רָעָה גְדוֹלָה (consequential)

1b וַיִּחַר לוֹ: (sequential)

2a וַיִּתְפַּלֵּל אֶל־יְהוָה (sequential)

2b וַיֹּאמַר (coincidental–request)

אָנָּה יְהוָה הֲלוֹא־זֶה דְבָרִי עַד־הֱיוֹתִי עַל־אַדְמָתִי עַל־כֵּן קִדַּמְתִּי לִבְרֹחַ תַּרְשִׁישָׁה כִּי יָדַעְתִּי כִּי אַתָּה אֵל־חַנּוּן וְרַחוּם אֶרֶךְ אַפַּיִם וְרַב־חֶסֶד וְנִחָם עַל־הָרָעָה: 3 וְעַתָּה יְהוָה קַח־נָא אֶת־נַפְשִׁי מִמֶּנִּי כִּי טוֹב מוֹתִי מֵחַיָּי:

4 וַיֹּאמֶר יְהוָה (sequential–reply)

הַהֵיטֵב חָרָה לָךְ:

5a וַיֵּצֵא יוֹנָה מִן־הָעִיר (foreground: parenthetical note)

5b וַיֵּשֶׁב מִקֶּדֶם לָעִיר (sequential)

5c וַיַּעַשׂ לוֹ שָׁם סֻכָּה (sequential)

5d וַיֵּשֶׁב תַּחְתֶּיהָ בַּצֵּל עַד אֲשֶׁר יִרְאֶה מַה־יִּהְיֶה בָּעִיר: (sequential)
6a וַיְמַן יְהוָה־אֱלֹהִים קִיקָיוֹן (sequential to 4)
6b וַיַּעַל מֵעַל לְיוֹנָה לִהְיוֹת צֵל עַל־רֹאשׁוֹ לְהַצִּיל לוֹ מֵרָעָתוֹ (sequential)
6c וַיִּשְׂמַח יוֹנָה עַל־הַקִּיקָיוֹן שִׂמְחָה גְדוֹלָה: (consequential)
7a וַיְמַן הָאֱלֹהִים תּוֹלַעַת בַּעֲלוֹת הַשַּׁחַר לַמָּחֳרָת (sequential)
7b וַתַּךְ אֶת־הַקִּיקָיוֹן (sequential)
7c וַיִּיבָשׁ: (consequential)
8a וַיְהִי כִּזְרֹחַ הַשֶּׁמֶשׁ (protasis)
8b וַיְמַן אֱלֹהִים רוּחַ קָדִים חֲרִישִׁית (apodosis–sequential)
8c וַתַּךְ הַשֶּׁמֶשׁ עַל־רֹאשׁ יוֹנָה (consequential)
8d וַיִּתְעַלָּף (consequential)
8e וַיִּשְׁאַל אֶת־נַפְשׁוֹ לָמוּת (sequential)
8f וַיֹּאמֶר (coincidental–request)
טוֹב מוֹתִי מֵחַיָּי:
9a וַיֹּאמֶר אֱלֹהִים אֶל־יוֹנָה (sequential–response)
הַהֵיטֵב חָרָה־לְךָ עַל־הַקִּיקָיוֹן
9b וַיֹּאמֶר (sequential–response)
הֵיטֵב חָרָה־לִי עַד־מָוֶת:
10 וַיֹּאמֶר יְהוָה (sequential–response)
אַתָּה חַסְתָּ עַל־הַקִּיקָיוֹן אֲשֶׁר לֹא־עָמַלְתָּ בּוֹ וְלֹא גִדַּלְתּוֹ שֶׁבִּן־לַיְלָה הָיָה וּבִן־לַיְלָה אָבָד: 11 וַאֲנִי לֹא אָחוּס עַל־נִינְוֵה הָעִיר הַגְּדוֹלָה אֲשֶׁר יֶשׁ־בָּהּ הַרְבֵּה מִשְׁתֵּים־עֶשְׂרֵה רִבּוֹ אָדָם אֲשֶׁר לֹא־יָדַע בֵּין־יְמִינוֹ לִשְׂמֹאלוֹ וּבְהֵמָה רַבָּה:

Jonah entered the city of Nineveh (3:4a) and preached his brief message (3:4c). The message stated that after forty days the city would be destroyed. All of Nineveh repented (vv. 5–9). In response to their repentance, verse 10 states that God relented. In response to the Lord's mercy on Nineveh, Jonah got angry and prayed that he might die, to which the Lord asked, "is it right for you to be angry?" (4:1–4). One must assume that there were forty days between 3:4c and 3:10. The report that God relented in verse 10 must be a reference to the end of the forty days and the absence of any judgment.

Then in 4:5 Jonah is said to leave the city "to see what would happen to the city." If this *wayyiqtol* clause were sequential, it would mean that Jonah stayed within the boundaries of the city during the forty days when there was a judgment on the city but left the city when there was no judgment on it. Nothing in his prayer in verses 2–3 suggests that he was hoping for the Lord to change his mind. His prayer was for him to die, not for the Lord to change his mind about Nineveh. Therefore, the *wayyiqtol* clause in verse 5a is temporally overlaid. It introduces a flashback to what happened right after Jonah preached in 3:4. All of the *wayyiqtol* clauses in 4:5 are part of this flashback. Then verse 6 takes the reader to the timeframe of 4:1–4. Jonah 4:6–11 captures an object lesson that the Lord taught Jonah after 4:1–4.

Jonah preached (3:4) and left the city, made a shelter for himself and stayed there (for forty days) to see what would happen to the city (4:5). What he built in verse 5 is gone by verse 6: "The booth Jonah constructed (v. 5) no doubt provided adequate shade for a short time in the oppressive Assyrian heat. The leaves on the brush used for the roof withered quickly, however, and no doubt fell off. It was then that the Lord God provided a vine to minister relief to Jonah."[7] This suggests some time elapsed between verse 5 and verse 6.

Genesis 5:6

1a זֶה סֵפֶר תּוֹלְדֹת אָדָם (title)
1b בְּיוֹם בְּרֹא אֱלֹהִים אָדָם (protasis)
1c בִּדְמוּת אֱלֹהִים עָשָׂה אֹתוֹ׃ (apodosis)
2a זָכָר וּנְקֵבָה בְּרָאָם (complementary)
2b וַיְבָרֶךְ אֹתָם (initiatory)
2c וַיִּקְרָא אֶת־שְׁמָם אָדָם בְּיוֹם הִבָּרְאָם׃ (complementary)
3a וַיְחִי אָדָם שְׁלֹשִׁים וּמְאַת שָׁנָה (sequential)
3b וַיּוֹלֶד בִּדְמוּתוֹ כְּצַלְמוֹ (sequential)
3c וַיִּקְרָא אֶת־שְׁמוֹ שֵׁת׃ (coincidental)
4a וַיִּהְיוּ יְמֵי־אָדָם אַחֲרֵי הוֹלִידוֹ אֶת־שֵׁת שְׁמֹנֶה מֵאֹת שָׁנָה (sequential)
4b וַיּוֹלֶד בָּנִים וּבָנוֹת׃ (simultaneous)
5a וַיִּהְיוּ כָּל־יְמֵי אָדָם אֲשֶׁר־חַי תְּשַׁע מֵאוֹת שָׁנָה וּשְׁלֹשִׁים שָׁנָה (summarizing)
5b וַיָּמֹת׃ (concluding)
6a וַיְחִי־שֵׁת חָמֵשׁ שָׁנִים וּמְאַת שָׁנָה (foreground)
6b וַיּוֹלֶד אֶת־אֱנוֹשׁ׃ (sequential)

---

7. Billy K. Smith and Frank S. Page, *Amos, Obadiah, Jonah*, NAC, ed. E. Ray Clendenen, vol. 19B (Nashville, TN: Broadman & Holman, 1995), 277.

7a וַיְחִי־שֵׁת אַחֲרֵי הוֹלִידוֹ אֶת־אֱנוֹשׁ שֶׁבַע שָׁנִים וּשְׁמֹנֶה מֵאוֹת שָׁנָה (sequential)
7b וַיּוֹלֶד בָּנִים וּבָנוֹת: (simultaneous)
8a וַיִּהְיוּ כָּל־יְמֵי־שֵׁת שְׁתֵּים עֶשְׂרֵה שָׁנָה וּתְשַׁע מֵאוֹת שָׁנָה (summarizing)
8b וַיָּמֹת: (concluding)

Genesis 5:1–32 is a genealogical list. Verse 5 ends with the death of Adam. Verse 6a uses the *wayyiqtol* to speak of Seth's giving birth to a son. Clearly Seth had his son before Adam's death (when Adam was 235). This same syntax applies in verses 9, 12, 15, 18, 21, and 28. The *wayyiqtol* clause in verse 6a (and in vv. 9, 12, 15, 18, 21, and 28) is temporally overlaid describing an event chronologically prior to the preceding clause, which in every case is the death of the father of the individuals mentioned in verse 6a (and in vv. 9, 12, 15, 18, 21, and 28).

APPENDIX 3

Outline of the Book of Joshua

Prologue 1:1–5:15 (cf. Epilogue 21:41–24:33)
A 1:1–18 Commission
    a 1:1–9 Promise and commission (cf. 21:41–45)[1]
    b 1:10–11 The preparation of people (cf. 22:7–24:28)
    c 1:12–18 Charge to the two and half tribes (cf. 22:1–6)
B Preparation 2:1–5:15 (cf. 22:7–24:33)
    a 2:1–24 Jericho feared: encouraging Joshua, not the people
    b 3:1–5 Cultic purity for the people
    c 3:6–5:1 Crossing the Jordan
    d 5:2–12 Cultic purity: circumcision and passover
    e 5:13–15 Encouraging Joshua

The Conquest 6:1–12:24
A Central 6:1–8:29
B Southern 9:1–10:43
C Northern 11:1–15
D Summary 11:16–12:34

Allotment of land 13:1–21:40
A 13:1–7 Need for allotment of land both conquered and yet to be conquered
B 13:8–33 Two and half tribes east of Jordan
C 14:1–17:18 Judah and Joseph: two and half tribes west of Jordan
D 18:1–19:51 Other tribes: seven tribes west of Jordan

---

1. The people are referred to in the second person masculine plural in vv. 3–4 but in second masculine singular elsewhere in vv. 1–9.

E 20:1–21:40 Appendix: Further allocations within the allocated land.
    a 20:1–9 Cities of refuge
    b 21:1–42 Levitical cities

Epilogue 21:43–24:33
A' 21:41–22:6 (cf. 1:1–18) Fulfillment of promise[2]
    a 21:41–45 The Lord kept his promise (cf. 1:3–4)[3]
    b 22:1–6 Two and half tribes kept their promise (cf. 1:12–18)
B' 22:7–24:32 Preparation[4] (cf. 2:1–5:15 and A1 1:1–9[5])
    a 22:7–34 Test for the people
    b 23:1–16 Commission of the people
    b' 24:1–28 Covenant for the people
    a' 24:29–32 Evaluation of the people

---

2. In A of the prologue, the Lord as well as the two and half tribes made promises; in A' of the epilogue these promises were fulfilled.

3. A2 1:10–11 is picked up in 2:1–5:15. So the parallel to A2 is same as the parallel to 2:1–5:15, which is 22:7–24:32.

4. In B Joshua prepared his generation for the conquest but in B' he prepared the next generation for the conquest and life in Canaan in his absence and in the absence of the elders who were his contemporaries.

5. Joshua's commission (1:1–9), without vv. 3–4, which was picked up in 2:1–5:15.

Bibliography

Aharoni, Yohanan. *The Land of the Bible: A Historical Geography*. Translated by A. F. Rainey. Philadelphia, PA: Westminster, 1967.

Amit, Yairah. *The Book of Judges: The Art of Editing*. Translated by Jonathan Chipman. Biblical Interpretation Series, edited by R. Alan Culpepper and Rolf Rendtorff, vol. 38. Leiden: Brill, 1999.

———. "Hidden Polemic in the Conquest of Dan: Judges 17–18." *Vetus Testamentum* 60, no. 1 (1990): 4–20.

———. *History and Ideology: An Introduction to Historiography in the Hebrew Bible*. Translated by Yael Lotan. Sheffield: Sheffield Academic Press, 1999.

———. *Reading Biblical Narratives: Literary Criticism and the Hebrew Bible*. Translated by Yael Lotan. Minneapolis: Fortress, 2001.

———. "The Use of Analogy in the Study of the Book of Judges." In *"Wünschet Jerusalem Frieden": Collected Communications to the XIIth Congress of the International Organization for the Study of the Old Testament, Jerusalem*, 387–394. Beiträge zur Erforschung des Alten Testaments und des antiken Judentums, edited by Matthias Augustin and Klaus-Dietrich Schunck, vol. 13. Frankfurt am Main: Peter Lang, 1986.

Anderson, A. A. *2 Samuel*. Word Biblical Commentary, edited by John D. W. Watts, vol. 11. Dallas: Word Books, 1989.

Andersson, G. "The Book and Its Narratives: A Critical Examination of Some Synchronic Studies of the Book of Judges." PhD diss., Örebro University, 2001.

———. *The Book and Its Narratives: A Critical Examination of Some Synchronic Studies of the Book of Judges*. Örebro Studies in Literary History and Criticism, edited by Joanna Israelsson-Kempinska and Heinz Merten, vol. 1. Örebro: Örebro University, 2001.

Andrason, Alexander. "Biblical Hebrew *Wayyiqtol*: A Dynamic Definition." *Journal of Hebrew Scriptures* 11, no. 8 (2011): 1–58.

Angel, Hayyim. "One Book, Two Books: The Joshua–Judges Continuum." *Jewish Bible Quarterly* 36, no. 3 (2008): 163–170.

Arnold, Bill T., and John H. Choi. *A Guide to Biblical Hebrew Syntax.* Cambridge: Cambridge University Press, 2003.

Asami, R. Shin. "The Origin of Holy War in the Book of Judges." ThM thesis, Western Conservative Baptist Seminary, 1985.

Assis, Elie. "'For It Shall Be a Witness Between Us': A Literary Reading of Josh 22." *Scandinavian Journal of the Old Testament* 18, no. 2 (2004): 208–231.

———. "The Position and Function of Jos 22 in the Book of Joshua." *Zeitschrift für die alttestamentliche Wissenschaft* 116, no. 4 (2004): 528–541.

Auld, A. Graeme. "The Deuteronomists and the Former Prophets, or What Makes the Former Prophets Deuteronomistic?" In *Those Elusive Deuteronomists: The Phenomenon of Pan-Deuteronomism*, edited by Linda S. Schearing and Steven L. McKenzie, 116–126. Journal for the Study of the Old Testament: Supplement Series, vol. 268. Sheffield: Sheffield Academic Press, 1999.

———. *Joshua, Judges, and Ruth.* Daily Study Bible: Old Testament, edited by John C. L. Gibson. Louisville, KY: Westminster John Knox, 1984.

———. "Judges 1 and History: A Reconsideration." *Vetus Testamentum* 25, no. 2 (1975): 261–285.

———. "Judges 1 and History: A Reconsideration." In *Joshua Retold: Synoptic Perspectives*, 79–101. Old Testament Series, edited by David J. Reimer. Edinburgh: T&T Clark, 1998.

Ayrolle, Christiane. "Le prologue du livre des Juges: Juges 1,1–3,6." *Etudes théologiques et religieuses* 84, no. 2 (2009): 189–204.

Baker, David Weston. "The Consecutive Non-perfective as Pluperfect in the Historical Books of the Hebrew Old Testament: Genesis–Kings." Master of Christian Studies thesis, Regent College, 1971.

Baldick, Chris. "Analypsis." In *Oxford Dictionary of Literary Terms.* Oxford: Oxford University Press, 2008.

Begg, C. "The Overture to the Period of the Judges according to Josephus." *Liber Annuus* 54, no. 1 (2004): 235–254.

Bekkum, Koert van. *From Conquest to Coexistence: Ideology and Antiquarian Intent in the Historiography of Israel's Settlement in Canaan.* Culture and History of the Ancient Near East, vol. 45. Leiden: Brill, 2011.

———. "Remembering and Claiming Ramesside Canaan: Historical-Topographical Problems and the Ideology of Geography in Joshua 13.1–7." In *The Book of Joshua*, edited by Ed Noort, 345–360. Bibliotheca Ephemeridum Theologicarum Lovaniensium, vol. 250. Leuven: Peeters, 2012.

Berlin, Adele. *Poetics and Interpretation of Biblical Narrative.* Winona Lake, IN: Eisenbrauns, 1994.

Bertheau, Ernst. *Das Buch der Richter und Ruth*. Exegetisches Handbuch zum Alten Testament, vol. 6. Leipzig: S. Hirzel, 1883.

Blass, F., A. Debrunner, and Robert W. Funk. *A Greek Grammar of the New Testament and Other Early Christian Literature*. Chicago and London: University of Chicago Press, 1961.

Block, Daniel I. *Judges, Ruth*. New American Commentary, edited by E. Ray Clendenen, vol. 6. Nashville, TN: Broadman & Holman, 1999.

Boda, Mark J. "Judges." In *Numbers – Ruth*, edited by Tremper Longman III and David E. Garland, vol. 2, 1043–1288. Expositor's Bible Commentary, rev. ed. Grand Rapids: Zondervan, 2012.

Boling, Robert G. *Joshua: A New Translation with Notes and Commentary*. Anchor Bible, edited by William Foxwell Albright and David Noel Freedman. Garden City, NY: Doubleday and Company, 1982.

———. *Judges: Introduction, Translation, and Commentary*. Anchor Bible, edited by William Foxwell Albright and David Noel Freedman, vol. 6A. Garden City, NY: Doubleday, 1975.

Bolinger, Dwight. *Meaning and Form*. English Language Series, vol. 11. London: Longman, 1977.

Bowman, Richard G. "Narrative Criticism." In *Judges and Method: New Approaches in Biblical Studies*, edited by Gale A. Yee, 19–45. Minneapolis: Fortress, 2007.

Brettler, Marc Zvi. *The Book of Judges*. Old Testament Readings, edited by Keith Whitelam. London and New York: Routledge, 2002.

———. "The Book of Judges: Literature as Politics." *Journal of Biblical Literature* 108, no. 3 (1989): 395–418.

———. "Judges 1,1–2,10: From Appendix to Prologue." *Zeitschrift für die alttestamentliche Wissenschaft* 101, no. 3 (1989): 433–435.

Burney, C. F. *The Book of Judges, with Introduction and Notes*. Rivingtons: University of Oxford, 1920.

Buth, Randall. "Methodological Collision between Source Criticism and Discourse Analysis: The Problem of 'Unmarked Temporal Overlay' and the Pluperfect/Nonsequential *Wayyiqtol*." In *Biblical Hebrew and Discourse Linguistics*, edited by Robert D. Bergen, 138–154. Dallas: Summer Institute of Linguistics, 1994.

Butler, Trent C. *Joshua 13–24*. 2nd ed. Word Biblical Commentary, edited by deClaissé-Walford, vol. 7B. Grand Rapids: Zondervan, 2014.

———. *Judges*. Word Biblical Commentary, edited by Bruce M. Metzger, David A. Hubbard, Glenn W. Barker, John D. W. Watts and James W. Watts, vol. 8. Nashville, TN: Thomas Nelson, 2009.

Calvin, John. *Commentaries on the Harmony on the Law: Extended Annotated Edition*. Translated by Charles William Bingham. vol. 4. Grand Rapids: Christian Classics Ethereal Library, 2012.

Campbell, Antony F., and Mark A. O'Brien. *Unfolding the Deuteronomistic History: Origins, Upgrades, Present Text*. Minneapolis: Fortress, 2000.

Childs, Brevard S. "A Study of the Formula, 'Until This Day.'" *Journal of Biblical Literature* 82, no. 3 (1963): 279–292.

Chisholm, Robert B. *A Commentary on Judges and Ruth*. Kregel Exegetical Library. Grand Rapids: Kregel, 2013.

———. "'For This Reason': Etiology and Its Implications for the Historicity of Adam." *Criswell Theological Review* 10, no. 2 (2013): 27–51.

———. "What's Wrong with This Picture? Stylistic Variation as a Rhetorical Technique in Judges." *Journal for the Study of the Old Testament* 34 (2009): 171–182. "יאל I." In *Dictionary of Classical Hebrew*, edited by David J. A. Clines, vol. 4, 71. Sheffield: Sheffield Academic Press, 1998.

Coleson, Joseph, Lawson G. Stone, and Jason Driesbach. *Joshua, Judges, Ruth*. Cornerstone Biblical Commentary, edited by Philip W. Comfort, vol. 3. Carol Stream, IL: Tyndale House, 2012.

Collins, C. John. "The Wayyiqtol as 'Pluperfect': When and Why." *Tyndale Bulletin* 46, no. 1 (1995): 117–140.

Cook, John A. "The Hebrew Verb: A Grammaticalization Approach." *Zeitschrift für Althebräistik* 14, no. 2 (2001): 117–143.

———. "The Semantics of Verbal Pragmatics: Clarifying the Roles of Wayyiqtol and Weqatal in Biblical Hebrew Prose." *Journal of Semitic Studies* 49, no. 2 (2004): 247–273.

———. *Time and the Biblical Hebrew Verb: The Expression of Tense, Aspect, and Modality in Biblical Hebrew*. Linguistic Studies in Ancient West Semitic, vol. 7. Winona Lake: Eisenbrauns, 2012.

Creach, Jerome F. D. "בעס." In *New International Dictionary of Old Testament Theology and Exegesis*, edited by Willem A. VanGemeren, vol. 2, 676–678. Grand Rapids: Zondervan, 1997.

Cross, Frank Moore, and George Ernest Wright. "Boundary and Province Lists of the Kingdom of Judah." *Journal of Biblical Literature* 75, no. 3 (1956): 202–226.

Dallaire, Hélène M. "Joshua." In *Numbers – Ruth*, edited by Tremper Longman III and David E. Garland, vol. 2, 815–1042. Expositor's Bible Commentary, rev. ed. Grand Rapids: Zondervan, 2012.

Davidson, A. B. *Hebrew Syntax*. 3rd. ed. Edinburgh: T&T Clark, 1901.

Declerck, Renaat. *When-Clauses and Temporal Structure*. London and New York: Routledge, 1997.

De Roche, Michael. "Yahweh's Rîb Against Israel: A Reassessment of the So-Called 'Prophetic Lawsuit' in the Preexilic Prophets." *Journal of Biblical Literature* 102, no. 4 (1983): 563–574.

Dozeman, Thomas B. "Joshua 1.1–9: The Beginning of a Book or a Literary Bridge?" In *The Book of Joshua*, edited by Ed Noort, 159–182. Bibliotheca Ephemeridum Theologicarum Lovaniensium, vol. 250. Leuven: Peeters, 2012.

Drews, Robert. "The 'Chariots of Iron' of Joshua and Judges." *Journal for the Study of the Old Testament* 45 (1989): 15–23.

Driver, S. R. *A Treatise on the Use of the Tenses in Hebrew and Some Other Syntactical Questions*. 4th ed. Biblical Resources Series, edited by Astrid B. Beck and David Noel Freedman. Grand Rapids: Eerdmans, 1998.

Dumbrell, W. J. "'In Those Days There Was No King in Israel; Every Man Did What Was Right in His Own Eyes.' The Purpose of the Book of Judges Reconsidered." *Journal for the Study of the Old Testament* 8, no. 25 (1983): 23–33.

Ederer, Matthias. *Ende und Anfang: Der Prolog des Richterbuchs (Ri 1,1–3,6) in "Biblischer Auslegung."* Herder's Biblical Studies, edited by Hans-Josef Klauck and Erich Zenger, vol. 68. Freiburg: Herder, 2011.

Engle, John Michael. "The Redactional Development of the Book of Judges." PhD diss., Hebrew Union College–Jewish Institute of Religion, 2002.

Ewald, Heinrich. *Syntax of the Hebrew Language of the Old Testament*. Translated by James Kennedy. First Gorgias Press ed. Edinburgh: T&T Clark, 1881. Reprint. Piscataway, NJ: Gorgias Press, 2005.

Fishbane, Michael. *Biblical Interpretation in Ancient Israel*. Oxford: Clarendon, 1985.

"Flashback." In *A Dictionary of Literary Terms and Literary Theory*, edited by J. A. Cuddon. Oxford: Blackwell, 1998.

Flinn, Charles G. "The Character of the Peshitta of the Book of Judges and Its Relation to Other Ancient Translations." PhD diss., The Catholic University of America, 2010.

Frolov, Serge. "Fire, Smoke, and Judah in Judges: A Response to Gregory Wong." *Scandinavian Journal of the Old Testament* 21, no. 2 (2007): 127–138.

———. "Joshua's Double Demise (Josh. 24:28–31; Judg. 2:6–9): Making Sense of a Repetition." *Vetus Testamentum* 58 (2008): 315–323.

———. *Judges*. Forms of the Old Testament Literature, edited by Rolf P. Knierim and Marvin A. Sweeney, vol. 18. Grand Rapids: Eerdmans, 2013.

Fuhs, H. F. "שׁאל." In *Theological Dictionary of the Old Testament*, edited by G. Johannes Botterweck, Helmer Ringgren and Heinz-Josef Fabry, vol. 14, 249–264. Grand Rapids: Eerdmans, 2004.

Garstang, John. *Joshua–Judges: The Foundations of the Bible*. Grand Rapids: Kregel, 1978.

Gaster, Theodor H. *Myth, Legend, and Custom in the Old Testament: A Comparative Study with Chapters from Sir James G. Frazer's Folklore in the Old Testament*. vol. 2. Gloucester, MA: Peter Smith, 2011.

Gesenius' Hebrew Grammar. Translated by A. E. Cowley and edited by E. Kautzsch. 2nd ed. Oxford: Oxford University, 1910.

Gibson, J. C. L. *Davidson's Introductory Hebrew Grammar-Syntax*. 4th ed. Edinburgh: T&T Clark, 1994.

Gillmayr-Bucher, Susanne. *Erzählte Welten im Richterbuch: Narratologische Aspekte eines polyfonen Diskurses*. Biblical Interpretation Series, edited by Paul Anderson and Yvonne Sherwood, vol. 116. Leiden: Brill, 2013.

———. "Framework and Discourse in the Book of Judges." *Journal of Biblical Literature* 128, no. 4 (2009): 687–702.

Globe, Alexander. "'Enemies Round About': Disintegrative Structure in the Book of Judges." In *Mappings of the Biblical Terrain: The Bible as Text*, edited by Vincent L. Tollers and John Maier, 233–251. Bucknell Review. Lewisburg, PA: Bucknell University, 1990.

Gooding, D. W. "The Composition of the Book of Judges." In *Harry M. Orlinsky Volume*, edited by Baruch A. Levine, and Abraham Malamat, 70*–79*. Eretz-Israel: Archaeological, Historical and Geographical Studies, vol. 16. Jerusalem: Israel Exploration Soceity, 1982.

Goshen-Gottstein, Moshe H. "Afterthought and the Syntax of Relative Clauses in Biblical Hebrew." *Journal of Biblical Literature* 68, no. 1 (1949): 35–47.

Greenspahn, Frederick E. "The Theology of the Framework of Judges." *Vetus Testamentum* 36, no. 4 (1986): 385–396.

Gregor, Geiger. "Erzählte Welt und *Wayyiqtol*." In Ἐν πάσῃ γραμματικῇ καὶ σοφίᾳ: *En pāsē grammatikē kai sophiā*, edited by Gregor Geiger, 129–152. SBF Analecta, vol. 78. Milan: Edizioni Terra Santa, 2011.

Groß, Walter. *Richter*. Herders Theologischer Kommentar zum Alten Testament, edited by Erich Zenger. Freiburg: Herder, 2009.

Guillaume, Philippe. "An Anti-Judean Manifesto in Judges 1?" *Biblische Notizen* 95 (1998): 12–17.

Hamlin, E. John. "Adoni-Bezek – What's in a Name (Judges 1:4–7)." In *Proceedings: Eastern Great Lakes and Midwest Biblical Societies* 4 (1984): 146–152.

———. "The Significance of Bethel in Judges 1:22–26." In *Proceedings: Eastern Great Lakes and Midwest Biblical Societies* 5 (1985): 67–72.

———. "Structure and Meaning of the Theological Essay in Judges 2:6–3:6." In *Proceedings: Eastern Great Lakes and Midwest Biblical Societies* 6 (1986): 114–119.

Hatav, Galia. "Past and Future Interpretation of Wayyiqtol." *Journal of Semitic Studies* 56, no. 1 (2011): 85–109.

Hauch, Gerhard. "Text and Contexts: A Literary Reading of the Conquest Narrative (Jos 1–11)." PhD diss., Princeton Theological Seminary, 1991.

Hazony, Y. "The Political Thought of the Biblical History." In *Judaic Sources and Western Thought: Jerusalem's Enduring Presence*, edited by Jonathan A. Jacobs. Oxford: Oxford University, 2011.

Heller, Roy L. *Narrative Structure and Discourse Constellations: An Analysis of Clause Function in Biblical Hebrew Prose*. Harvard Semitic Studies, edited by Jo Ann Hackett and John Huehnergard, vol. 55. Winona Lake, IN: Eisenbrauns, 2004.

Hess, Richard S. "Judges 1–5 and Its Translation." In *Translating the Bible: Problems and Prospects*, edited by Stanley E. Porter and Richard S. Hess, 142–160. Journal for the Study of the New Testament: Supplement Series, vol. 173. Sheffield: Sheffield Academic Press, 1999.

Howard, David M. *Joshua*. New American Commentary, edited by E. Ray Clendenen, vol. 5. Nashville, TN: Broadman & Holman, 1998.

Ingram, Everette Wayne. "The Peculiar Judgment on God's People with Special Reference to the Book of Judges." PhD diss., University of KwaZulu-Natal, 2004.

Joosten, Jan. *The Verbal System of Biblical Hebrew: A New Synthesis Elaborated on the Basis of Classical Prose*. Jerusalem Biblical Studies, vol. 10. Jerusalem: Simor, 2012.

Joüon, Paul, and T. Muraoka. *A Grammar of Biblical Hebrew*. 2nd ed. Subsidia biblica, vol. 27. Rome: Editrice Pontificio Instituto Biblico, 2006.

Junkkaala, Eero. *Three Conquests of Canaan: A Comparative Study of Two Egyptian Military Campaigns and Joshua 10–12 in the Light of Recent Archaeological Evidence*. Finland: Abo Akademi University Press, 2006.

Kaiser, Walter C. *A History of Israel: From Bronze Age through the Jewish Wars*. Nashville, TN: Broadman & Holman, 1998.

Klein, Lilian R. "Structure, Irony and Meaning in the Book of Judges." In *Proceedings of the 10th World Congress of Jewish Studies: Division A*, 83–90. Jerusalem: Magnes Pr., 1990.

———. *Triumph of Irony in the Book of Judges*. Bible and Literature Series, edited by David M. Gunn, vol. 14. Sheffield: Sheffield Academic Press, 1989.

Kooij, A. van der. "'And I Also Said': A New Interpretation of Judges 2:3." *Vetus Testamentum* 45, no. 3 (1995): 294–306.

Levin, Yigal. "Conquered and Unconquered: Reality and Historiography in the Geography of Joshua." In *The Book of Joshua*, edited by Ed Noort, 361–370. Bibliotheca Ephemeridum Theologicarum Lovaniensium, vol. 250. Leuven: Peeters, 2012.

Licht, Jacob. *Storytelling in the Bible*. 2nd ed. Jerusalem: Magnes Press, 1986.

Lilley, J. P. U. "A Literary Appreciation of the Book of Judges." *Tyndale Bulletin* 18 (1967): 94–102.

Lindars, Barnabas. *Judges 1–5: A New Translation and Commentary*. Edited by A. D. H. Mayes. Edinburgh: T&T Clark, 1995.

Long, V. Philips. *The Reign and Rejection of King Saul: A Case for Literary and Theological Coherence*. Society of Biblical Literature: Dissertation Series, edited by David L. Petersen, vol. 118. Atlanta, GA: Scholars Press, 1989.

Longacre, Robert E. *Joseph – A Story of Divine Providence: A Text Theoretical and Textlinguistic Analysis of Genesis 37 and 39–48*. 2nd ed. Winona Lake, IN: Eisenbrauns, 2003.

———. "*Weqatal* Forms in Biblical Hebrew Prose: A Discourse-Modular Approach." In *Biblical Hebrew and Discourse Linguistics*, edited by Robert D. Bergen, 50–98. Dallas, TX: Summer Institute of Lingusitics, 1994.

Lubbe, John. "The Danite Invasion of Laish and the Purpose of the Book of Judges." *Old Testament Essays* 23, no. 3 (2010): 681–692.

Marais, Jacobus. *Representation in Old Testament Narrative Texts*. Biblical Interpretation Series, edited by R. Alan Culpepper and Rolf Rendtorff, vol. 36. Leiden: Brill, 1998.

Martin, Lee Roy. "From Gilgal to Bochim: The Narrative Significance of the Angel of Yahweh in Judges 2:1." *Journal for Semitics* 18, no. 2 (2009): 331–343.

———. *The Unheard Voice of God: A Pentecostal Hearing of the Book of Judges*. Journal of Pentecostal Theology Supplemental Series, edited by John Christopher Thomas, Rickie Moore and Steven J. Land, vol. 32. Blandford Forum: Deo Publishing, 2008.

———. "'Where Are All His Wonders?' The Exodus Motif in the Book of Judges." *Journal of Biblical and Pneumatological Research* 2 (2010): 87–109.

———. "Yahweh Conflicted: Unresolved Theological Tension in the Cycle of Judges." *Old Testament Essays* 22, no. 2 (2009): 356–372.

Martin, W. J. "'Dischronologized' Narrative." In *Congress Volume: Rome 1968*, 179–186. Supplements to Vetus Testamentum, edited by G. W. Anderson, P. A. H. De Boer, G. R. Castellino, Henry Cazelles, E. Hammershaimb, H. G. May and W. Zimmerli, vol. 17. Leiden: Brill, 1969.

Mayes, A. D. H. *Judges*. Sheffield: Sheffield Academic Press, 1995.

McCann, J. Clinton. *Judges*. Interpretation: A Bible Commentary for Teaching and Preaching, edited by James Luther Mays. Louisville: John Knox, 2001.

Mead, Charles Marsh. "Examination of Exodus xxxiii. 7–11." *Journal of the Society of Biblical Literature and Exegesis* 1, no. 2 (1881): 155–168.

Merrill, Eugene H. *Kingdom of Priests: A History of Old Testament Israel*. 2nd ed. Grand Rapids: Baker Academic, 2008.

Merwe, N. C. van der. "The Identification and Function of Whole and Unwhole Bodies in the Book of Judges." DLitt et Phil. diss., University of Johannesburg, 2009.

Miller, C. L. "Ellipsis." In *Dictionary of the Old Testament: Wisdom, Poetry and Writings*, edited by Tremper Longman III and Peter Enns, 156–160. Downers Grove, IL: InterVarsity Press, 2008.

———. *The Representation of Speech in Biblical Hebrew Narrative: A Linguistic Analysis*. Harvard Semitic Museum Monographs, edited by Lawrence E. Stager and Peter Machinist, vol. 55. Atlanta: Scholars Press, 1996.

Moore, George F. *A Critical and Exegetical Commentary on Judges*. International Critical Commentary, edited by S. R. Driver, A. Plummer and C. A. Briggs. Edinburgh: T&T Clark, 1895.

Mullen, E. Theodore. "Judges 1:1–36: The Deuteronomistic Reintroduction of the Book of Judges." *The Harvard Theological Review* 77, no. 1 (1984): 33–54.

Nelson, Richard D. *The Double Redaction of the Deuteronomistic History*. Journal for the Study of the Old Testament: Supplement Series, edited by David J. A. Clines, Philip R. Davies and David M. Gunn, vol. 18. Sheffield: Sheffield Academic Press, 1981.

Niccacci, Alviero. "Basic Facts and Theory of the Biblical Hebrew Verb System in Prose." In *Narrative Syntax and the Hebrew Bible: Papers of the Tilburg Conference 1996*, edited by Ellen Van Wolde, 167–202. Biblical Interpretation Series, vol. 29. Leiden: Brill, 1997.

———. *The Syntax of the Verb in Classical Hebrew Prose*. Edited by W. G. E. Watson. Journal for the Study of the Old Testament: Supplement Series, edited by David J. A. Clines and Philip R. Davies, vol. 86. Sheffield: Sheffield Academic Press, 1990.

Niditch, Susan. *Judges: A Commentary*. Old Testament Library, edited by William P. Brown, Carol A. Newsom and David L. Petersen. Louisville, KY: Westminster John Knox, 2008.

———. "Reading Story in Judges 1." In *The Labour of Reading: Desire, Alienation, and Biblical Interpretation*, edited by Fiona C. Black, Roland Boer and Erin Runions. Society of Biblical Literature: Semeia Studies, vol. 36. Atlanta, Georgia: Society of Biblical Literature, 1999.

———. "The 'Sodomite' Theme in Judges 19–20: Family, Community, and Social Disintegration." *Catholic Biblical Quarterly* 44, no. 3 (1982): 365–378.

Nielsen, Kirsten. *Yahweh as Prosecutor and Judge: An Investigation of the Prophetic Lawsuit (Rîb-Pattern)*. Edited by Frederick Cryer. Journal for the Study of the Old Testament: Supplement Series, vol. 9. Sheffield: University of Sheffield Press, 1978.

Noth, Martin. *The Deuteronomistic History*. Translated by D. Orton. 2nd ed. Journal for the Study of the Old Testament: Supplement Series, edited by David J. A. Clines, Philip R. Davies and David M. Gunn, vol. 15. Sheffield: Sheffield Academic Press, 1991.

O'Brien, Mark A. "Judges and the Deuteronomistic History." In *History of Israel's Traditions: The Heritage of Martin Noth*, edited by Steven L. McKenzie and M. Patrick Graham, 235–259. Journal for the Study of the Old Testament: Supplement Series, vol. 182. Sheffield: Sheffield Academic Press, 1994.

O'Connell, Robert H. *The Rhetoric of the Book of Judges*. Supplements to Vetus Testamentum, vol. 63. Leiden: E. J. Brill, 1996.

O'Doherty, Eamonn. "Literary Problem of Judges 1:1–3:6." *Catholic Biblical Quarterly* 18, no. 1 (1956): 1–7.

O'Reilly, Marc J., and Wesley B. Renfro. "Like Father, Like Son? A Comparison of the Foreign Policies of George H. W. Bush and George W. Bush." *Historia Actual Online* 10 (2006): 17–36.

Osborne, Grant R. *The Hermeneutical Spiral: A Comprehensive Introduction to Biblical Interpretation*, revised and expanded. Downers Grove, IL: IVP Academic, 2006.

Paris, Christopher T. *Narrative Obtrusion in the Hebrew Bible*. Minneapolis: Fortress, 2014.

Penchansky, David. "Up For Grabs: A Tentative Proposal for Doing Ideological Criticism." *Semeia* 59 (1992): 35–41.

Polzin, Robert. *Moses and the Deuteronomist: A Literary Study of the Deuteronomic History; Part One: Deuteronomy, Joshua, Judges*. Indiana Studies in Biblical Literature, edited by Herbert Marks and Robert Polzin. New York: Seabury, 1980.

Prince, Gerald. *A Dictionary of Narratology*. Lincoln, NE: University of Nebraska Press, 1987.

Qimron, Elisha. "Consecutive and Conjunctive Imperfect: The Form of the Imperfect with Waw in Biblical Hebrew." *The Jewish Quarterly Review* 77, no. 2–3 (1986): 149–161.

Rake, Mareike. *Juda wird aufsteigen! Untersuchungen zum ersten Kapitel des Richterbuches*. Beihefte zur Zeitschrift für die alttestamentliche Wissenschaft, edited by John Barton, Reinhard G. Kratz, Choon-Leong Seow and Markus Witte, vol. 367. Berlin and New York: Walter de Gruyter, 2006.

Ramsey, George W. "Speech-Forms in Hebrew Law and Prophetic Oracles." *Journal of Biblical Literature* 96, no. 1 (1977): 45–58.

Revell, E. J. "The Battle with Benjamin (Judges xx 29–48) and Hebrew Narrative Techniques." *Vetus Testamentum* 35, no. 4 (1985): 417–33.

Robar, Elizabeth. *The Verb and the Paragraph in Biblical Hebrew: A Cognitive-Linguistic Approach.* Studies in Semitic Languages and Linguistics, vol. 78. Leiden: Brill, 2015.

Robertson, A. T. *A Grammar of the Greek New Testament in the Light of Historical Research.* Nashville, TN: Broadman, 1934.

Roehrs, Walter R. "Conquest of Canaan according to Joshua and Judges." *Concordia Theological Monthly* 31, no. 12 (1960): 746–760.

Sailhamer, John H., Walter C. Kaiser, and Richard S. Hess. *Genesis–Leviticus.* Expositor's Bible Commentary, edited by Tremper Longman III and David E. Garland. Grand Rapids: Zondervan, 2008.

Sasson, Jack M. *Judges 1–12: A New Translation with Introduction and Commentary.* Anchor Yale Bible, edited by John J. Collins, vol. 6D. New Haven: Yale University Press, 2014.

Satterthwaite, P. E. "Judges," In *Dictionary of the Old Testament Historical Books: A Compendium of Contemporary Biblical Scholarship*, edited by Bill T. Arnold and H. G. M. Williamson, 580–592. Downers Grove, IL: InterVarsity Press, 2005.

Satterthwaite, Philip E., and Gordon J. McConville. *A Guide to the Historical Books.* Exploring the Old Testament, vol. 2. Downers Grove, IL: InterVarsity Press, 2007.

Schneider, Tammi J. *Judges.* Berit Olam: Studies in Hebrew Narrative & Poetry, edited by David W. Cotter. Collegeville, MN: Liturgical, 2000.

Ska, Jean Louis. *"Our Fathers Have Told Us": Introduction to the Analysis of Hebrew Narratives.* Subsidia biblica, vol. 13. Rome: Editrice Pontificio Instituto Biblico, 2000.

Smith, Billy K., and Frank S. Page. *Amos, Obadiah, Jonah.* New American Commentary, edited by E. Ray Clendenen, vol. 19B. Nashville, TN: Broadman & Holman, 1995.

Smith, Michael John. "The Failure of the Family as a Theme in the Book of Judges." PhD diss., Dallas Theological Seminary, 2004.

Sommers, L. Javed. "A World in Which Things Are Not As They Should Be: How the Deuteronomistic Ideology Is Reinforced in the Book of Judges by the Portrayal of Women and Domestic Space." MA thesis, McGill University, 2011.

Sonnet, Jean-Pierre. *The Book within the Book: Writing in Deuteronomy.* Biblical Interpretation Series, vol. 14. Leiden: Brill, 1997.

Spronk, Klaas. "From Joshua to Samuel: Some Remarks on the Origin of the Book of Judges." In *The Land of Israel in Bible, History, and Theology: Studies in Honour of Ed Noort*, edited by Jacques van Ruiten and J. Cornelis de Vos. Supplements to Vetus Testamentum, vol. 124. Leiden: Brill, 2009.

Stemmer, Nathan. "The Introduction to Judges, 2,1–3,4." *Jewish Quarterly Review* 57, no. 3 (1967): 239–241.

Stevenson, Jeffery S. "Judah's Successes and Failures in Holy War: An Exegesis of Judges 1:1–20." *Restoration Quarterly* 44, no. 1 (2002): 43–54.

Stone, Lawson G. "Book of Judges," In *Dictionary of the Old Testament: Historical Books*, edited by Bill T. Arnold and H. G. M. Williamson, 592–606. Downers Grove, IL: InterVarsity Press, 2005.

———. "From Tribal Confederation to Monarchic State: The Editorial Perspective of the Book of Judges." PhD diss., Yale University, 1988.

Sweeney, M. A. "Davidic Polemics in the Book of Judges." *Vetus Testamentum* 47, no. 4 (1997): 517–529.

———. *Isaiah 1–39: With an Introduction to Prophetic Literature*. Forms of the Old Testament Literature, edited by Rolf P. Knierim and Gene M. Tucker, vol. 16. Grand Rapids: Eerdmans, 1996.

Talstra, Eep. "A Hierarchy of Clauses in Biblical Hebrew Narrative." In *Narrative Syntax and the Hebrew Bible: Papers of the Tilburg Conference 1996*, edited by Ellen Van Wolde, 85–105. Biblical Interpretation Series, vol. 29. Leiden: Brill, 1997.

Van Bekkum, Koert. "De Historiografie van Israëls vestiging in Kanaän aan de hand van Richteren 1: 1–2: 5." *Nederlandsch theologisch tijdschrift* 54, no. 4 (2000): 295–309.

Van Dam, Cornelis. "גורל." In *New International Dictionary of Old Testament Theology and Exegesis*, edited by Willem A. VanGemeren, vol. 1, 825–827. Grand Rapids: Zondervan, 1997.

Wallace, Daniel B. *Greek Grammar Beyond the Basics: An Exegetical Syntax of the New Testament with Scripture, Subject, and Greek Word Indexes*. Grand Rapids: Zondervan, 1996.

Walsh, Jerome T. *Old Testament Narrative: A Guide to Interpretation*. Louisville, KY: Westminster John Knox, 2009.

Waltke, Bruce K., and M. O'Connor. *An Introduction to Biblical Hebrew Syntax*. Winona Lake, IN: Eisenbrauns, 1990.

Webb, Barry G. *The Book of Judges*. New International Commentary on the Old Testament, edited by R. K. Harrison and Robert L. Hubbard. Grand Rapids: Eerdmans, 2012.

———. *The Book of the Judges: An Integrated Reading*. Journal for the Study of the Old Testament: Supplement Series, vol. 44. Eugene, OR: Wipf & Stock, 2008.

Weinfeld, M. "Judges 1.1–2.5: The Conquest under the Leadership of the House of Judah." In *Understanding Poets and Prophets: Essays in Honour of George Wishart Anderson*, edited by A. Graeme Auld. Journal for the Study of the

Old Testament: Supplement Series, vol. 152. Sheffield: Sheffield Academic Press, 1993.

Wenham, Gordon J. *Genesis 16–50*. Word Biblical Commentary, edited by David A. Hubbard, Gleen W. Baker and John D. W. Watts, vol. 2. Dallas, TX: Word, 1994.

Wessels, J. P. H. "Persuasions in Judges 2.20–3.6: A Celebration of Differences." In *The Rhetorical Analysis of Scripture: Essays from the 1995 London Conference*, edited by Stanley E. Porter and Thomas H. Olbricht, 120–136. Journal for the Study of the New Testament: Supplement Series, vol. 146. Sheffield: Sheffield Academic Press, 1997.

———. "'Postmodern' Rhetoric and the Former Prophetic Literature." In *Rhetoric, Scripture and Theology: Essays from the 1994 Pretoria Conference*, edited by Stanley E. Porter and Thomas H. Olbricht, 182–194. Journal for the Study of the New Testament: Supplement Series, vol. 131. Sheffield: Sheffield Academic Press, 1996.

Williams, Jay G. "The Structure of Judges 2.6–16.31." *Journal for the Study of the Old Testament* 49 (1991): 77–85.

Wong, Gregory T. K. *Compositional Strategy of the Book of Judges: An Inductive, Rhetorical Study*. Supplements to Vetus Testamentum, vol. 111. Leiden: Brill, 2006.

———. "Is There a Direct Pro-Judah Polemic in Judges?" *Scandinavian Journal of the Old Testament* 19, no. 1 (2005): 84–110.

Wright, G. Ernest. "The Literary and Historical Problem of Joshua 10 and Judges 1." *Journal of Near Eastern Studies* 5, no. 2 (1946): 105–114.

Yee, Gale A. "Ideological Criticism: Judges 17–21 and the Dismembered Body." In *Judges and Method: New Approaches in Biblical Studies*, edited by Gale A. Yee, 146–170. Minneapolis: Fortress, 1995.

Younger, K. Lawson. "The Configuring of Judicial Preliminaries: Judges 1.1–2.5 and Its Dependence on the Book of Joshua." *Journal for the Study of the Old Testament* 68 (1995): 75–92.

———. "Joshua." In *Eerdmans Commentary on the Bible*, edited by James D. G. Dunn and John W. Rogerson, 174–189. Grand Rapids: Eerdmans, 2003.

———. "Judges 1 in Its Near Eastern Literary Context." In *Faith, Tradition, and History: Old Testament Historiography in Its Near Eastern Context*, edited by A. R. Millard, James K. Hoffmeier and David W. Baker, 207–227. Winona Lake, IN: Eisenbrauns, 1994.

———. *Judges, Ruth*. NIV Application Commentary: From Biblical Text to Contemporary Life, edited by Terry Muck. Grand Rapids: Zondervan, 2002.

Zertal, Adam. "Bezek." In *Anchor Bible Dictionary*, edited by David Noel Freedman, vol. 1, 717–718. New York: Doubleday, 1992.

Zevit, Ziony. *The Anterior Construction in Classical Hebrew*. Society of Biblical Literature Monograph Series, edited by Terence E. Fretheim, vol. 50. Atlanta, GA: Scholars Press, 1998.

Langham Literature and its imprints are a ministry of Langham Partnership.

Langham Partnership is a global fellowship working in pursuit of the vision God entrusted to its founder John Stott –

> *to facilitate the growth of the church in maturity and Christ-likeness through raising the standards of biblical preaching and teaching.*

Our vision is to see churches in the majority world equipped for mission and growing to maturity in Christ through the ministry of pastors and leaders who believe, teach and live by the Word of God.

Our mission is to strengthen the ministry of the Word of God through:
- nurturing national movements for biblical preaching
- fostering the creation and distribution of evangelical literature
- enhancing evangelical theological education

especially in countries where churches are under-resourced.

Our ministry

Langham Preaching partners with national leaders to nurture indigenous biblical preaching movements for pastors and lay preachers all around the world. With the support of a team of trainers from many countries, a multi-level programme of seminars provides practical training, and is followed by a programme for training local facilitators. Local preachers' groups and national and regional networks ensure continuity and ongoing development, seeking to build vigorous movements committed to Bible exposition.

Langham Literature provides majority world preachers, scholars and seminary libraries with evangelical books and electronic resources through publishing and distribution, grants and discounts. The programme also fosters the creation of indigenous evangelical books in many languages, through writer's grants, strengthening local evangelical publishing houses, and investment in major regional literature projects, such as one volume Bible commentaries like *The Africa Bible Commentary* and *The South Asia Bible Commentary*.

Langham Scholars provides financial support for evangelical doctoral students from the majority world so that, when they return home, they may train pastors and other Christian leaders with sound, biblical and theological teaching. This programme equips those who equip others. Langham Scholars also works in partnership with majority world seminaries in strengthening evangelical theological education. A growing number of Langham Scholars study in high quality doctoral programmes in the majority world itself. As well as teaching the next generation of pastors, graduated Langham Scholars exercise significant influence through their writing and leadership.

To learn more about Langham Partnership and the work we do visit **langham.org**

w.ingramcontent.com/pod-product-compliance
ng Source LLC
burg PA
4230426
0017B/2485